Library of
Davidson College

EXCISE TAXATION OF MONOPOLY

COLUMBIA STUDIES IN ECONOMICS

3

Excise Taxation of Monopoly

N. SHILLING

COLUMBIA UNIVERSITY PRESS
NEW YORK and LONDON 1969

NED SHILLING is Associate Professor
in the College of Business Administration
at The Pennsylvania State University

Copyright © 1968, 1969 Columbia University Press
SBN 231-03178-5
Library of Congress Catalog Card Number: 70-76620
Printed in the United States of America

To my Mother
    and
to the Memory of my Father

Acknowledgments

Several persons provided valuable assistance during the development and writing of this manuscript. Carl S. Shoup offered a number of suggestions and improved the exposition in many places; I am very grateful for his help. Thanks are due Thomas Iwand and Warren C. Robinson for their comments on an earlier draft of the manuscript. The responsibility for whatever faults remain rests, of course, with the author.

Thanks are also due Ossian MacKenzie, Dean of the College of Business Administration, Pennsylvania State University, for releasing me from other duties, when time was badly needed.

My wife, Carolyn Recht Shilling, performed cheerfully many of the tasks entailed in making the book, and I would like to express my appreciation to her here.

N.S.

Contents

Part I

Introduction

1	Scope and Method of Study	3
	A. Area of Inquiry	5
	B. Scope and Limitations of the Conclusions	6
2	Excise Tax Functions and Their Characteristics	9
	A. Tax Functions	9
	B. Characteristics of Excise Tax Functions	15
	C. Progression in Excise Tax Functions	19
	D. Some Definitions	22

Part II

Effects of Excise Taxes on Price and Output

3	Pre-tax Equilibrium: Monopoly	25
	A. Theory of Monopoly Price	25
	B. Theoretical Treatment of Excise Taxes	33
4	After-tax Equilibrium: General Statement	37
	A. Direction of Price Change	37
	B. Amount of Price Change	45
5	After-tax Equilibrium: Power Tax Function	51
	A. Limitations on Parameters	51
	B. Tax Elasticity	52
	C. Examples	52
	D. Direction of Price Change	52
	E. Amount of Price Change	64
6	After-tax Equilibrium: Proportional Tax on Excess Price	73
	A. Limitations on Parameters	73
	B. Tax Elasticity	74

xi

	C. Examples	75
	D. Direction of Price Change	75
	E. Amount of Price Change	80
7	After-tax Equilibrium: Bracketed Taxes	87
	A. Upward Step	88
	B. Downward Step	94
	C. No Step Effect	95
	D. Gap in After-tax Prices	96
8	After-tax Equilibrium: Bounties	99
9	Other Market Structures	103
	A. Monopsony	103
	B. Pure Competition	108
	C. Monopolistic Competition	111
	D. Oligopoly	116
10	Summary of Part II	121

Part III

Effects of Excise Taxes on Selling Effort

11	Pre-tax Equilibrium: Price, Output, and Selling Effort	127
12	After-tax Equilibrium: General Statement	139
	A. Description of Equilibrium	139
	B. Types of Demand Functions	141
13	After-tax Equilibrium: Specific Tax	145
	A. Tax-Induced Shift in N-S Ridge Line	145
	B. Tax-Induced Shift in W-E Ridge Line	146
	C. Net Effect	146
14	After-tax Equilibrium: Ad Valorem Tax	153
	A. Tax-Induced Shift in N-S Ridge Line	153
	B. Tax-Induced Shift in W-E Ridge Line	154
	C. Net Effect of Both Shifts	155
15	After-tax Equilibrium: Progressive Tax	163
	A. Tax-Induced Shift in N-S Ridge Line	163
	B. Tax-Induced Shift in W-E Ridge Line	165
	C. Net Effect of Both Shifts	166
16	After-tax Equilibrium: Highly Regressive Tax	173
	A. Tax-Induced Shift in N-S Ridge Line	173
	B. Tax-Induced Shift in W-E Ridge Line	174
	C. Net Effect of Both Shifts	174
17	Some Comparisons between "Equal" Taxes	177
	A. Taxes That Lead to the Same After-tax Output	177
	B. Taxes That Are Equal at the Pre-tax Price	178
18	Extension of Results	187
	A. The General Tendencies	187

Contents   *xiii*

	B. Scope of Results	193
19	Summary of Part III	197

Part IV

Effects of Excise Taxes on Product Quality

20	Before-tax and After-tax Equilibrium	201
	A. Before-tax Equilibrium	203
	B. After-tax Equilibrium	208
21	Durability as a Dimension of Quality	211
	A. Before-tax Equilibrium	212
	B. After-tax Equilibrium	216

Part V

Conclusion

22	Implications of the Results	223
	A. Excise Taxation for Revenue	224
	B. Excise Taxation for Non-fiscal Purposes	225
	C. Problems Associated with Progressive Excise Taxes	227

Appendixes

I	Joint Maximization and Marginal Revenue	233
II	Relation between Slopes of the Ridge Lines	235
III	Effects of a Tax Based on Advertising Outlays	238
IV	Relation between Classifications of Demand Functions	242
V	Effect of an Excise Tax on the Elasticity of Industry Demand with Respect to Price Net of Tax	246

Bibliography   249

Index   253

Charts

1	Bracketed ad valorem tax schedules	13
2	Bracketed specific tax schedules	14
3	Continuously graduated excise taxes	15
4a	Effect on output and price, increase in marginal revenue	28
4b	Effect on output and price, decrease in marginal revenue	29
5a	Average revenue, marginal revenue, marginal cost, and optimum output and price	31
5b	Total revenue, total cost, and optimum output	32
6	Before- and after-tax profit and total tax bill, specific tax of $1 per unit	34
7a	Marginal cost and before- and after-tax marginal revenue, tax that does not change price	40
7b	Before- and after-tax profit and total tax bill, tax that does not change price	41
8a	Marginal revenue, decreased or increased by an excise tax	43
8b	Profits before and after taxes that raise or lower price	43
9a	Effect of increasing and decreasing costs on amount of price change, a tax that reduces price	45
9b	Effect of increasing and decreasing costs on amount of price change, a tax that increases price	46
10a	Effect of heavier tax rate on amount of price change, a tax that reduces price	47
10b	Effect of heavier tax rate on amount of price change, a tax that increases price	48
11	Effect of "heavy" tax on price and output: tax elasticity equals demand elasticity	60
12a	Effect of "heavy" tax on price: tax elasticity smaller than demand elasticity	63
12b	Effect of "heavy" tax on price: tax elasticity greater than demand elasticity	63

Charts xv

13a	Effect of increased tax elasticity on amount of price change: taxes equal at pre-tax price and both taxes reduce price	68
13b	Effect of increased tax elasticity on amount of price change: taxes equal at pre-tax price and both taxes increase price	68
14	Effect of weight of tax on marginal revenue curves	70
15a	Effect on marginal revenue, output, and price: proportional tax on excess price; "c" exceeds marginal cost at pre-tax output	77
15b	Effect on marginal revenue, output, and price: proportional tax on excess price; "c" smaller than marginal cost at pre-tax output	77
16a	Proportional tax on excess price: effect on marginal revenue	78
16b	Increasing the weight of tax need not produce further price change	79
17a	Effect of higher elasticity on amount of price change: taxes equal at pre-tax price and both taxes lower price	84
17b	Effect of higher elasticity on amount of price change: pairs of taxes equal at pre-tax price and each pair raises price	85
18a	Effect on marginal revenue, output, and price of bracketed specific tax	89
18b	Before-tax profit, after-tax profit, and tax bill: bracketed specific tax	90
19a	Effect on marginal revenue, output, and price of bracketed ad valorem tax	92
19b	Effect on marginal revenue of several price brackets: specific tax	93
20a	Effect of downward step in tax: price may rise farther than without step	95
20b	Effect of downward step in tax: price may rise less than without step	96
21a	Monopsony equilibrium: price and purchases	104
21b	Effect on "tax on price deficiency" on monopsony price and purchases	105
22	Effect of any excise tax on price and output: pure competition	110
23a	Pre-tax equilibrium: monopolistic competition, excess profit	112
23b	Pre-tax equilibrium: monopolistic competition, no excess profit	113

24	Contours of profit surface and ridge lines: specific demand and cost functions	135
25	Constant price lines and ridge lines: same functions as Chart 24	137
26	Contours of profit surface, ridge lines, and constant price lines: demand function type ii	142
27	Contours of profit surface and ridge lines: demand function type iii	143
28	Effects of specific tax on selling outlays and output: three types of demand functions	147
29	Effect of ad valorem tax on selling outlays and output: three types of demand functions and two marginal cost conditions. (Left-hand panels, $MC = 0$; right-hand panels, $MC \neq 0$)	156
30	Effect of progressive tax $\{E_t(p) > -E_x(p)\}$ on selling outlays and output: three types of demand functions	168
31	Effect of highly regressive tax $\{E_t(p) < 0\}$ on selling outlays and output: three types of demand functions	175
32	Relative effects of taxes equal at pre-tax price: upper panel – both taxes increase price. Lower panel – both taxes reduce price	182
33	Effects of various taxes and bounties on selling outlays and output: demand function of type ii	188
34	Cross-section, at a fixed price, of revenue, cost and profit surfaces (durability and price as independent variables)	214
35	Contours of profit surface, three ridge lines, constant price lines: demand function type ii	243

Tables

Table 1	Profit at Different Levels of Output	32
Table 2	Tax per Unit, at Various Prices, for Different Combinations of n and k: Power Tax	53
Table 3	Tax per Unit, at Various Prices, for Different Combinations of r and c: Proportional Tax on Excess Price	75

EXCISE TAXATION OF MONOPOLY

Part I. *Introduction*

The purpose of this study and the main line of approach are sketched out in Chapter 1. In Chapter 2 a general excise tax function is formulated, and the important characteristics of excise tax functions are described.

Chapter 1. *Scope and Method of Study*

Excise taxes on individual commodities have typically been levied either as a fixed amount per unit sold or as a fixed percentage of the price of the product per unit sold. The effects of such taxes have been treated extensively in the literature on tax incidence, where perhaps the most noteworthy results of an excise tax are shown to be an almost invariable increase in the price of the good to the consumer and a consequent reduction in consumption and production of the taxed commodity. One of the major criticisms of excise taxes as revenue-raising devices is that, by increasing the price of the taxed good, consumer preferences and the resulting allocation of resources to the production of various products are distorted from their natural (optimum) form. Whether the good is marketed competitively or monopolistically is not considered to be essential to the validity of the criticism.

Of course, extreme conditions are possible, under which an excise tax could lead to no increase in price (e.g., an inelastic supply curve). In addition some writers have demonstrated that, under ordinary circumstances, an excise tax might actually reduce the price (including the tax) of the taxed good rather than increase it. For a price reduction to occur, either (1) the tax would have to be levied on one or more related commodities, or (2) the taxed commodity must be monopolized to some extent, and the form of tax must be different from the usual specific or ad valorem tax. With the exception of Edgeworth, who showed that, when related goods are taxed, one or more prices may fall, tax theorists have by and large ignored these possibilities, or dismissed them without further inquiry as insignificant or as raising serious administrative problems.

One aspect of the present study that may be new is the extension of the analysis to any form of excise tax.[1] This extension permits the identification of the characteristics of the tax that are important in determining its effects. The form of tax needed to reduce monopoly price is not as complex as might be imagined, and a number of existing taxes take this form. Generally speaking, the distinguishing feature of such taxes is variation in the rate at different prices. More specifically, if the average rate of tax increases for any rise in price, the tax may lower price. All taxes of this type are referred to here as "graduated" taxes. The use of exemptions, exclusions, and graduations in tax schemes is not unusual and can produce effects that differ strikingly from those of the usual excises. The price may fall, with the seller still responsible for the tax payment out of the reduced price.

If this is so, the accepted criticism of excise taxes does not apply to all types of tax. It becomes theoretically possible to achieve all of the following effects with one tax: (1) produce some tax revenue, (2) reduce a monopolist's excess profit, (3) increase the consumers' surplus through a lower price, and (4) increase the demand for the factors of production. A tax on monopoly profit could produce the first two effects but not the last two; an ad valorem or specific excise could also produce the first two, but the third and fourth results would be reversed in direction; a price ceiling would produce the last three but not the first. Many other devices have been proposed to control, or at least influence, monopoly price.

The proof that a tax can reduce price does not require any "new" assumption, nor does it depend upon possible demand or production relationships with goods other than the taxed one. It is simply an unsuspected implication of the conditions for profit maximization.

The effect of a tax on product price and the resulting consequences have received the predominant emphasis in the analysis of excise taxes. This emphasis is perhaps not unnatural in view of the early development of economic theory around the problem of price determination. However, according to recent theories of value, product quality and selling effort may be as important as price or even more important, from the point of view of the firm, as "para-

---

[1]For the purposes of this study, an "excise tax" is defined as a tax on the sale of a good or service such that the amount of tax due per unit sold is a function—possibly a constant—of price only.

Scope and Method of Study

meters of action" in profit maximization. Excise taxes change not only the most profitable price but also the most profitable quality of product and the most profitable volume of selling expenditure. Furthermore, if the tax does induce quality or other changes, additional price adjustments may be required. Thus a price theory that neglects non-price changes will not predict the same after-tax price as will a price theory that takes these changes into account. The effects of a tax on product quality and selling effort have received very little attention from tax theorists. Since almost any form of excise tax is likely to lead to some quality or selling-outlay variation, such changes are studied here in some detail.

A. *Area of Inquiry*

A major portion of the following pages is given to a study of the effects of different types of excise taxes. The most important effects are those on product price, output, selling outlay, or product quality. Other effects include the raising of revenue and a reduction of profits in the taxed industry. Since graduated taxes are now being levied in the United States and in other countries, their consequences should be known as far as possible, especially since firms may not be aware of the optimal reaction to a tax. Furthermore, graduated excises may be proposed in the future for reasons other than the desirability of any of these effects. An awareness of all likely economic results of such taxes is essential to the formulators of tax policy. Particular emphasis will be placed on effects that are different from those of the more common types of excise tax.

Although the raising of revenue has been the single most important stated purpose for excise taxation, other aims have not been absent. Taxes have consequences other than producing revenue. When these consequences are believed to be desirable and more easily brought about by taxation than by other means, a tax is often imposed. Although in the United States there are legal and other limitations to the use of taxes as control mechanisms, within the scope of these limitations the principle of taxation for control is generally, if not unanimously, accepted. As a means of raising revenue, graduated taxes are perhaps better, or perhaps worse, than conventional excises. In any event the primary emphasis here will be on other effects. Given the price lowering effect that they may provide, such taxes may be used for the fiscal control of monopoly and oligopoly. Under certain circumstances they may work to reduce or inhibit large advertising or other selling expenditures. They have been and may again be used to divert consumer expenditures from expensive, high-quality commodities to cheaper goods.

B. *Scope and Limitations of the Conclusions*

The effects of excise taxes are analyzed in terms of the familiar static partial equilibrium framework to show the manner in which the tax changes the conditions of profit maximization with respect to price, output, and selling outlay or quality. That is, on the assumption that firms maximize profits before the tax is levied, what changes will be necessary in order to maximize profits after the tax is levied?

The demand and cost conditions underlying the proofs are general, being restricted no more than is necessary to identify different market structures and to assure that the conditions required for maximization are fulfilled. Apart from the continuity and stability of demand and cost functions, the only assumption made about the demand curves is that they are not positively sloped. In addition, the good or goods on which a tax is levied are assumed to be "unimportant" in the economy as a whole, so that the secondary effects of price and other changes induced by the tax on consumers' real incomes, the demand structure, and expenditure patterns may safely be ignored, as well as the effects of the tax on general price levels and on the demand for the factors of production.

No attention will be given to the possible consequences (e.g., the migration of firms) of a tax being levied by a state or smaller political jurisdiction. The existence of the tax is assumed not to change the pre-tax demand curve; that is, public expenditures that change as a result of the collection of tax revenue are assumed to be made in ways that do not change the demand curve for the taxed good. It is also assumed that the existence of the tax and the resulting changes in public expenditures, if any, do not affect cost functions. For time periods shorter than the "long run," the fixed costs of production are ignored—profit maximization may mean the minimization of losses.

Scope and Method of Study

The proofs are generally analytical rather than geometrical or verbal. It is often not clear to what extent a geometrical proof depends upon the shape of the drawn curves; also, analytical expression is much more flexible and, perhaps, more easily manipulated rigourously. Edgeworth's long note (34 lines), translating into ordinary language a mathematical proof of a simple theorem of tax incidence, is telling evidence for the point he was making: "I don't know that much has been effected by this cumbrous simplification, except to show the great superiority of the genuine mathematical method."[2]

[2]F. Y. Edgeworth, *Papers Relating to Political Economy* (London, 1925), II, 91.

Chapter 2. *Excise Tax Functions and Their Characteristics*

In this chapter excise taxes are examined from the point of view of the formulae that define them. Different forms of graduated taxes are presented algebraically. The mathematical characteristics of tax formulae are discussed, including the concepts of continuity and differentiability. Possible definitions of *progression* in taxes are examined, and a choice is made among them largely on the grounds of analytical usefulness in subsequent chapters.

A. *Tax Functions*

1. "A tax scheme addressed to any taxpayer is a list of statements relating quantities of payments required from him to selected objective conditions."[1] For example, the payments may be the total amounts due per time period and the conditions may be the possible levels of income per time period. For an excise tax, the conditions may be the numbers of units of a single commodity sold per time period or the possible amounts of gross revenue received from the sale of a good per time period. Alternatively, the payments may be the amount due *per unit sold* and the conditions may be the possible prices per unit.

There are no necessary limitations on the form of the relationship between the payments and the conditions. Generally speaking, however, it is desirable that the relationship be relatively simple and consistent if capricious and unintended effects are to be avoided. It seems also desirable that the tax schedule should not add to the uncertainty of taxpayers as to how future net returns will be affected

---

[1] A. C. Pigou, *A Study in Public Finance* (3rd ed.; London, 1951) p. 46.

by their behavior. As a rule, the conditions chosen to determine the tax liability should be at least partly under the control of the taxpayer.

For the present, the most useful formulation of an excise tax is one that relates the amount due per unit sold, t, to the price per unit, p. The general mathematical statement of the tax function is

$$t = t(p), \quad p > 0 \tag{1}$$

where p is the total price collected by the seller of the good[2,3]

---

[2]Insofar as possible, a variable is denoted by the first letter of its name; thus p represents price, t tax per unit sold, etc. E is used to represent the elasticity of a function, for example, $E_t(p)$ is the elasticity of the per unit tax with respect to price, $-E_x(p)$ the elasticity of demand with respect to price.

Functions are represented with as few symbols as possible. The demand function with price as the dependent variable is written as $p = p(x)$; with output as the dependent variable it would be $x = x(p)$. Thus any symbol followed by parentheses that include one or more other symbols will generally represent a function and not multiplication. The exact meaning will usually be clear from the context.

Derivatives of functions are indicated by adding the appropriate number of primes to the function notation. For example, the first derivative of the demand function, $p = p(x)$, is written as $p'(x)$. This is equivalent to the usual notation, dp/dx. The second derivative is written as $p''(x)$, etc.

For reference, some mathematical expressions are numbered consecutively through all chapters.

[3]The statement of the per unit tax as a general function of price represents, it is believed, a useful departure from the usual procedure in studies of the effects of excise taxes in that it permits the analysis of *any* type of tax, as long as the per unit tax is a function of price only. In addition, it becomes possible to discover the characteristics of the tax function that determine (or influence) the direction and magnitude of the effects of a tax. As a rule, the only excise taxes considered in the literature of tax incidence are the specific and the ad valorem tax, although some isolated exceptions will be noted below.

The price variable in the tax function need not be the actual transaction price. It may be a "suggested retail price" or even an appraised value of the good. The definition of the price variable will determine how the effects of the tax are analyzed. The tax per unit is the tax liability of the seller or producer of the goods. Those costs to the firm that are increased by the existence of the tax (e.g., collection, accounting, and cash transfers) should be included if they vary with price or output. They have generally been ignored, however, in the theory of tax incidence. Several reasons for this neglect can be tentatively offered. Such costs may be believed to be small enough to be unimportant, although some studies of retail sales tax collection costs show them to be a significant proportion of tax collections.

Instead, collection costs may be considered to be largely fixed rather than variable. If these costs are completely independent of sales or price, they are irrelevant to a decision on price, but they are not irrelevant to the decision to produce an untaxed or a taxed good. When a bracketed tax is levied—for example, one with no tax on a low-priced good—the latter decision arises more often than under the usual form of excise tax, for then a decision to raise price can also be a decision to produce a taxed, rather than an untaxed, good.

Excise Tax Functions and Their Characteristics

Of course, the seller is more interested in the quantity $(p-t)$, the *net* proceeds of each unit sold. It is equally possible to symbolize the net proceeds to the seller and to carry out the analysis in terms of this net price. However, the demand function is most conveniently expressed in terms of the total price to the buyer. Thus proofs of the effects of taxes are simpler and some expressions are easier to interpret if the price variable in the tax function is also the total price to the buyer. Conclusions about the effects of taxes are not affected by this choice.

The tax function, $t(p)$, is not necessarily restricted to positive values; if $t(p)$ is negative, the "tax" is in fact a bounty.[4]

It will be noted that the above tax function is not sufficient to determine the total tax liability of the taxpayer, for it shows only the amount of tax per unit sold. However, with the addition of a known demand function, relating price and units sold per time period, the tax bill is known. In practice, excise tax functions are invariably expressed in terms of the per unit tax rather than the tax bill, if only because of uncertainty about the demand function for a good.

The tax function need not be expressed in terms of price. Since the demand function

$$p = p(x)$$

relates price to sales per time period, the amount of tax per unit could be treated as a function of a function of sales per time period:

$$t = t[p(x)]$$

Both tax functions will be used below in working out proofs. The concepts of graduation and progression are presented in terms of tax function (1), if only because this form emphasizes the fact that the price determines the tax per unit.

A "graduated" excise tax might be considered as any tax function such that the amount of tax per unit, t, varies as the price varies. By this criterion all excise taxes, except specific taxes, but including ad valorem taxes, are graduated. Alternatively, the criterion might be variation in the average tax rate, r, that is, the amount of tax per unit as a proportion of the price, as the price varies. By this standard

---

[4] A. Cournot was apparently the first writer to note this symmetry between taxes and bounties [*Recherches sur les principes mathematiques de la théorie des richesses* (Paris, 1938) 76–77].

all excise taxes except the proportional ad valorem tax are graduated. Neither specific nor proportional ad valorem taxes are excluded from occasional consideration in this study; however, the major emphasis, particularly in Part II, will be on excise taxes that apply varying average tax rates according to changes in the price of the commodity.

2. Many different forms of tax schedule are possible. Some of those that will receive particular attention are briefly described.

Bracketed ad valorem tax. The usual ad valorem tax can be generalized by applying a different tax rate to different price brackets:

Price Brackets	Tax per Unit	Average Tax Rate	
$p \leq p^*$	pr^*	r^*	
$p^* < p \leq p^{**}$	pr^{**}	r^{**}	
$p^{**} < p \leq p^{***}$	pr^{***}	r^{***}	(2)
$p^{***} < p \leq p^{****}$	pr^{****}	r^{****}	
etc.	etc.	etc.	

As long as the price remains within a single bracket, the tax appears to apply in the same manner as a proportional ad valorem tax (hereafter referred to simply as "ad valorem tax"). However, the existence of a different tax rate in other price brackets may lead to effects that differ from those of the ad valorem tax. The tax rate may increase with rising prices, or it may decrease.

The schedule may have only two price brackets, and there may or may not be a tax levied in the lower bracket. In Chart 1 several different forms of bracketed ad valorem schedules are shown.

Bracketed specific tax. The applicable tax within a price bracket may be a flat amount per unit instead of a stated proportion of the price:

Price Brackets	Tax per Unit	Average Tax Rate	
$p \leq p^*$	t^*	t^*/p	
$p^* < p \leq p^{**}$	t^{**}	t^{**}/p	
$p^{**} < p \leq p^{***}$	t^{***}	t^{***}/p	(3)
$p^{***} < p \leq p^{****}$	t^{****}	t^{****}/p	
etc.	etc.	etc.	

Excise Tax Functions and Their Characteristics

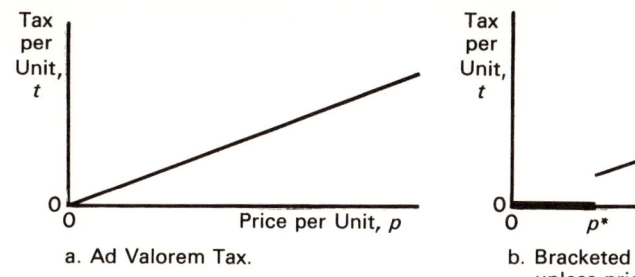
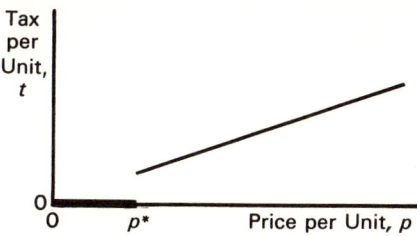
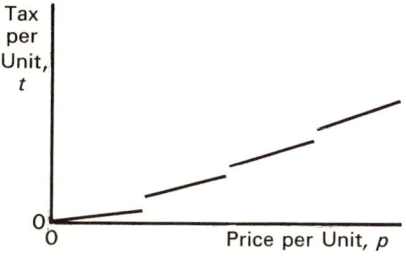
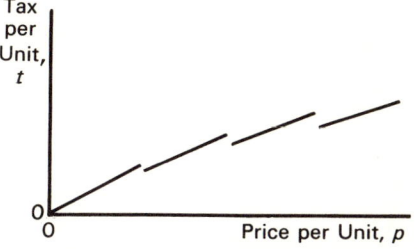

a. Ad Valorem Tax.

b. Bracketed Ad Valorem Tax: no tax unless price exceeds p^*.

c. Bracketed Ad Valorem Tax: rising average rate of tax.

d. Bracketed Ad Valorem Tax: falling average rate of tax.

CHART 1.
Bracketed ad valorem tax schedules.

As before, the average tax rate may tend to increase or decrease as the price increases, or it may remain approximately constant. In Chart 2 several forms of bracketed specific tax schedules are shown. If the price brackets become narrower and more numerous, tax (3) and tax (2) become indistinguishable and in the limit could be replaced by some formula that relates the tax per unit to the price in a continuous manner.

Tax (3) often results from the levy of an ad valorem tax. The schedule is derived by increasing the tax per unit from one bracket to the next in such a fashion that the rate per unit is approximately the same from one bracket to the next (Chart 2, Panel d). The schedule is intended to serve two purposes: (1) to substitute for an actual calculation of tax due when a transaction is settled, and (2) to round off the amount of tax due to the nearest cent.

3. Graduated excise taxes may be defined by some function relating the per unit tax to price.

Proportional tax on excess price. The tax rate, r, may be applied, not to the entire price, but only to the amount by which the price exceeds

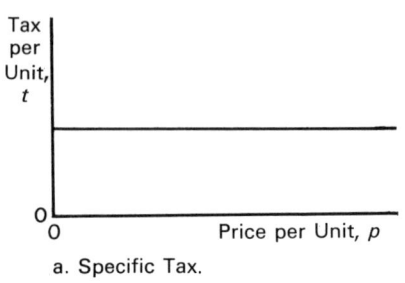
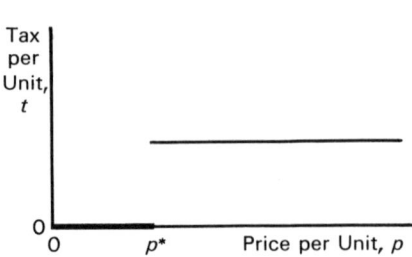
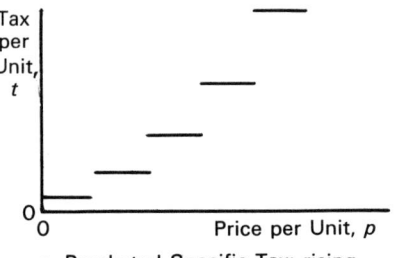
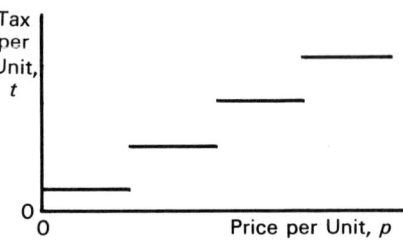

CHART 2.
Bracketed specific tax schedules.

some predetermined level, c. As before, several price brackets are possible. With no explicit price brackets, the tax formula is

$$t = r(p-c) \tag{4}$$

There are two variants of this tax, depending upon the result when the price is smaller than the constant, c. One possibility (4a), exemplified by the tax in New York City on motion picture theater admissions, is to give the tax function the value of zero whenever p is equal to or less than c. The other possibility (4b) is to award a bounty of amount $r(p-c)$ whenever the price is less than the constant c. Both variants of this tax are shown in Chart 3.

Power tax. There is a very general tax formula that, by the proper selection of parameters, can be used to generate a wide variety of excise tax schedules:

$$t = kp^n \tag{5}$$

With n equal to unity, tax (5) is equivalent to the usual ad valorem tax. With n equal to zero, it is a specific tax of amount k per unit.

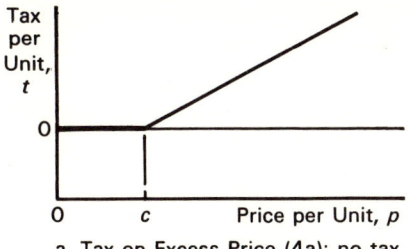
a. Tax on Excess Price (4a): no tax unless price exceeds c.

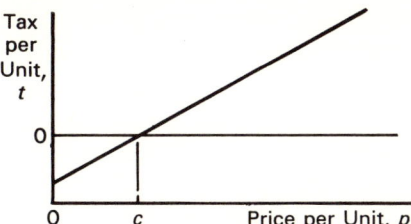
b. Tax on Excess Price (4b): bounty paid if price is less than c.

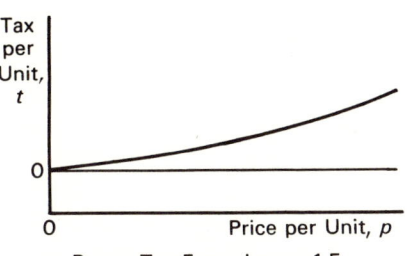
c. Power Tax Formula: $n = 1.5$.

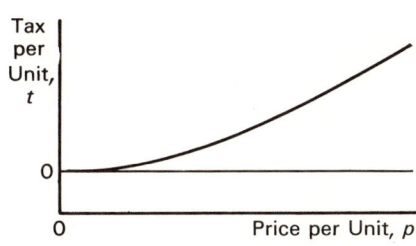
d. Power Tax Formula: $n = 2$.

CHART 3.
Continuously graduated excise taxes.

Values of k and n can be chosen to approximate a wide variety of tax schedules. Chart 3 illustrates two forms of this tax.

B. *Characteristics of Excise Tax Functions*

Tax functions have several mathematical characteristics that are pertinent to the following chapters. Two of these characteristics are used to define *progression* in an excise tax.

1. A per unit tax function may be either continuous or discontinuous. In general, continuity exists when there are no "jumps" in the function. Taxes (2) and (3) are discontinuous at the prices at the ends of the price brackets. The amount of tax per unit increases substantially when the price rises infinitesimally above p^*, p^{**}, etc. Taxes (4b) and (5) are continuous at all prices.

2. A continuous tax function may also be either smooth or kinked. A kink is a sudden change in the direction of the tangent to the function. For example, the tangent to tax function (4a) is horizontal at prices equal to or less than c (see Chart 3); at any price above c, the tangent takes the value of r. The smoothness of a tax function is

related to the concept of the derivative. If the first derivative exists at all non-negative prices, the tax curve is smooth; if at some price or prices the first derivative of the tax function does not exist, the curve will show a kink.[5] The first derivative of tax function (4a) is not defined when price is equal to c. The limit, as Δp approaches zero, of the ratio

$$\frac{t(c+\Delta p)-t(c)}{\Delta p}$$

does not exist; for if Δp is positive, the ratio is equal to r, and if Δp is negative, the ratio is equal to zero. If a tax function is both continuous and "smooth," the effects of the tax on price and product quality can be studied by the methods of the differential calculus; if the function is discontinuous, or if the first derivative does not exist at all non-negative prices, less familiar methods must be used.

At the extreme of logical nicety, all excise tax functions are bracketed and thus discontinuous. If the tax is levied on the "transaction," no matter how many units are sold at one time to one buyer, the tax liability is not expressed in units smaller than the cent. Thus even a mathematically continuous per unit tax becomes, in actual effect, a bracketed tax where the implicit brackets are determined by the range of price that would increase the tax liability by one cent.

Just as demand functions are sometimes assumed to be continuous for the purpose of facilitating the analysis of characteristics of demand that are believed to be important, the emphasis here will sometimes be placed on the continuous tax formula which in practice leads to a discontinuous tax schedule.

On occasion, however, the express or implied discontinuities in a tax schedule may be of sufficient magnitude to warrant specific study. Indeed, it is possible for an ideally continuous tax to have one theoretical effect on, say, price, while the schedule used to simplify the administration of the tax may include discontinuities that have the opposite effect.

3. Reference has already been made to the "average rate of tax." In all except ad valorem taxes, the average rate varies from one price to another. Graphically, the average rate is shown by the slope of the line drawn from the origin of the graph to the tax function at that

---

[5]For a detailed discussion of continuity and smoothness, see R. G. D. Allen, *Mathematical Analysis for Economists* (London, 1953), pp. 98–100, 147.

Excise Tax Functions and Their Characteristics

price. Tax (2), as represented in Chart 1, panel c, shows an increasing average rate from one price bracket to another but a constant average rate within any one price bracket. Tax (3), Chart 2, panel d, shows a roughly constant average rate from one bracket to a higher one but a decreasing average rate within any one price bracket. As indicated in Chart 3, taxes (4) and (5) can be devised to have increasing average rates as price increases. Analytically, the average rate of tax is the ratio of the amount of tax per unit at any price to that same price:

$$\frac{t(p)}{p}$$

The average rate of tax (4b) is given by

$$\frac{r(p-c)}{p} \quad \text{or} \quad r(1-c/p)$$

Thus variations in price cause variations in the average rate of tax. If c is negative, increases in price reduce the average rate; if c is positive, increases in price raise the average rate.

Similarly, the average rate of tax (5) is given by

$$\frac{kp^n}{p} = kp^{n-1}$$

If n has any value except unity, the price determines the average rate. As already noted, the only tax that does *not* show variation in the average rate is the usual ad valorem tax. The average rate of tax is equal to the constant r (Chart 1, panel a).

4. One last characteristic of an excise tax function, which will serve to classify continuous and smooth excise taxes according to their effect on monopoly price, is the elasticity of the per unit tax with respect to price. This elasticity is analogous to the usual elasticity of demand with respect to price. For any given tax function, the elasticity measures the limit of the ratio of the proportionate increase in tax per unit to a proportionate increase in price. Algebraically, the elasticity is

$$\frac{dt/t}{dp/p} \quad \text{or} \quad \frac{pt'(p)}{t(p)} \tag{6}$$

where $t'(p)$ is the first derivative of the tax function with respect to price, or the marginal rate of per unit tax. Thus the elasticity is defined only for prices at which the first derivative is defined.

Expression (6) can be rewritten by dividing both the numerator and the denominator by p:

$$E_t(p) = \frac{t'(p)}{t(p)/p}$$

and the per unit tax elasticity is seen to be simply the ratio of the marginal per unit tax to the average per unit tax.[6]

The ad valorem tax

$$t = rp$$

has an elasticity

$$\frac{pr}{rp} \quad \text{or} \quad \text{unity}$$

An x per cent increase in price raises the tax per unit by x per cent.

The elasticity of the bracketed tax (2) is defined only within the price brackets, where, like that of the ad valorem tax, it is unity.

The elasticity of the bracketed specific tax (3) is zero within the price brackets and is not defined otherwise.

The elasticities of taxes (4a) and (4b) are the same at all prices higher than the constant c and are equal to

$$\frac{pr}{r(p-c)} \quad \text{or} \quad \frac{p}{p-c}$$

If c is positive, the elasticity is greater than unity; if c is negative, the elasticity is less than unity. If the elasticity is greater than unity, a small, y per cent increase in price will increase the per unit tax by more than y per cent, and vice versa.

The tax formula

$$t = kp^n$$

---

[6]The concept of the elasticity of a function has had a long and fruitful history of application in many sciences. Introduced into economics as the elasticity of demand with respect to price by A. Marshall in the late nineteenth century [*Principles of Economics* (8th ed.; New York, 1949), pp. 102, 839–40], the concept has since proven to be a useful characteristic of many economic functions. Yet no suggestion that the elasticity of a per unit tax function has any significance has been discovered in the literature of economics.

where k and n are positive constants, has elasticity

$$\frac{p \cdot nkp^{n-1}}{kp^n} \quad \text{or} \quad n$$

It may be noted that there is no invariable relation between the average rate of tax and the elasticity. It is possible, by adjusting the parameters in the tax function, to design a "heavy" tax with a low elasticity or a "light" tax with a high elasticity.

C. Progression in Excise Tax Functions

1. If an excise tax function is both continuous and smooth, progression is defined in terms of the elasticity of the per unit tax with respect to price. If the elasticity is greater than unity over some range of price, the tax is progressive. If the elasticity equals unity, the tax must be a straight ad valorem tax, which is proportional. If the elasticity is less than unity, the tax is regressive. The specific tax has an elasticity of zero and is regressive.

The importance of the elasticity of the per unit tax can be indicated as follows (proofs will be given in Chapter 4).

> *a.* If a good sold under conditions of monopoly is subject to an excise tax, and if the elasticity of the per unit tax is greater than the elasticity of demand at the pre-tax price, the price will fall, even though the seller must still pay the tax.[7]
> *b.* If the elasticity of the tax is equal to the elasticity of demand, the price will not change as a result of the tax.
> *c.* If the elasticity of the tax is smaller than the elasticity of demand, the price will rise.

The selection of unitary elasticity of the per unit tax function as the dividing line between progressive and regressive excise taxes thus has practical significance. Under conditions of maximum monopoly profit, given that the elasticity of demand is always equal to or larger than unity, a progressive excise tax *may* lower price, a proportional tax *cannot* lower price, and a regressive tax *must* raise price.

---

[7]Note that for the purpose of simplifying the exposition, the elasticity of demand, which has the same sign as the slope (negative) of the demand function, has been defined as $-E_x(p)$ to change it to a positive number. In the analysis, $E_x(p)$ is, of course, a negative quantity.

2. Unfortunately, elasticity cannot always be used to characterize an excise tax. Where price brackets are stated, or where discontinuities exist, the first derivative of the per unit tax is not defined at some prices. At these prices the elasticity of the tax also is not defined.

An alternative criterion of progression is thus required for discontinuous taxes. The following will be adopted, again because it serves to classify taxes by their possible effects on monopoly price: if an increase in price, over any range of prices, leads to an increase in the average rate of tax, the tax is progressive over that range. By this definition both the graduated ad valorem tax (2) and the graduated specific taxes (3) can be devised to be progressive at some prices.

The effect of a discontinuous tax on monopoly price is more difficult to specify than that of a continuous tax. It depends upon conditions not only *at* the pre-tax equilibrium position but also over a range of positions where they may differ markedly from those at the pre-tax position. Furthermore, the effect will differ according to the form of the tax function within the price brackets and to the level of the per unit tax. In Chapter 7 it will be shown that, if a discontinuous tax is progressive at any price or prices, the tax *may* reduce monopoly price.

3. The above definitions of progression in an excise tax function are based solely on the tax function itself. A progressive tax remains progressive regardless of other circumstances. However, the direction of the price effect of an excise tax depends not only upon the tax but also on demand and cost conditions. In addition, it will be recalled that the per unit tax function (1) does not specify the total liability of the taxpayer unless the corresponding demand function is known.

The characteristics of the demand and per unit tax functions can be integrated into a more comprehensive concept of progression that describes the relationship between price and the total tax liability.[8] The total tax bill, T, per time period is the product of the per unit tax function (1) and the demand function that relates sales per time period to price:

---

[8] This approach to progression of an excise tax was suggested by Professor C. S. Shoup when an earlier version of this study was presented to a Public Finance Seminar at Columbia University.

Excise Tax Functions and Their Characteristics

$$T = t(p) \cdot x(p) \tag{7}$$

Allen has shown that the elasticity of the product of two functions is the sum of the elasticities of the two functions.[9] Thus the elasticity of the total tax bill is equal to the sum of the elasticity of the per unit tax and the (negative) elasticity of demand, both with respect to price. The statements made in the second paragraph of Section C-1 rely on comparisons of these two elasticities. The equivalent statements based on the elasticity of the tax bill are as follows.

  a. If a good sold under conditions of monopoly is subject to an excise tax, and if the elasticity of the total tax bill is positive, the price will fall.
  b. If the elasticity of the tax bill is zero, the price will not change.
  c. If the elasticity of the tax bill is negative, the price will rise.

Thus the two concepts of progression can be used interchangeably as long as it is recognized that the elasticity of the per unit tax is independent of demand, whereas the elasticity of the tax bill takes demand conditions into account.

[9]For continuous and smooth tax functions, the elasticity of the total tax bill with respect to price is derived as follows. The absolute amount of change in the tax bill per unit change in price is the first derivative of (7) or

$$T' = t'(p) \cdot x(p) + t(p) \cdot x'(p) \tag{8}$$

The relative amount of change in the tax bill per unit change in price is the ratio of (8) to the tax bill itself, or

$$\frac{T'}{T} = \frac{t'(p) \cdot x(p) + t(p) \cdot x'(p)}{t(p) \cdot x(p)}$$

This reduces to

$$\frac{T'}{T} = \frac{t'(p)}{t(p)} + \frac{x'(p)}{x(p)} \tag{9}$$

The absolute amount of change in price is 1 unit. The relative amount of change in price is

$$1/p. \tag{10}$$

The elasticity of the tax bill is the ratio of (9) to (10), or simply (9) multiplied by p:

$$E_T(p) = \frac{p \cdot t'(p)}{t(p)} + \frac{p \cdot x'(p)}{x(p)} \tag{11}$$

Expression (11) is the sum of the elasticity of the tax function and the (negative) elasticity of demand. If the elasticity of the tax bill is positive, an increase in price increases the per unit tax relatively more than the number of units sold decreases and the tax bill accordingly increases. If the elasticity of the tax bill is negative, an increase in price increases the per unit tax relatively less than the number of units sold sold decreases and the tax bill declines.

See Allen, *Mathematical Analysis*, pp. 252-53.

D. *Some Definitions*

In order to lessen the possibility of confusion among different meanings for common terms, some of the definitions used in this study will now be given.

GRADUATED TAX

An excise tax function so devised that, for some changes in price, the average tax per unit, $t(p)/p$, changes. The only tax that is not graduated in this sense is the ad valorem tax.

BRACKETED TAX

An excise tax function such that different tax formulae apply to each of two or more price ranges (brackets).

PROGRESSIVE TAX

A graduated tax such that an increase in price raises the average rate of tax. Thus the marginal tax must exceed the average rate (if the average is rising) and the tax elasticity must exceed unity.

REGRESSIVE TAX

A graduated tax such that an increase in price *reduces* the average rate of tax. The tax elasticity is less than unity.

HIGHLY REGRESSIVE TAX

A graduated tax such that a price increase reduces not only the average rate of tax but also the per unit tax.

Part II. *Effects of Excise Taxes on Price and Output*

In Part II the adjustments that a firm must make to maximize profit after an excise tax is levied are derived, in relation to the form of the tax and to the external conditions faced by the firm. The possibility that the optimum adjustment to a tax may include changes in factors other than price and output is postponed to Parts III and IV.

Several different types of excise taxes, including bounties, are examined. The possible structure of the market in which the firm is assumed to operate includes pure monopoly (and monopsony), monopolistic competition, oligopoly, and pure competition.

Chapter 3. *Pre-tax Equilibrium: Monopoly*

In this chapter the traditional theory of monopoly price, on which much of the subsequent analysis rests, is briefly reviewed. Then there is a short discussion of the best way to introduce an excise tax into the structure of this theory, followed by some comments on the generality of the assumptions that are either dictated by the chosen scope of the study or made necessary by our lack of perfect knowledge of various economic relations.

A. *Theory of Monopoly Price*

1. The study of the effects of excise taxes on commodity prices cannot begin without a specific theory of price determination. Such a theory should include both a description of the circumstances under which price is determinate and a statement of the conditions that determine price. It must be possible also to derive from the theory the effects on price of changes in these conditions. The imposition of a tax or a change in the structure of a tax formula modifies the price-determining conditions and therefore generally leads to a change in price. This resulting price change can be studied within the framework of the underlying price theory.

Although the last word of the theory of price has not yet been written, the theory based on the assumption of long-run profit maximization has proven far more satisfactory than any other in terms of the variety, generality, and accuracy of the conclusions that can be derived from it. The implications of the profit maximization assumption can be readily derived by means of the differential calculus.

As an illustration of the basic structure of the theory, a firm producing and selling a single product in a single market will be considered. The many different forces that are believed to bear upon price and output can be classified into two groups: (1) those influencing the amount of product that would be purchased per time period at each price; and (2) those influencing the costs of producing and selling each amount of product.

The first set of forces is understood to determine a demand schedule facing the firm. This demand schedule is often expressed as a general function in either of two forms: (*a*) with price as the dependent variable,

$$p = p(x)$$

or, with amount purchased per time period as the dependent variable,

$$x = x(p)$$

The choice of expression is largely dictated by convenience. In order that the firm have monopoly power, it is assumed that the product has no "close" substitutes; thus the demand function is downward sloping, that is, the higher the price, the less product will be sold, and vice versa.

The second set of forces determine the cost function,

$$c = c(x)$$

or if the analysis is to be performed with price as the independent variable,

$$c = c[x(p)]$$

Both the demand and the cost functions are considered to be continuous and smooth. The slight loss of realism incurred is recovered several times over by the analytical advantages gained.

The total profit of the firm per time period (π) will then be the difference between the gross income from sales and the gross amount of costs, or (taking sales as the independent variable),

$$\pi = x \cdot p(x) - c(x) \tag{12}$$

For this total profit function to be maximized, three conditions must be satisfied:

Pre-tax Equilibrium: Monopoly

1. The first derivative of the function must be equal to zero.
2. The second derivative of the function must be negative.[1]
3. As the first two conditions may be satisfied at several levels of sales, particularly when the demand or cost functions have some irregular form, there must be a single level of sales that provides profit as great as at any other level of sales, or greater.

The first derivative of the profit function is

$$\pi' = x \cdot p'(x) + p(x) - c'(x) \tag{13}$$

The first two terms on the right side represent the "marginal revenue," that is, the hypothetical addition to total sales revenue that would have occurred if sales per time period had been slightly larger. It will be noted that, since the slope of the demand function, $p'(x)$, is negative, the marginal revenue from an increase of sales is always less than the price per unit, $p(x)$. This is so because, in order to increase sales slightly, the price of all units must be decreased somewhat. As long as the decrease in revenue over all units sold is less than the revenue from increased sales, marginal revenue will be positive. Marginal revenue may also be negative with respect to output but not at a level of sales that maximizes profit.

The last term on the right of expression (13) represents marginal cost in the conventional sense. This is the addition to total cost that would have been incurred if production and sales per time period had been increased slightly. Marginal cost is always positive although it is sometimes assumed to be zero in order to show the effect on price of "very small" marginal costs, or just to simplify the analysis.

To satisfy condition 1, (13) is set equal to zero:

$$\pi' = x \cdot p'(x) + p(x) - c'(x) = 0$$

or $\tag{14}$

$$x \cdot p'(x) + p(x) = c'(x)$$

Thus, for profit to be a maximum, marginal revenue must be equal to marginal cost. For if marginal revenue is greater than marginal cost at some level of sales, increasing sales will add more to gross revenue than to gross outlay and profit will be increased. If marginal revenue is less than marginal cost, decreasing sales will reduce

---
[1] Allen, *Mathematical Analysis*, pp. 196 ff.

gross revenue by less than the reduction in gross costs, again increasing profits. Since marginal cost is always positive, marginal revenue at the profit-maximizing output will also always be positive. It will be seen from (14) that the production and selling costs that do not vary with output have no influence upon the optimum output or price, and changes in these costs would not change either the optimum output or the optimum price.

To satisfy condition 2 for a maximum, the second derivative of the profit function must be negative:

$$\pi'' = x \cdot p''(x) + 2p'(x) - c''(x) < 0$$

or

$$x \cdot p''(x) + 2p'(x) < c''(x) \tag{15}$$

The left side of the inequality (15) represents the "slope" of the marginal revenue function, and the right side represents the slope of the marginal cost function. Whereas the marginal cost function may be horizontal or sloping upward or downward, the marginal revenue function usually slopes downward. Expression (15) indicates that, for profit to be a maximum, the slope of the marginal cost function must be algebraically greater than the slope of the marginal revenue function. Or, as larger outputs are considered, the marginal revenue curve must intersect the marginal cost curve from above. Therefore, at equilibrium, as shown on Charts 4a and 4b, regardless of the slope of the marginal cost curve, a change in

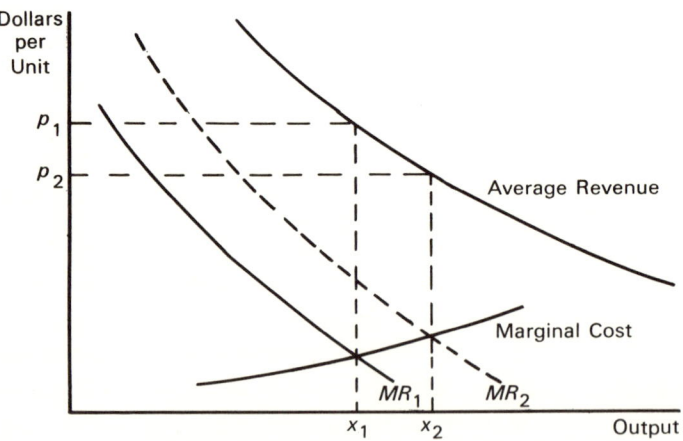

CHART 4a.
Effect on output and price, increase in marginal revenue.

Pre-tax Equilibrium: Monopoly

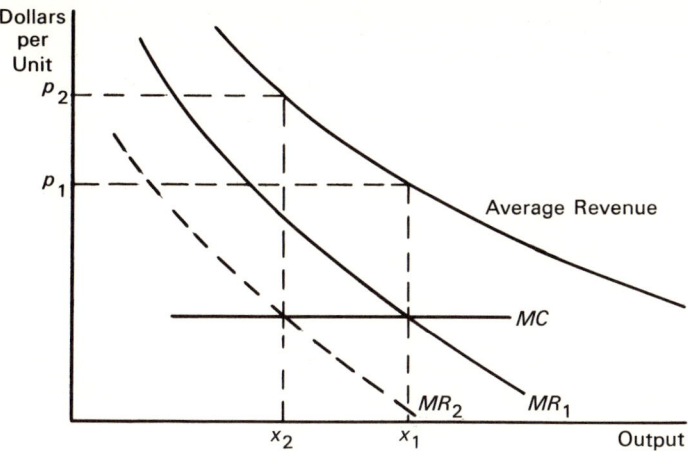

CHART 4b.
Effect on output and price, decrease in marginal revenue.

any factor that leads to a rise in the marginal revenue function must increase the optimum output (and reduce the optimum price), and, conversely, any change that lowers the marginal revenue function must reduce the optimum output (and increase the optimum price).[2]

When conditions 1 and 2 are met, profits are maximized for variations in output in the neighborhood of the optimum output.

Condition 3, which assures that the largest of several maximum profit positions is achieved, is not so easy to satisfy. It is usually met by slightly restricting the form of the demand and cost functions. The demand function is assumed to be of "normal" form, implying not only that its slope is negative, but also that the elasticity of demand varies smoothly from a value of $-\infty$ at an output of zero toward a value of zero as output increases.[3] This assumption assures that the gross revenue curve will increase smoothly to a maximum and then, at higher outputs, decline. The restriction on the shape of the total cost curve is based on grounds of simplicity. With constant returns to scale, the total cost curve is a straight line. With increasing or decreasing returns to scale, it seems unreasonable to suppose that if, say, increasing returns are observed over one range

---

[2] As long as the marginal cost curve is not vertical, as it would be if the producer had encountered an absolute limitation to *any* expansion of output.

[3] Allen, *Mathematical Analysis*, p. 258.

of outputs, at a higher range decreasing returns suddenly set in, only to be followed by increasing returns at still higher outputs. As long as the demand and cost functions are not highly irregular in form, there will be only one output at which the first and second conditions for a maximum obtain.

2. As an example, specific functions have been chosen to represent the demand and cost schedules. Let the total cost function be

$$c = \$1x + \$0.01x^2 \tag{16}$$

where c represents the total cost of production and sales per day, and x the volume of production and sales per day. Let the demand function be

$$p = \$7 - \$0.005x \tag{17}$$

where p represents the price per unit to the buyer. Condition 1 for maximum profits will be satisfied if the equality shown in (14) holds, that is, if marginal revenue equals marginal cost. The *total revenue* from sales is given by the volume of sales per day, x, multiplied by (17), or

$$\$7x - \$0.005x^2 \tag{18}$$

The marginal revenue function is, then, the first derivative of (18) with respect to x, or

$$\$7 - \$0.01x \tag{19}$$

The marginal cost function is simply the first derivative of the total cost function, (16), or

$$\$1.00 + \$0.02x \tag{20}$$

Both the marginal revenue (19) and marginal cost (20) functions are graphed in Chart 5a. If these two expressions are set equal to each other and solved for x, there is a unique solution (meeting condition 3); $x = 200$ units per day. This solution is also shown on the graph. In order that 200 units per day may maximize rather than minimize profits, condition 2 must also be satisfied; that is, the slope of the marginal revenue function, at an output of 200 units, must be less than the slope of the marginal cost function at that output. The slope of the marginal revenue function, the first derivative of (19),

Pre-tax Equilibrium: Monopoly

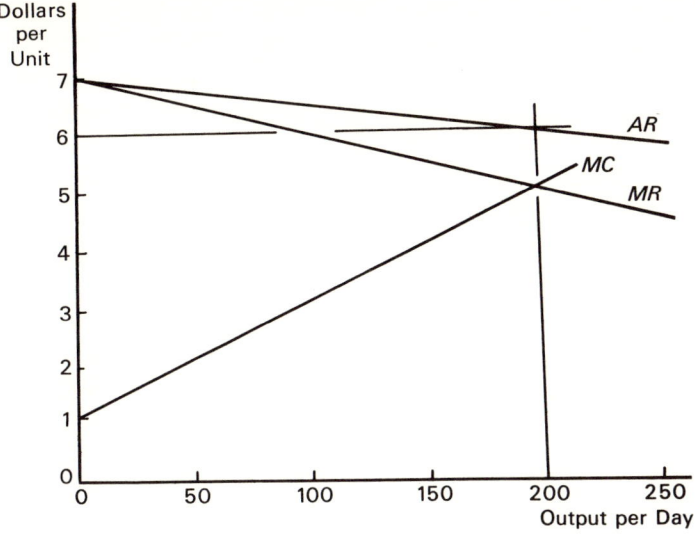

CHART 5a.
Average revenue, marginal revenue, marginal cost, and optimum output and price.

equals −$0·01; while the slope of the marginal cost function, the first derivative of (20), equals +$0·02. Thus the marginal revenue curve intersects the marginal cost curve from above, and profits are maximized at an output of 200 units per day. The optimum price is obtained from the demand function, also shown in Chart 5a, and is $6 per unit.

In Chart 5b the total revenue and total cost curves are shown. The difference between the two curves represents profit, which is seen to be as large as possible at the same output, 200 units. At this output, daily revenue is $1200 and daily costs are $600. The resulting profit, $600, cannot be exceeded at any other output.

3. It should be noted that, although there may be only a single output that produces the maximum profit, a substantial range of outputs may produce very nearly the maximum profit. When the three conditions for a single maximum are met, the profit curve is very nearly "flat" in the neighborhood of the maximum. A slight change in output from the optimum value will reduce profit by an imperceptible amount. Table 1 shows the price, total revenue, total cost, and profit associated with several different output levels.

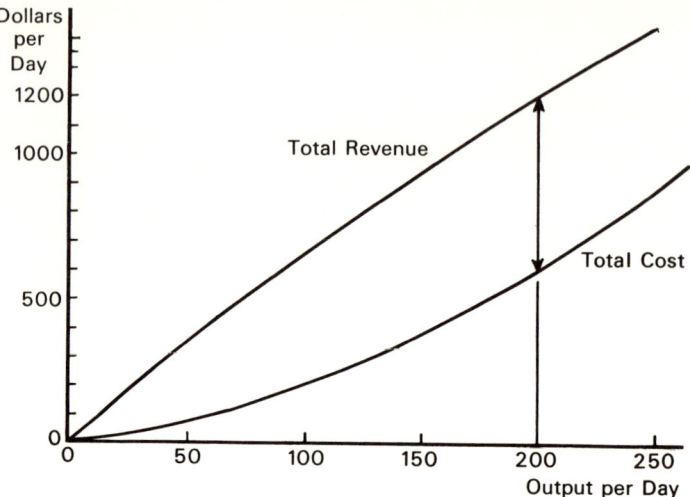

CHART 5b.
Total revenue, total cost, and optimum output.

TABLE 1. *Profit at Different Levels of Output*

Output	Price	Total Revenue	Total Costs	Profit
150	$6.250	$ 937.500	$375.000	$562.500
...				
190	6.050	1149.500	551.000	598.500
...				
198	6.010	1189.980	590.040	599.940
199	6.005	1194.995	595.010	599.985
200	6.000	1200.000	600.000	600.000
201	5.995	1204.995	605.010	599.985
202	5.990	1209.980	610.040	599.940
...				
210	5.950	1240.500	651.000	598.500
...				
250	5.750	1437.500	875.000	562.500

It will be seen that within an output range of 190 to 210, that is, an output deviation from optimum of 5%, the variation in profit is extremely small, being only ¼%. Smaller output deviations result in very much smaller profit variation. Large changes in output will, of course, cause profit to fall noticeably. It is clear that a similar argument applies to changes in price.

Pre-tax Equilibrium: Monopoly

The flatness of the profit function near the optimum output and price serves as the basis for conclusions about the direction of output or price change caused by an excise tax. Suppose a specific tax of $1.00 per unit to be levied. If the firm retains the 200 unit output level, profit will be $600.00 less the $200.00 tax bill. If the firm increases output to 201 units, not only will before-tax profit be reduced, although very slightly (by $0.015), but also the tax bill will increase by $1.00, further reducing profit. But if output is reduced to 199 units, before-tax profit is reduced again by only $0.015 whereas the tax bill is reduced by $1.00, for a net increase in after-tax profit of $0.985. Further reductions in output (and increases in price) are in order as long as the reduction in the tax bill exceeds the reduction in before-tax profit. How far output should be reduced generally to maximize after-tax profit is a more difficult question to answer.

The same effect may be paraphrased as follows. Slight reductions in output produce insignificant reductions in before-tax profit but significantly lower the tax bill. Therefore output restriction will increase after-tax profit.

In still other words, the before-tax profit function is "flat" near the optimum output or price; however, the total tax function for this type of tax is not flat—it has a definite slope. Changing output in the direction of a lower tax bill must, up to a point, increase after-tax profits. Chart 6 shows, for the demand and cost functions treated above and for a specific tax of $1.00 per unit, the before-tax profit function, the total tax bill (as a function of output), and the after-tax profit function. It will be seen that the after-tax function is maximized at a lower output (and higher price) than the before-tax function.

The same type of argument will be used in this book on several occasions. It applies not only to the effects of various kinds of excise taxes on the price of the product but also to some aspects of their effects on product quality and selling effort.

B. *Theoretical Treatment of Excise Taxes*

The method by which the tax is introduced into the framework of price theory would appear to be a matter of indifference. A symbol for the per unit tax or for the total tax bill can be added to the total profit function (*12*). The per unit tax can be considered as a

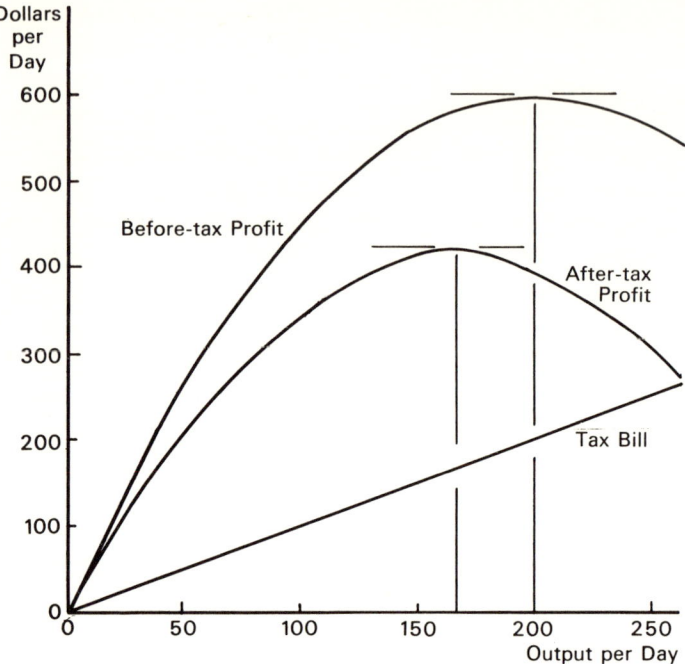

CHART 6.
Before- and after-tax profit and total tax bill, specific tax of $1 per unit.

deduction from the price,[4] or it can be treated as an addition to cost and, if appropriate, to marginal cost. The traditional practice has been to regard a specific tax as an addition to cost,[5] and an ad valorem tax as a deduction from revenue. This procedure made it extremely difficult to answer a question concerning tax incidence that arose in the United States during the 1930's, namely, under monopoly which tax will produce the greater increase in price, the specific or the ad valorem tax?[6] Some procedural roadblocks are averted if all excise taxes are treated as reducing the revenue of the

[4]It will be recalled that the price variable is defined to include any excise taxes.
[5]This practice is an old one, going back at least to the time of Cournot, who first studied the effect on monopoly price of an increase in marginal cost, and then considered the imposition of a specific tax as one example of a cost increase [*Principes Mathematiques,* Sections 31, 36, and 37].
[6]The problem was neatly disposed of in a manner similar to that suggested in the text by R. Musgrave and D. B. Suits, "Ad Valorem and Unit Taxes Compared," *Quarterly Journal of Economics,* LXVII, 589-604. See, also, R. Musgrave, *The Theory of Public Finance,* (New York, 1959), pp. 304-6.

Pre-tax Equilibrium: Monopoly

firm. Then, before- and after-tax conditions or the effects of two different types of taxes may be readily compared without any immediate concern over costs. In much of the discussion that follows, the influence of excise taxes on price will be examined through their effects on the marginal revenue function. As noted in Chart 4, as long as conditions 2 and 3 for profit maximization are satisfied, any change (including a tax) that raises the marginal revenue curve with respect to output will lead to a higher output and a lower price.

Taxes that are not based on actual output or the actual transaction price cannot readily be analyzed within the framework of traditional price theory and hence are not considered in this study.

Chapter 4. *After-tax Equilibrium: General Statement*

In the subsequent chapters in Part II, several different forms of excise taxes and their effects on price and output are treated. In this chapter, some results are obtained for *any* form of excise tax, as long as the per unit tax is a function of price only, in a single-price market. The characteristics of the per unit tax function that determine the direction of price change from the tax are derived in Section A; some of the factors that influence the amount of price change are examined in Section B.

A. *Direction of Price Change*

If an excise tax is considered as a deduction from revenue, it has been shown above that the manner in which a tax shifts the marginal revenue function will determine whether the tax increases or lowers price, or leaves price unchanged. More specifically, if marginal revenue *with respect to output* is lowered at the pre-tax output, output will fall and price will rise; if marginal revenue with respect to output is increased, output will rise and price will fall. The tax-induced change in the marginal revenue function will now be shown.

The demand (or average revenue) function is

$$p = p(x)$$

The total revenue function before tax is

$$R = x \cdot p(x) \tag{21}$$

The tax bill is the product of the per unit tax (which is now an implicit function of output)

$$t = t[p(x)]$$

and sales, or

$$T = x \cdot t[p(x)]$$

The total revenue function net of tax is then

$$R_t = x \cdot p(x) - x \cdot t[p(x)] \qquad (22)$$

The before-tax marginal revenue function is the first derivative of (21), or

$$MR = x \cdot p'(x) + p(x) \qquad (23)$$

The after-tax marginal revenue function is the first derivative of (22):

$$MR_t = x \cdot p'(x) + p(x) - \{xt'[p(x)]p'(x) + t[p(x)]\} \qquad (24)$$

It may be noted that, except for the bracketed portion of (24), expressions (23) and (24) are identical; the bracketed portion represents the first derivative of the tax bill function—that is to say, the marginal tax bill with respect to output. The tax will lower marginal revenue at any output if the marginal tax bill is positive at that output, will leave marginal revenue unchanged if the marginal tax bill is zero, and will raise marginal revenue if the marginal tax bill is negative.

Some albegraic manipulation of the bracketed portion of (24) will be revealing. If this portion is both multiplied and divided by $x \cdot t[p(x)]$, the result is

$$x \cdot t[p(x)] \left\{ \frac{x \cdot t'[p(x)]p'(x)}{x \cdot t[p(x)]} + \frac{t[p(x)]}{x \cdot t[p(x)]} \right\}$$

or

$$x \cdot t[p(x)] \left\{ \frac{t'[p(x)]p'(x)}{t[p(x)]} + \frac{1}{x} \right\}$$

If multiplication and division by $p'(x)$ is performed,

$$x \cdot t[p(x)]p'(x) \left\{ \frac{t'[p(x)]p'(x)}{t[p(x)]p'(x)} + \frac{1}{x \cdot p'(x)} \right\}$$

or

$$x \cdot p'(x)t[p(x)] \left\{ \frac{t'[p(x)]}{t[p(x)]} + \frac{1}{x \cdot p'(x)} \right\} \qquad (25)$$

After-tax Equilibrium: General Statement

The last step is to multiply and divide by $p(x)$:

$$\frac{x \cdot p'(x)t[p(x)]}{p(x)} \left\{ \frac{p(x)t'[p(x)]}{t[p(x)]} + \frac{p(x)}{x \cdot p'(x)} \right\}$$

With output as the independent variable, the price elasticity of demand becomes

$$E_x(p) = \frac{dx}{dp} \cdot \frac{p}{x} = \frac{1}{(dp/dx)(x/p)} = \frac{1}{[x \cdot p'(x)]/p(x)} = \frac{p(x)}{x \cdot p'(x)}$$

The price elasticity of the per unit tax becomes

$$E_t(p) = \frac{dt}{dp} \cdot \frac{p}{t}$$

$$= \frac{dt}{dx} \cdot \frac{dx}{dp} \cdot \frac{p}{t}$$

$$= \frac{dt}{dx} \cdot \frac{1}{dp/dx} \cdot \frac{p}{t}$$

$$= \frac{t'[p(x)]p'(x) \cdot p(x)}{t[p(x)]p'(x)}$$

$$E_t(p) = \frac{t'[p(x)] \cdot p(x)}{t[p(x)]}$$

When the appropriate elasticities are substituted for their equivalents, (25) becomes:

$$\frac{t[p(x)]}{E_x(p)} \left[E_t(p) + E_x(p) \right]$$

or

$$t[p(x)] - t[p(x)] \left[\frac{E_t(p)}{-E_x(p)} \right] \tag{26}$$

Thus the after-tax marginal revenue at any output will fall short of (exceed) the pre-tax marginal revenue by the amount in (26) if that amount is positive (negative); the difference, if any, is equal to (*a*) the per unit tax at that output, less (*b*) the product of the per unit tax and the ratio of the tax and demand elasticities. If the tax elasticity is negative or zero, (26) will be positive and the tax will *lower* the marginal revenue; if the tax elasticity is positive and equals the demand elasticity, (26) will be zero and the marginal revenue is unchanged by the tax; if the tax elasticity exceeds the demand elasticity, the right half of (26) is negative and larger in absolute value than the left half, and (26) is negative, raising the marginal revenue.

The direction of output and price change from a tax depends upon the relative sizes (ratio) of the tax and demand elasticities at the pre-tax price, or output. If the ratio is unity, output and price will not change; if the ratio is less than unity, output will fall and price will rise; if the ratio is greater than unity, output will rise and price will fall.

Chart 7a shows before- and after-tax marginal revenue curves and a marginal cost curve, all drawn to illustrate the effect of an

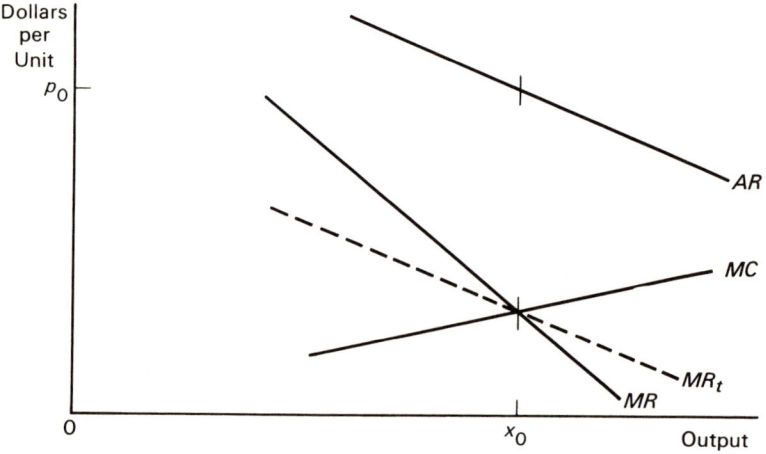

CHART 7a.
Marginal cost and before- and after-tax marginal revenue, tax that does not change price.

excise tax that has an elasticity *equal* to the demand elasticity at x_0. Since the demand elasticity is typically assumed to vary monotonically along the demand function, the before- and after-tax marginal revenue curves will intersect at only one output. The effects of the tax would be exactly the same as those of a net profits tax: the firm would find a certain portion of its income siphoned off as tax revenue but would have no profit incentive to change output or price.

The same situation is depicted in a different form in Chart 7b, showing before- and after-tax profits and the tax bill as a function of output. The tax bill curve is horizontal at output x_0 (i.e., the mar-

After-tax Equilibrium: General Statement

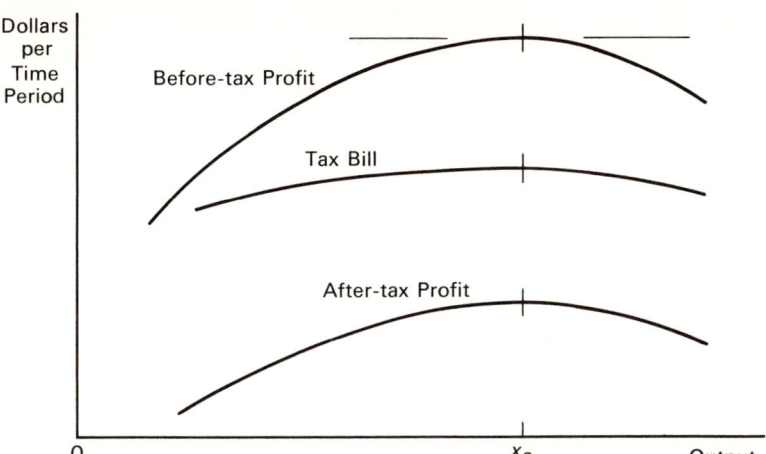

CHART 7b.
Before- and after-tax profit and total tax bill, tax that does not change price.

ginal tax bill is zero), and no change from the pre-tax output can increase after-tax profit. A lump-sum tax function, also being horizontal, would similarly leave output and price unchanged. Such a tax is equivalent, at the pre-tax output, to an excise tax with an elasticity equal to the demand elasticity.

Since under monopoly the elasticity of demand is always positive and larger than unity,[1] the elasticity of the per unit tax function must, if no price or output shift is to occur, also be positive and larger than unity.[2]

---

[1] At the maximum point of a total revenue function the elasticity of demand equals +1. For at that output, very small percentage changes in output are exactly offset by equal (but opposite) percentage changes in price, and total sales revenue is tending not to change. The ratio of these percentages (roughly speaking, the negative of the elasticity of demand) is +1. At lower outputs and higher prices, the total revenue function is rising, indicating that a small increase in output is accompanied by a smaller relative decrease in price, and the elasticity is larger than unity. As still lower outputs are considered, the elasticity increases without limit. Since the total *cost* function cannot have a negative slope, the output that maximizes profit cannot be larger than the output that maximizes total sales revenue. At equilibrium the elasticity of demand must be larger than +1.

[2] If the marginal costs are so low that they may be ignored, the elasticity of demand at the pre-tax price will be +1, and the ordinary ad valorem tax, which has an elasticity of +1, will lead to no change in price. See Cournot, *Principes Mathematiques*, Section 41.

If the elasticities of the per unit tax and demand functions are not equal. (*a*) the slope of the total tax function at the pre-tax output will not be zero; (*b*) the before- and after-tax marginal revenue functions will be raised or lowered at the pre-tax output; and (*c*) price and output will change as a result of the tax (as long as the marginal cost curve is not vertical). Whether the price will rise or fall depends upon the relative values of the tax and demand elasticities.

Chart 8a shows the effect on output and price of a rise or fall in marginal revenue with respect to output. If a tax shifts the marginal revenue curve downward (for example, from MR_1 to MR_2 in the chart), output will fall. The marginal revenue curve will be shifted downward if expression (26) is positive, that is, if the tax elasticity is smaller than the demand elasticity. The marginal revenue and total tax curves designated as 2 in Charts 8a and 8b represent the effects of a graduated tax with an elasticity smaller than the elasticity of demand. Since the elasticity of demand at equilibrium is greater than unity, both the ad valorem and specific taxes, with elasticities of +1 and zero, respectively, will generally lower output and raise price. Furthermore, *any* tax with an elasticity smaller than the demand elasticity will also raise price (a possible exception to this statement will be noted in Chapter 5).[3]

---

[3]That any tax with an elasticity smaller than the demand elasticity would raise price was apparently understood (although not in those terms) by previous writers. Note that, if a tax meets this description, the total tax bill will rise as price falls (and output increases).

After demonstrating that a tax "proportional to the amount produced" (i.e., a specific tax) would increase monopoly price, Marshall makes the comment that the argument does not require any particular form of per unit tax, but requires only that the total tax bill increase as production increases. "In the text it is supposed that the tax... is directly proportional to the sales: but the argument, when closely examined, will be found to involve no further assumption than that the aggregrate tax... increases with every increase in that amount: the argument does not really require that it should increase in exact proportion to that amount" (*Principles of Economics*, p. 483, note).

Edgeworth also shows that a specific tax, u, will raise price and adds, "Analogous propositions may be proved for an *ad valorem* tax which is not regressive by inserting in the expression for the tax [i.e., tax bill], instead of u, x as just now, any function of x [output], (or p) which increases (or diminishes) with the increase (or decrease) of x (*Political Economy*, I, 113). This statement is correct, except that the comma between u and x should be a centered dot to indicate multiplication, and is consistent with the conclusions presented here. For if the tax bill increases as output increases, the total tax function will correspond to total tax 2 in Chart 8b. Edgeworth apparently did not investigate the types of per unit tax function that would lead to price declines.

After-tax Equilibrium: General Statement

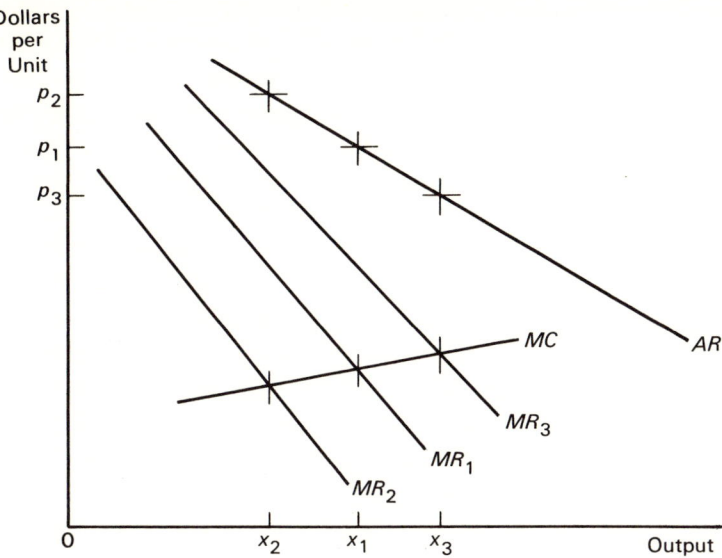

CHART 8a.
Marginal revenue, decreased or increased by an excise tax.

On the other hand, if the tax elasticity exceeds the demand elasticity, the marginal revenue function will be shifted upward; and the price which maximizes after-tax profits will be lower than the pre-tax price. This situation is shown by the marginal revenue and total tax curves labeled 3 in Charts 8a and 8b. Thus many

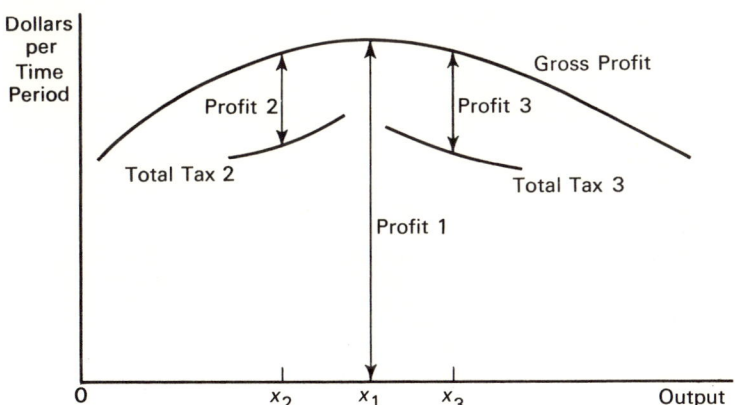

CHART 8b.
Profits before and after taxes that raise or lower price.

excise tax functions can be designed to produce a decline in monopoly price. The only essential feature of such a tax function is that its elasticity be larger than the elasticity of demand.[4]

The profitability of the firm, after any tax is levied, cannot be predicted with certainty unless both demand and cost conditions are known. What has been demonstrated above is that, if the firm is maximizing profit before the tax is levied, there is some after-tax price that will either maximize profits or minimize losses. There is also a possibility that the tax will destroy the conditions for equilibrium and the firm will "minimize" losses by not producing at all.

The commonly accepted belief that all excise taxes worsen the allocation of resources by "driving a wedge" between the real costs of production and the price paid by buyers must then be modified when monopolized goods are taxed. The exercise of monopoly power itself constitutes such a "wedge" and a graduated tax can reduce or even eliminate the discrepancy between costs and prices to the benefit of consumers (both as buyers of the taxed good and as possible recipients of an increased volume of public services) and to the detriment of the monopolist's surplus profit. To the extent that the surplus profit serves no desirable economic functions, a reduction in monopoly price by a graduated excise tax will improve

[4]That an excise tax might reduce monopoly price was briefly noted by Dalton: "There is also a ... possibility, that of a tax whose total amount diminishes as the monopolist's output increases. Such a tax, if its imposition were practicable, would in some cases cause the monopolist to increase his output and lower his price. An example would be a tax whose total amount was proportionate to the price of the commodity per unit, or a lump sum with a rebate proportionate to output." He explains the qualification "in some cases" as follows: "In those cases, namely, in which, as his output increases, his tax payments diminish faster than his monopoly profits, apart from the tax" [*Principals of Public Finance* (3rd ed.; London, 1951), pp. 60–61].

The qualification is unnecessary. If the monopolist was maximizing profits before the tax was imposed, his profits were *not* tending to diminish as output increases (see Chart 8b). If the monopolist was not maximizing profits before the tax, his reaction to the tax is unpredictable.

The first of the examples suggested by Dalton, "a tax whose total amount was proportionate to the price of the commodity per unit," would lower price. For if the tax bill is proportional to price, the total tax function is a straight line through the origin, with a positive slope with respect to price. But the elasticity of a positively sloped linear function that passes through the origin is +1. Since the total tax elasticity equals the sum of the tax and demand elasticities, any per unit tax function whose elasticity exceeds the demand elasticity by unity would satisfy the condition that Dalton specified.

The lump-sum tax with a rebate proportional to output will also lower monopoly price. This tax-bounty combination will be discussed in Chapter 8.

After-tax Equilibrium: General Statement

rather than worsen the allocation of resources to various economic ends.

B. Amount of Price Change

A few remarks on the amount of price change induced by a tax may be in order at this point. Of course, if the demand and cost functions are known, the before- and after-tax prices can be computed and the difference noted. However helpful this procedure may be in specific instances, it seldom affords much insight into the factors that determine the amount of price change.

1. Charts 9a and 9b illustrate the effect of increasing versus decreasing costs on the amount of price change. On both charts MR represents the before-tax marginal revenue curve; MC_1, an increasing marginal cost curve; and MC_2, a decreasing marginal cost curve. The pre-tax price in both cases is p_0.

In Chart 9a, MR_t is the marginal curve resulting from a tax that lower price to p_1 if costs are increasing and further to p_2 if costs are decreasing. Similarly, in Chart 9b, if costs are decreasing, the price change (an increase) is greater than if costs are increasing.

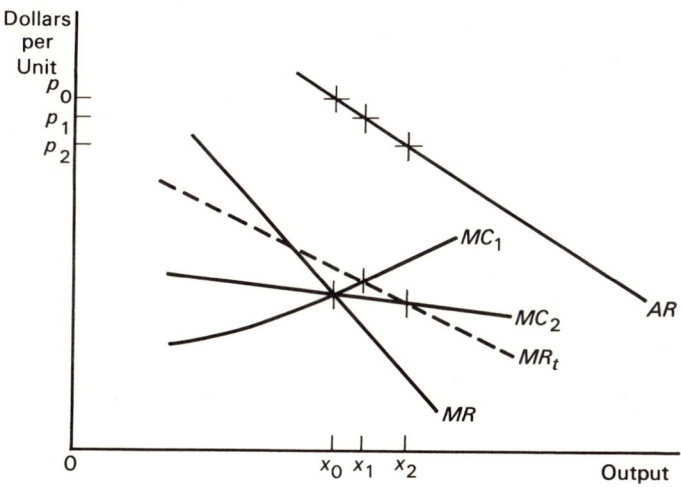

CHART 9a.
Effect of increasing and decreasing costs on amount of price change, a tax that reduces price.

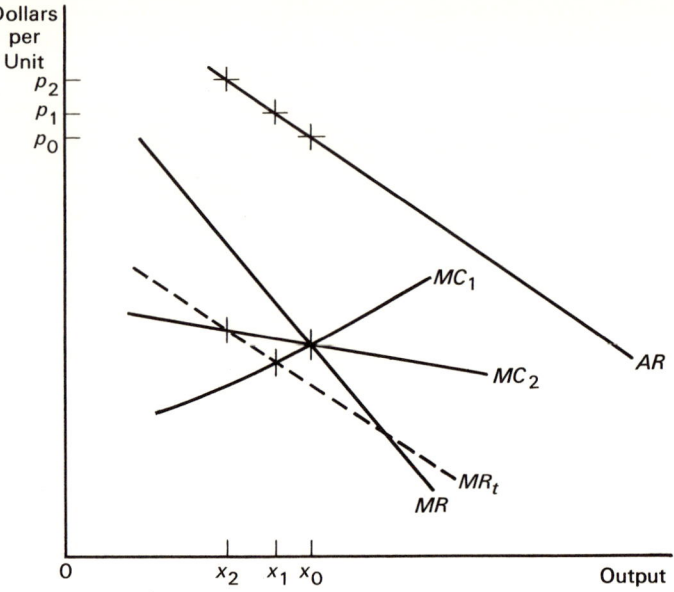

CHART 9b.
Effect of increasing and decreasing costs on amount of price change, a tax that increases price.

The general rule then is that, if costs are increasing at the pre-tax equilibrium, the amount of price change (if any) resulting from a tax will be smaller than if costs are decreasing.[5]

2. To show the effect of the weight or average rate of the tax on the amount of price and output change, the marginal tax bill, given in terms of the tax and demand elasticities in (26), may be rewritten slightly as

$$t[p(x)]\left[1 - \frac{E_t(p)}{-E_x(p)}\right] \tag{27}$$

It will be recalled that this expression is the difference, at any output, between the before- and after-tax marginal revenue functions.

---

[5]With the usual proviso—that the second-order conditions for a maximum continue to be fulfilled.

Edgeworth, in treating the extent of price rise from a specific or an ad valorem tax, states, "Accordingly in the long run the rise of price consequent on any assigned increase in taxation is likely to be greater the smaller c [i.e., the slope of the marginal cost curve] is" (*Political Economy*, II, 167–68).

After-tax Equilibrium: General Statement

First, consider a tax so designed that output rises and price falls. The tax elasticity must be greater than the demand elasticity at the pre-tax output, and (27) will be negative; the tax raises the marginal revenue function (compare MR and MR_t in Chart 10a). If the weight of the tax, $t[p(x)]$ is increased, the marginal revenue curve, $MR_{t'}$, will rise even further, lowering the price from p_1 to p_2. Provided it is possible to increase the tax without changing its elasticity at output x_1, the added decline in price from p_1 to p_2 can be attributed entirely to the increase in the tax.

Similarly, if the tax elasticity is smaller than the elasticity of demand (so that the price will rise), (27) will be positive; the marginal revenue curve is lowered by the tax from MR to MR_t, as in Chart 10b, and the price increases from p_0 to p_1. Increasing the per unit tax again lowers the marginal revenue curve to $MR_{t'}$, increasing the price to p_2.

To show that it is possible to change the per unit tax while holding constant the elasticity of the tax, a comparison of the expressions for the per unit tax and the tax elasticity is made. For all excise tax functions, the per unit tax is given by $t[p]$.

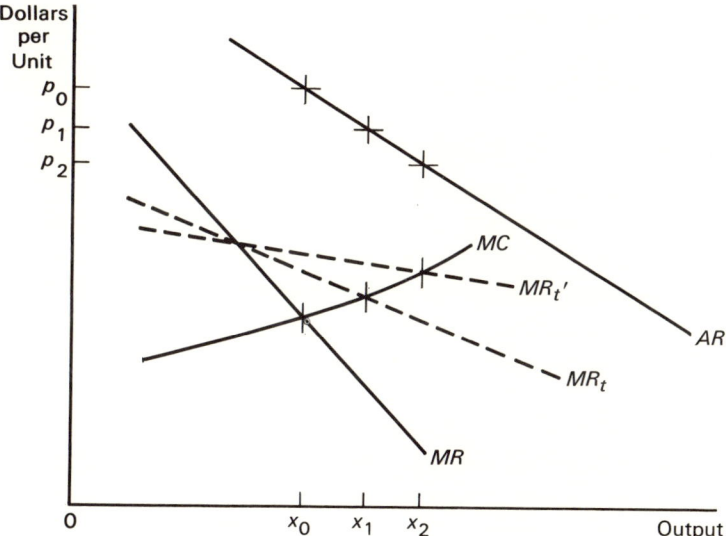

CHART 10a.
Effect of heavier tax rate on amount of price change, a tax that reduces price.

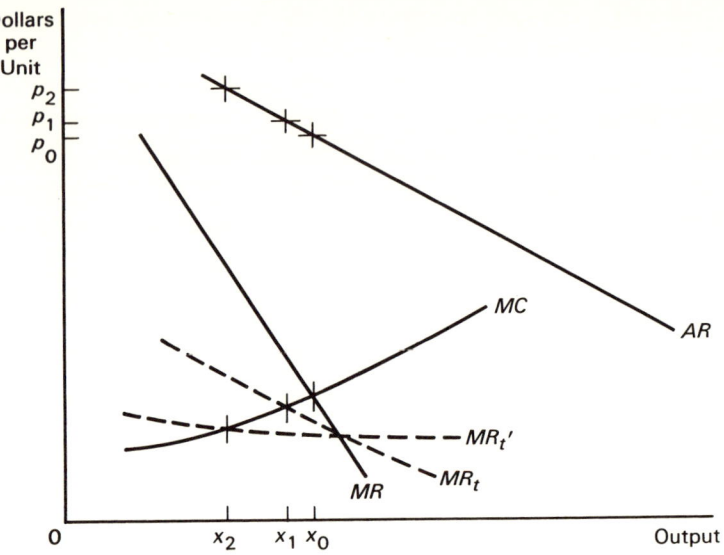

CHART 10b.
Effect of heavier tax rate on amount of price change, a tax that increases price.

The elasticity of the tax is

$$E_t(p) = p\frac{t'(p)}{t(p)} \qquad (6)$$

Any increase in $t(p)$ that also results in an equal, proportionate increase in $t'(p)$ will increase the weight of the tax but will increase the numerator and the denominator of (6) equally and hence leave the tax elasticity unchanged.

The type of change in $t(p)$ that will alter $t'(p)$ in the same proportion is a multiplicative change. If $t(p)$ is multiplied by a factor c, $t'(p)$ will also be multiplied by the same factor, for it is true that[6]

$$t'\{c[t(p)]\} = ct'(p)$$

Therefore, it is always possible to change the per unit tax, while keeping the tax elasticity constant.

It can be concluded that a change which increases the per unit tax without affecting the tax elasticity will increase the amount of

---

[6]Allen, *Mathematical Analysis*, p. 165.

After-tax Equilibrium: General Statement   49

price and output change from the tax, whether the effect of the tax is to increase or to reduce the price.

3. It is far more difficult to make general and useful statements about the effect of the elasticity of the per unit tax function on the amount of price change. It is clear that any increase in the value of $E_t(p)$ in (27) that did not compel changes in any other terms would raise the marginal revenue curve and lead to a lower price. However, continuous tax formulae are such that a change in one parameter to change the elasticity will, *pari passu*, change the per unit tax. If both the tax elasticity and the per unit tax are increased, the marginal revenue curve will rise and the price will fall, but the problem remains of determining which of two taxes, equal at the pre-tax price but with different elasticities, will cause the greater price change. To change the tax elasticity without altering the per unit tax would require that a second parameter in the tax formula also be changed in some specific manner so that the per unit tax (at, say, the pre-tax output) did not change. But the manner in which the two parameters have to be adjusted to achieve the desired change cannot be determined without specifying the form of the tax function.

In any event it appears that the effect of the tax elasticity on the amount of price change is not a simple one. Musgrave and Suits have shown that the price change from a given ad valorem tax may be greater or less than that from a specific tax where both taxes are equal at the pre-tax.[7] Both of these tax functions are special cases of the power tax, with elasticities of 1 and 0 respectively. Thus, increasing the elasticity from 0 to 1 and making a corresponding change in the tax formula to keep the per unit tax the same at the pre-tax price may produce a greater or smaller change in price, depending upon other factors.

4. It is possible, however, to draw more precise conclusions about the effect of the elasticity of an excise tax on the amount of price change, if the basis for comparison of the two taxes is equality, not at the price prevailing before either tax is levied, p_0, but rather at the price after one of the taxes is levied, p_1.[8] After tax 1 is levied, some price, p_1, will prevail which may be different from the pre-tax

---

[7] *Quarterly Journal of Economics*, LXVII, 602.

[8] This comparison is the appropriate one to make when a change in an existing tax is being considered.

price, p_0. Whatever price p_1 may be, it will be possible to change the values of the parameters of tax 1 to yield a second tax function, tax 2, such that

$$t_2(p_1) = t_1(p_1)$$

and that the elasticities of the two taxes are *not* the same. This can always be done by choosing for tax 2 an elasticity different from that of tax 1 and then modifying the per unit tax without changing the elasticity (it was shown on p.   that this second step is possible) until the above equality holds.

To see how the differing elasticity affects price and output, first suppose that tax 2 is more elastic than tax 1, that is,

$$E_{t_2}(p_1) > E_{t_1}(p_1)$$

It is clear from (27) that the marginal revenue function for tax 2 will be higher than that for tax 1, and hence the output after tax 2, x_2, will be greater than x_1. Thus, if tax 1 had lowered price from p_0 to p_1, increasing the elasticity of the tax would, *ceteris paribus*, lower the price further. Or, if tax 1 had increased price, tax 2 would have produced a smaller price increase (or, if the tax elasticity is sufficiently large, a price decrease).

In general, then, if two taxes are equivalent in the sense defined here, the tax with the larger elasticity will produce the smaller price increase or the greater price decline. This effect will be examined in greater detail in the chapters on particular forms of graduated taxes.

Chapter 5. *After-tax Equilibrium: Power Tax Function*

This particular form of excise tax function has been touched upon in several of the preceding sections. The expression for the per unit tax is

$$t(p) = kp^n \tag{5}$$

The parameters n and k determine the tax function, and their values can, if the demand elasticity is known, be selected by the tax authorities according to the effect that is desired.

A. *Limitations on Parameters*

The limitations on these values are not severe. The parameter k can take either positive or negative values; if the latter, the tax becomes a bounty or subsidy. The larger the value of k for any given value of n, the greater is the tax (or bounty) at each price. If the price is quoted in various units, different values of k will be necessary if the effect of the tax is to be the same in each case. The value assigned to n need not be an integer.

The value given to n can also be positive or negative, although a more important distinction is whether the value is greater or less than unity. If n is set equal to or less than one, the tax cannot lower monopoly price. If n exceeds 1, the tax is progressive and may lower monopoly price. If n is less than 1, or even negative, the tax is regressive.

There is also a limit on the combination of values k and n. If the average tax rate, given by

$$kp^{n-1}$$

exceeds 1.00 at the after-tax price, the firm will not only obtain no net revenue from the sale of the product, but will, in addition, have to pay the excess of tax over price. Such a tax would force a single-product firm out of business, although a firm with diversified output might find it profitable to continue production and sale of the taxed product at an apparent loss. There is, of course, no necessary objection to an average rate above 1.00 at the pre-tax price if the tax is designed to lower price.

B. Tax Elasticity

As noted previously, the elasticity of this per unit tax is equal to the parameter n. Thus, for a given value of n, the elasticity remains the same at all prices, regardless of the value assigned to k.

C. Examples

Examples of power tax schedules for various values of n and k are shown in Table 2. These schedules illustrate the wide variety of taxes that may be generated by the power tax formula. In column 1 is shown a specific tax of $0.10 per unit, which results from values of 0 and 0.10 for n and k, respectively. Schedule 3 represents a 10% ad valorem tax. Schedule 2 shows a tax intermediate between the specific and the ad valorem tax; that it is regressive is indicated either by the value of n, which is less than 1, or by the fact that the average rate of tax falls from 10% at a price of $1.00 to 5.8% at a price of $3.00. Schedule 7 is even more regressive than schedule 1; the per unit tax *declines* as the price increases, with the rate falling from 20% at a price of $1.00 to 2.2% at a price of $3.00.

Schedules 4, 5, and 6 are all progressive, the average rate of tax increasing as the price rises. Schedules 4 and 5 differ only in the value of k, and tax schedule 4 is double schedule 5 at all prices. Although schedules 4 and 6 are equal at a price of $1.00, the higher elasticity of schedule 6 means that its average rate increases more rapidly, as price increases, than the average rate of schedule 4.

D. Direction of Price Change

The direction of price change from any tax of this type depends almost entirely upon the value of the parameter n, relative to the elasticity of demand, since n determines the elasticity of the tax function.

After-tax Equilibrium: Power Tax Function

TABLE 2. *Tax Per Unit, at Various Prices, for Different Combinations of n and k: Power Tax*

Price per Unit	(1) n = 0.0 k = 0.10	(2) n = 0.5 k = 0.10	(3) n = 1.0 k = 0.10	(4) n = 2.0 k = 0.10	(5) n = 2.0 k = 0.05	(6) n = 3.0 k = 0.10	(7) n = −1.0 k = 0.20
$1.00	$0.10	$0.100	$0.10	$0.100	$0.050	$0.100	$0.200
1.10	0.10	0.105	0.11	0.121	0.060	0.133	0.182
1.20	0.10	0.110	0.12	0.144	0.072	0.173	0.167
1.30	0.10	0.114	0.13	0.169	0.085	0.220	0.154
1.40	0.10	0.118	0.14	0.196	0.098	0.274	0.143
1.50	0.10	0.122	0.15	0.225	0.112	0.338	0.133
1.60	0.10	0.126	0.16	0.256	0.128	0.410	0.125
1.70	0.10	0.130	0.17	0.289	0.145	0.491	0.118
1.80	0.10	0.134	0.18	0.324	0.162	0.583	0.111
1.90	0.10	0.138	0.19	0.361	0.181	0.686	0.105
2.00	0.10	0.141	0.20	0.400	0.200	0.800	0.100
2.10	0.10	0.145	0.21	0.441	0.220	0.926	0.095
2.20	0.10	0.148	0.22	0.484	0.242	1.065	0.091
2.30	0.10	0.152	0.23	0.529	0.265	1.217	0.087
2.40	0.10	0.155	0.24	0.576	0.288	1.382	0.083
2.50	0.10	0.158	0.25	0.625	0.312	1.563	0.080
2.60	0.10	0.161	0.26	0.676	0.338	1.758	0.077
2.70	0.10	0.164	0.27	0.729	0.364	1.968	0.074
2.80	0.10	0.167	0.28	0.784	0.392	2.195	0.071
2.90	0.10	0.170	0.29	0.841	0.420	2.439	0.069
3.00	0.10	0.173	0.30	0.900	0.450	2.700	0.067

1. Tax elasticity exceeds demand elasticity. Thus, according to the results shown in Chapter 4, if n is greater than the elasticity of demand at the pre-tax price, the price will fall. This conclusion holds for all demand and cost functions that are theoretically admissible and for all power taxes.

That this type of tax could reduce monopoly price appears to have been discovered by R. Garver.[1] He showed that, given specific demand and cost functions, a power tax (he referred to it as a "graduated" tax) with n set equal to 2 would lower price.

[1] R. Garver, "The Effect of Taxation on a Monopolist," *American Economic Review*, XXII, 463–65.

Effects of Excise Taxes on Price and Output

The assumed demand function is

$$p = 78¢ - 0.1x$$

The assumed total cost function is

$$c = 2x + 7000 \tag{28}$$

The pre-tax price is obtained by equating the marginal revenue and marginal cost functions and solving for price.

The total revenue function is the product of sales and price or

$$\begin{aligned} R &= x(78 - 0.1x) \\ &= 78x - 0.1x^2 \end{aligned} \tag{29}$$

The marginal revenue function is the first derivative of (29) or

$$MR = 78 - 0.2x \tag{30}$$

the marginal cost function is the first derivative of (28) or

$$MC = +2¢$$

that is to say, an increase in output of 1 unit will increase total costs by 2 cents.

Setting MR equal to MC and solving for x,

$$\begin{aligned} 78 - 0.2x &= 2 \\ 0.2x &= 76 \\ x &= 380 \end{aligned}$$

The equilibrium output is 380 units per time period; by referring to the average revenue function, it is seen that the corresponding price is 40 cents.

That this output maximizes rather than minimizes profits may be seen by noting that the marginal revenue function is steeper (its slope is -0.2) than the marginal cost function (which is horizontal), and thus the former intersects the latter from above as output is increased to 380 units.

The total profit per time period at a price of 40 cents is

$$380(78 - 0.1 \cdot 380) - (2 \cdot 380) + 7000 \quad \text{or} \quad \$74.40$$

The elasticity of demand at this price is

After-tax Equilibrium: Power Tax Function

$$E_x(p) = -\frac{p(x)}{x \cdot p'(x)}$$

$$= \frac{40}{380 \cdot 0.1}$$

$$\approx 1.05$$

Garver next proposes a per unit tax of the form

$$t = 0.001 p^2$$

$$t = 0.001(78 - 0.1x)^2$$

It is clear from the conclusions given above that, since the value of n (in this case, 2) in the tax function exceeds the elasticity of demand, this tax must lower price. Garver states correctly that the best after-tax price is 39.25 cents.

It can be shown that 39.25 cents maximizes after-tax profits. Total profit is equal to the following:

Total revenue or

$$x(78 - 0.1x)$$

less the per unit tax, times the quantity sold, or

$$0.001(78 - 0.1x)^2 x$$

less total costs

$$c = 2x + 7000$$

or

$$\pi = x(78 - 0.1x) - 0.001(78 - 0.1x)^2 x - (2x + 7000) \qquad (31)$$

This expression can be simplified to

$$\pi = 0.00001 x^3 - 0.0844 x^2 + 69.916 x - 7000$$

The first derivative of the profit function is

$$\pi' = -0.00003 x^2 - 0.1688 x + 69.916 \qquad (32)$$

and the second derivative is

$$\pi'' = -0.00006 x - 0.1688 \qquad (33)$$

Profits will be maximized when the first derivative equals zero, provided that the second derivative is negative at that price.

Setting (32) equal to zero and solving the resulting quadratic equation yields

$$x = 387.5$$
$$x = -6194$$

Only the positive root is relevant; the best after-tax price is

$$p = 78 - 0.1 \cdot 387.5$$
$$= 78 - 38.75$$
$$= 39.25¢$$

The output, 387.5, maximizes rather than minimizes profits since the value of (33), for any positive value of x, is negative.

The tax rate has fallen from 4% at the pre-tax price to 3.925% at the after-tax price. Similarly, the per unit tax has declined from 1.6 to 1.54 cents. If the price is maintained at 40 cents after the tax is imposed, profit will be $74.40 less the tax bill or

$$7440 - 380\,[0.001(1600)] = 7440 - 608 \quad \text{or} \quad \$68.32$$

If the price is reduced to 39.25 cents, profit will be [substituting 387.5 in (31)]

$$\pi = 387.5(78 - 38.75) - 0.001(39.25)^2 387.5 - 7775$$
$$= \$68.38$$

Garver remarked that "the difference [in profit between adjusting to and ignoring the tax] would naturally not be great, for the tax we have assumed is a very small tax." Thus the incentive to reduce price under the assumed conditions is slight; nevertheless, the best price after the tax is lower than the pre-tax price, even though the seller must pay the tax from the proceeds of the reduced price. Garver did not generalize this result to other demand and cost conditions or to other tax functions.

If a heavier tax, with the same elasticity, is levied, such as

$$t = 0.01 p^2$$

the price decline from the tax will be greater. Expression (31) becomes

$$\pi = -0.0001 x^3 + 0.056 x^2 + 15.16 x - 7000$$

After-tax Equilibrium: Power Tax Function

Expressions (32) and (33) become, respectively

$$\pi' = -0.0003x^2 + 0.112x + 15.16 \tag{34}$$
$$\pi'' = -0.0006x + 0.112 \tag{35}$$

Setting (34) equal to zero and solving for x yields

$$x = 478.8$$
$$x = -105.5$$

As before, only the positive root is relevant, and, again, substituting this output in (35) gives a negative quantity; an output of 478.8 units maximizes rather than minimizes profit.

The after-tax price is

$$p = 78 - 0.1x$$
$$= 30.12¢$$

The tax rate has fallen from 40% at the pre-tax price to 30.12% at the after-tax price, and the per unit tax is reduced (by the price reduction) from 16 to about 9 cents.

If the seller persists in charging 40 cents, profit will be reduced to

$$7440 - 480(0.01 \cdot 1600) \quad \text{or} \quad \$13.60$$

By reducing the price to 30.12 cents, the profit will be increased to \$21.20; in this instance the incentive to reduce price as a result of this tax is stronger than before.

2. *Tax elasticity equals demand elasticity.* If the elasticity of the tax (in this case, the value of n in the tax function) is equal to the elasticity of demand at the pre-tax price, the marginal revenue function will be changed by the tax roughly as indicated in Chart 7a. At all outputs below the pre-tax output, marginal revenue is lowered; at higher outputs (short of the output that reduces price to zero) marginal revenue is increased; and at the pre-tax output marginal revenue is unchanged. As long as the after-tax marginal revenue function continues to intersect the marginal cost curve from above, the pre-tax output and price will still maximize the after-tax profit, although this profit will be reduced by the amount of tax revenue collected. Output and price will be unchanged. The effect of the tax is exactly the same as that of a tax on monopoly profit.[2]

[2] Among the obvious differences between an excise and a profit tax is the fact that the excise tax bill could easily amount to more than monopoly profit at the after-tax equilibrium, whereas a pure profit tax typically would not.

To illustrate this possibility, consider a modification of the example used in the preceding section. Let the demand function remain unchanged but change the cost function to:

$$c = 26x + 2000$$

The marginal revenue function is still

$$MR = 78 - 0.2x \tag{30}$$

while marginal costs are now 26 cents. Setting (30) equal to 26 cents gives

$$78 - 0.2x = 26$$

$$x = 260 \text{ units} \quad \text{and} \quad p = 52 \text{¢}$$

Price is now higher as a result of higher marginal costs. At this higher price the elasticity of demand is

$$-E_x(p) = -\frac{52}{260(-0.1)} = 2$$

If a per unit tax of the form $0.005p^2$ is now levied, the profit function will be

$$\pi = x(78 - 0.1x) - 0.005(78 - 0.1x)^2 x - 26x - 2000$$

which reduces to

$$\pi = -0.00005x^3 - 0.022x^2 + 21.58x - 2000 \tag{36}$$

The first derivative of (36) is set equal to zero and solved for x:

$$\pi' = -0.00015x^2 - 0.044x + 21.58 = 0$$

$$x = 260 \text{ units}$$

and

$$p = 78 - 0.1x$$
$$= 52 \text{¢}$$

Neither output nor price is changed by the tax. At this output the second derivative of (36)

$$\pi'' = -0.00030x - 0.044$$

is negative and profits are maximized.

After-tax Equilibrium: Power Tax Function

The only effect of the tax is to reduce profit by the amount of the tax bill, which is:

$$0.005(52)^2 \cdot 260 \text{ units} \quad \text{or} \quad \$35.15.$$

3. *Tax elasticity is smaller than demand elasticity.* If the value of the parameter n in the power tax formula is smaller than the elasticity of demand, the new marginal revenue function intersects the old at an output below the pre-tax level. At still lower outputs, marginal revenue is raised by the tax; at outputs higher than that at the point of intersection, marginal revenue is lowered by the tax (see Chart 8a). As long as the second-order conditions for a maximum continue to be fulfilled at outputs lower than the pre-tax level, output will fall and price will rise as a result of the tax.

Consider the following illustration:

Demand function: $\quad p = 78 - 0.1x$
Marginal revenue function: $\quad MR = 78 - 0.2x$
Total cost function: $\quad c = 39x$
Marginal cost function: $\quad MC = +39 \text{ c}$

Setting marginal revenue equal to marginal cost yields

$$78 - 0.2x = 39$$
$$-0.2x = -39$$
$$x = \frac{39}{0.2} = 195 \text{ units}$$
$$p = 78 - 0.1 \cdot 195 = 58.5 \text{ ¢}$$

The elasticity at the pre-tax output is

$$E_x(p) = -\frac{58.5}{195 \cdot (-0.1)} = 3$$

Suppose the tax function to be

$$t[p(x)] = 0.002[p(x)]^2$$

Total profit is now

$$\pi = x(78 - 0.1x) - 0.002x(78 - 0.1x)^2 - 39x$$
$$= -0.00002x^3 - 0.0688x^2 + 26.822x$$

The first derivative of the after-tax profit function is

$$\pi' = -0.00006x^2 - 0.1376x + 26.822$$

and $x = 180.5$ units
$$p = 78 - 0.1(180.5)$$
$$= 59.95 ¢$$

Output falls and price rises as a result of the tax.

4. Tax may disturb second-order conditions for maximization. The conclusions of the three preceding sections concerning the effect of the tax elasticity on the direction of output and price change are all subject to an important qualification: the power tax, if sufficiently heavy, may distort the shape of the marginal revenue curve to such an extent that there are two after-tax outputs, at which marginal revenue (after-tax) and marginal cost are equal.

This possibility is illustrated in Chart 11 which shows marginal revenue before and after a "heavy" tax is levied and the marginal cost curve. (Should the after-tax marginal revenue curve appear extreme, two points may be recalled: first, the output at which these

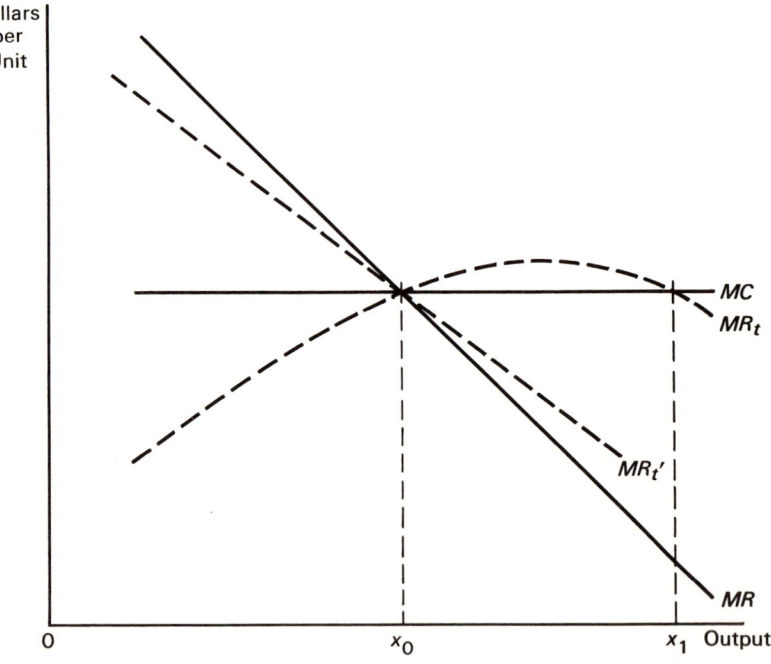

CHART 11.
Effect of "heavy" tax on price and output: tax elasticity equals demand elasticity.

After-tax Equilibrium: Power Tax Function

two marginal revenue curves intersect is determined by the tax and demand elasticities and will not change unless the tax elasticity is changed; second, the vertical distance between the curves at each output depends directly upon the weight of the tax.) It is clear from the chart that, if costs are as shown by *MC* (hence the tax elasticity must have been set to equal the demand elasticity at the pre-tax output and a "light" tax would leave output and price unchanged), the output, x_1, different from x_0, is an equilibrium output.

Although it may be easy to draw curves, it may not always be easy to draw curves that represent real possibilities, and up to this point the conditions necessary for the after-tax marginal revenue curve to turn downward at high outputs have not been established. Both necessary and sufficient conditions cannot be given, for the specific shape of the after-tax marginal revenue curve depends upon the tax function, as well as upon certain characteristics of the demand function, such as curvature, that are not part of the restrictions on the demand function. However, certain clues concerning the shape of the after-tax marginal revenue curve, at outputs above the pre-tax output, can be obtained by comparing before- and after-tax marginal revenue at an output so high that price is zero (if there is such an output).

A comparison of (23) and (24) shows marginal revenue after-tax to differ from that before tax by the marginal tax bill, or

$$-\{xt'[p(x)]p'(x)+t[p(x)]\} \tag{37}$$

If, at an output so high that price is zero, both $t[p(x)]$ and $t'[p(x)]$ are zero, (37) will also be zero; the before- and after-tax marginal revenue curves will be equal at a price of zero, and the latter must fall as the price is lowered to zero to reach this equality; also, if the tax is heavy enough, there is some equilibrium output, x_1, higher than x_0. (A lighter tax, producing $MR_{t'}$ on the chart, would have left the pre-tax output unchanged.) Whether both $t(p)$ and $t'(p)$ become zero at zero price depends on the value of the parameter n in the tax function

$$t(p) = kp^n \tag{5}$$

where

$$t'(p) = nkp^{n-1}$$

The various possibilities are as follows:

n	$t(0)$	$t'(0)$	Type of Tax
Negative	∞	∞	Highly regressive
Zero	k	Zero	Regressive (specific tax)
$0 < n < 1$	Zero	∞	Mildly regressive
Unity	Zero	k	Proportional (ad valorem)
$n > 1$	Zero	Zero	Progressive

(Only a progressive tax will leave the price unchanged, as assumed in this example.)

Thus the marginal revenue curve resulting from a progressive power tax *must*, from these considerations, eventually turn downward as output is increased above the pre-tax output. Hence a tax that is intended to leave price and output unchanged may actually increase output and reduce price.

Exactly how heavy a tax designed not to change output and price must be in order to produce disequilibrium at the pre-tax output cannot be determined without knowledge of demand and cost conditions. However, the behavior of costs bears upon the matter. If the marginal cost curve is falling, a light tax may be sufficient to bring the after-tax marginal revenue curve above marginal cost at outputs just above x_0. If marginal costs are rising, a heavier tax will be required to produce disequilibrium at the pre-tax output. In any event, regardless of demand and cost conditions, there is some "light" tax that will leave output unchanged.

Even if the tax is specifically designed to lower output (through the selection of the appropriately small tax elasticity), there is the possibility that output will rise instead. If the demand and cost conditions assumed in Chart 11 are retained but the tax elasticity is reduced, the general effect on the after-tax marginal revenue curve will be to move the point of intersection with the before-tax marginal revenue curve to a higher output (where the tax and demand elasticities are again equal) and in the neighborhood of the pre-tax output to lower the after-tax marginal revenue curve, as in Chart 12a. Thus the tax increases output to x_1, even though the tax elasticity is smaller than the demand elasticity.

If the tax is designed to increase output, it is quite likely to do so. Chart 12b represents the same demand and cost conditions as those

After-tax Equilibrium: Power Tax Function

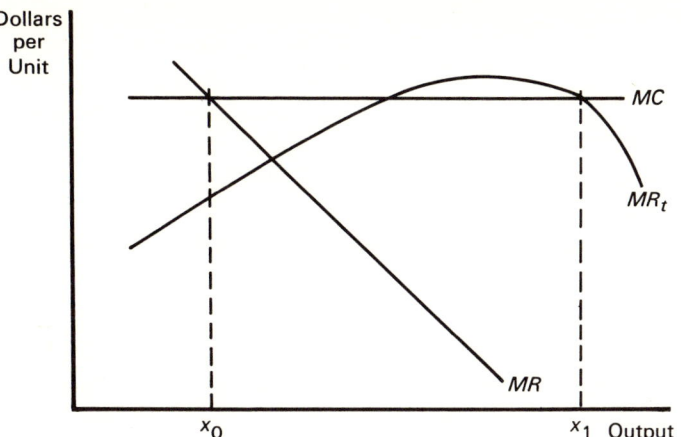

CHART 12a.
Effect of "heavy" tax on price: tax elasticity smaller than demand elasticity.

in Chart 11. Only the tax elasticity has been increased so that it is greater than the demand elasticity at the pre-tax output, and a light tax would certainly lower price. The heavy tax shown is also certain to increase output and lower price.

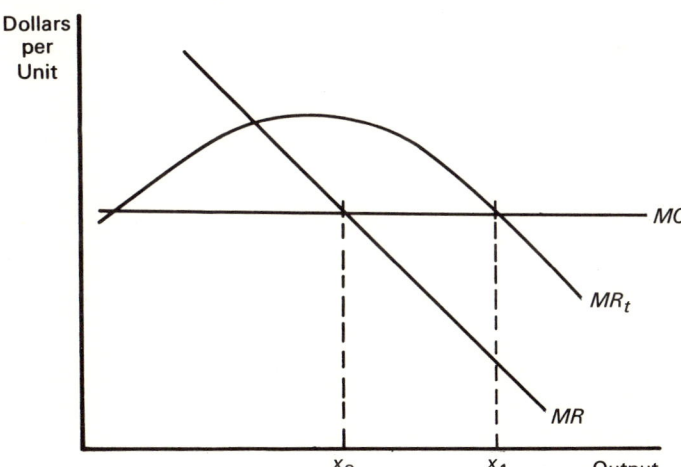

CHART 12b.
Effect of "heavy" tax on price: tax elasticity greater than demand elasticity.

The unexpected price effects may be summarized as follows.

1. If a tax is sufficiently heavy, the direction of price change that results may not be the same as given in the general conclusions above.
2. If marginal costs are rising, the likelihood of a perverse price effect is smaller than if costs are falling.
3. If the tax is clearly designed to raise output (i.e., if the tax and demand elasticities differ substantially), the likelihood of a perverse price effect is reduced.
4. Other forms of progressive excise tax (see Chapter 6) do not, and modifications of the power tax may not, lead to an unexpected direction of price change.
5. If the marginal revenue curve is so distorted that the conditions for an equilibrium price are not met, no price maximizes profit or minimizes loss and the firm minimizes losses by ceasing production.

It may be noted again that, lacking demand and cost data, any form of excise tax, whatever the elasticity or the weight of the tax, can conceivably amount to more than the profit from the production and sale of the taxed item. The weight of a progressive tax heavy enough to produce a perverse price effect may also be sufficient to put the firm out of business.

E. *Amount of Price Change*

In Chapter 4 the factors that influence the amount of price change from any type of excise tax were examined. The following results were obtained:

1. If marginal costs are increasing, the output and price change (either a rise of a fall) will be smaller than if costs are constant or decreasing, provided the tax changes output and price at all.
2. If the average rate of tax is increased, the change in price, either a rise or a fall, will be increased.
3. If, after an excise tax is levied, the tax formula is modified so that the revised tax is equivalent in weight to the initial tax at the price prevailing after the initial tax and so that the elasticity of the revised tax is greater than the elasticity of the initial tax, then (*a*) if the initial tax increased price, the revised tax will

After-tax Equilibrium: Power Tax Function

produce a smaller price increase; (b) if the initial tax decreased price, the revised tax will produce a greater price decline.

Remaining to be discussed here is the effect on the amount of price change of the tax elasticity, when the high- and low-elasticity taxes being compared are equal, not at the price prevailing after one of the taxes is levied, but rather at the price prevailing before *either* tax is imposed. If two tax functions have different elasticities, it is possible for one of the taxes to increase price and the other to decrease it, or for one to change price and the other to leave it unchanged. It is presumed, however, that the question of the relative amount of price change from such pairs of taxes is not very likely to arise, and the following discussion is accordingly limited to a comparison of pairs of taxes, both of which either increase or decrease price.

Let the two per unit taxes be

$$t_1(p) = kp^n$$

The elasticity of this tax is equal to the parameter n.

$$t_2(p) = \frac{kp^{n+\alpha}}{p_0^\alpha}$$

The elasticity of tax 2 is larger (α may be defined as greater than zero) than that of tax 1, and at price p_0, the pre-tax price, the two taxes are equal. It may be noted that at prices below p_0 tax 2 is lighter than tax 1 and at prices above p_0 tax 2 is the heavier tax. In Table 2 [compare taxes 3 and 5, which are equal at a price of $2.]

The following analysis will be much simplified if price is taken as the independent variable, so that

Demand function:	$x = x(p)$
Per unit tax function:	$t = t(p)$
Total tax function:	$T = x(p) \cdot t(p)$
Total revenue function (before-tax):	$R = p \cdot x(p)$
Marginal revenue function (before-tax):	$MR = px'(p) + x(p)$
Total revenue function (after-tax):	$R_t = p \cdot x(p) - t(p) \cdot x(p)$
Marginal revenue function (after-tax):	

$$MR_t = px'(p) + x(p) - \{x(p) \cdot t'(p) + x'(p) \cdot t(p)\} \qquad (38)$$

Expression (38) can be rearranged by multiplying each of the two terms in brackets by

$$\frac{p \cdot t(p) \cdot x(p)}{p \cdot t(p) \cdot x(p)}$$

and by canceling terms to yield

$$MR_t = p \cdot x'(p) + x(p) - \frac{t(p) \cdot x(p)}{p} \left[\frac{p \cdot t'(p)}{t(p)} + \frac{p \cdot x'(p)}{x(p)} \right]$$

But the terms inside the brackets are the tax and demand elasticities with respect to price, so that

$$MR_t = p \cdot x'(p) + x(p) - \frac{t(p) \cdot x(p)}{p} \left[E_t(p) + E_x(p) \right]$$

Note that, if a tax lowers the marginal revenue function *with respect to price*, price will fall (e.g., if the tax elasticity exceeds the demand elasticity[3]); if a tax raises the marginal revenue function with respect to price, price will rise (e.g., if the tax elasticity is less than the elasticity of demand).

The marginal revenue functions for the two power taxes will be

$$MR_{t_1} = px'(p) + x(p) - \frac{x(p)}{p} \cdot kp^n [n + E_x(p)]$$

$$MR_{t_2} = px'(p) + x(p) - \frac{x(p)}{p} \cdot \frac{k}{p_0^\alpha} \cdot p^{n+\alpha} [n + \alpha + E_x(p)]$$

At the pre-tax price, p_0, MR_{t_2} must lie below MR_{t_1}, that is, $MR_{t_2} - MR_{t_1}$ is negative at that price, as will now be shown:

$$MR_{t_2} - MR_{t_1} = -\frac{x(p)}{p} \cdot \frac{k}{p_0^\alpha} p^{n+\alpha} [n + \alpha + E_x(p)]$$

$$+ \frac{x(p)}{p} \cdot kp^n [n + E_x(p)]$$

$$= \frac{x(p) \cdot kp^n}{p} \left\{ -\frac{p^\alpha}{p_0^\alpha} [n + \alpha + E_x(p)] \right.$$

$$\left. + [n + E_x(p)] \right\} \quad (39)$$

---

[3]See note 7, p. 19.

After-tax Equilibrium: Power Tax Function

The *sign* of (39) will not be changed if positive quantities or functions are deleted, leaving

$$-\frac{p^\alpha}{p_0^\alpha}[n+\alpha+E_x(p)] + [n+E_x(p)] \qquad (40)$$

At $p = p_0$, (40) becomes

$$-[n+\alpha+E_x(p)] + [n+E_x(p)]$$

or simply $-\alpha$. Since α is always positive, the marginal revenue curve resulting from the more elastic tax will, *at the pre-tax price*, lie below that resulting from the less elastic tax.

If MR_{t_2} were below MR_{t_1} *at all prices*, it would follow that the tax with the greater elasticity would produce the greater price decline or the smaller price increase. Nevertheless, this conclusion is not true (as shown by the study of Musgrave and Suits); therefore these two marginal revenue curves may be equal at one or more prices.

It can be shown that at some prices the marginal revenue curve produced by the more elastic tax must lie *above* that produced by the less elastic tax. For example, at a price slightly above zero (where the elasticity of demand is slightly larger than zero), (40), which has the same sign as $(MR_{t_2} - MR_{t_1})$, must be positive. Both bracketed terms of this expression are positive and only the first is multiplied by a negative fraction; there must be some low price p at which (40) is positive. Since MR_{t_2} is below MR_{t_1} at the pre-tax price and is above MR_{t_1} at some low price, there is some price below the pre-tax price at which the two after-tax marginal revenue curves are equal.

In addition, at some high price above p_0, where the elasticity of demand becomes large (greater than $n+\alpha$), (40) is again positive. The two bracketed terms in this expression are now both negative and differ only by the constant α. Since the smaller (in absolute value) of these two terms in multiplied by a negative ratio larger than unity, that is, $-p^\alpha/p_0^\alpha$, expression (40) must, at a sufficiently high price, become positive, and marginal revenue from the more elastic tax again exceeds that from the less elastic tax at some high price.

Thus, the pre-tax and the two after-tax marginal revenue curves are related as shown in Chart 13a. If marginal costs are as shown by MC in the chart, both taxes would have reduced price, the more elastic tax to a greater degree (compare p_1 and p_2).

68   *Effects of Excise Taxes on Price and Output*

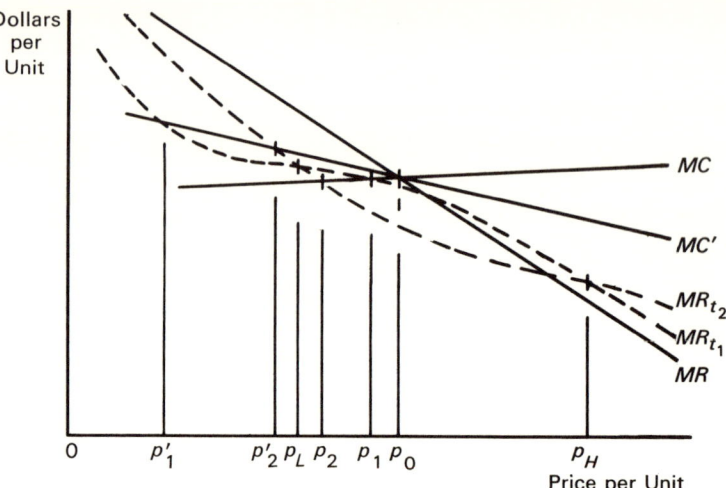

CHART 13a.
Effect of increased tax elasticity on amount of price change: taxes equal at pre-tax price and both taxes reduce price.

If both taxes had been designed to increase price, the after-tax marginal revenue curves would have been shifted upward, as in Chart 13b. The two prices at which the after-tax marginal revenue curves are equal have both been reduced (as will be seen below).

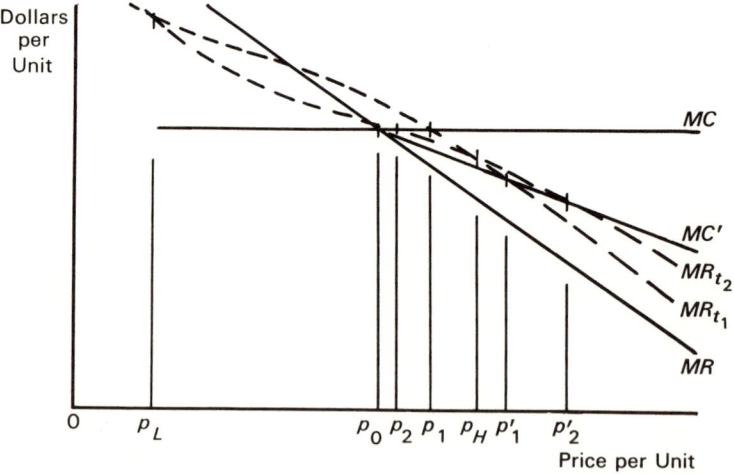

CHART 13b.
Effect of increased tax elasticity on amount of price change: taxes equal at pre-tax price and both taxes increase price.

After-tax Equilibrium: Power Tax Function

In this instance the more elastic tax produces the smaller price increase; p_2 is below p_1.

In both cases illustrated in Charts 13a and 13b, it will be noted that, if the marginal cost curve has a sufficient small slope, for example, MC', the effect of the elasticity on the relative amount of price change will be opposite to that described above.

Therefore, it may or may not be true to conclude as follows: if two taxes are equal at the pre-tax price and both taxes change price in the same direction, but one tax is more elastic than the other, the more elastic tax will produce a greater price decline or a smaller price increase. However something can be said about the conditions under which the conclusion holds.

1. If the conclusion holds under given cost conditions, there is some less steeply sloped marginal cost function such that the pre-tax price is the same but the conclusion does not hold (compare Charts 13 and 14).

2. The weight of the pair of taxes being compared also bears upon the conclusion in a fairly simple way. The sign of (40) represents the sign of the difference between the two after-tax marginal revenue functions. To investigate the conditions that determine the prices at which these two functions are equal, the latter are expressed as equivalent, that is, (40) is set equal to zero:

$$-\frac{p^\alpha}{p_0^\alpha}[n + E_x(p) + \alpha] + [n + E_x(p)] = 0$$

$$\frac{p^\alpha}{p_0^\alpha} = \frac{n + E_x(p)}{n + E_x(p) + \alpha}$$

(41)

where n is the elasticity of tax 1;

$(n + \alpha)$ is the (higher) elasticity of tax 2;

$E_x(p)$ is the elasticity of demand, which is a function of price, varying from a value of zero when price is zero toward $-\infty$ as price increases;

p_0 is the pre-tax price, that is, the price at which the two taxes are constructed to be equivalent.

Since the parameter k in both tax functions does not appear in (41), it follows that the value assigned to k has no effect on the prices at which the two after-tax marginal revenue curves are equivalent. If then the weight of both taxes is increased by raising the value of k (the taxes will still be equal at the pre-tax price), the marginal revenue curves for the heavier pair will be shifted generally as discussed above, but they will be equivalent at the same prices at which the marginal revenue curves for the lighter pair of taxes are equal, as shown in Chart 14. If both taxes are very light, both after-

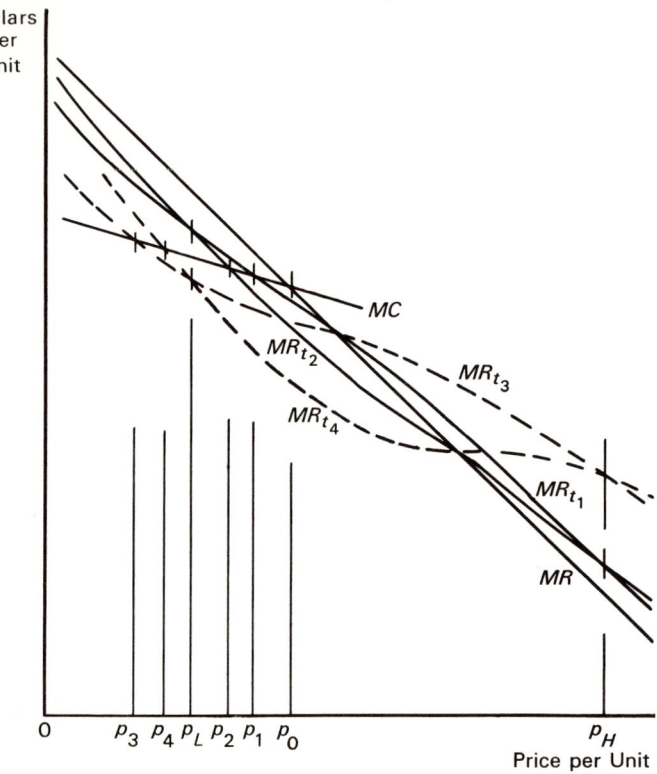

CHART 14.
Effect of weight of tax on marginal revenue curves.

tax marginal revenue curves will lie very close to the pre-tax marginal revenue curve. Marginal cost and pre-tax marginal revenue must be equal at some price between p_L and p_H, and the statement on p. 69 is true. If both taxes are heavy, as shown by MR_{t_3} and MR_{t_4}, the conclusion is false.

Therefore, if the conclusion holds for a given weight of the pair of taxes (at, say, the pre-tax price), there is some heavier pair of taxes such that the conclusion is false.

After-tax Equilibrium: Power Tax Function

An examination of (41) makes clear that, although the two per unit taxes being compared are equal at the pre-tax price, p_0, the two after-tax marginal revenue curves cannot be. For at p_0 the left-hand side of (41) equals unity, but the right-hand side does not; therefore the equality shown by (41) cannot hold at the pre-tax price.

Chapter 6. *After-tax Equilibrium: Proportional Tax on Excess Price*

A second tax function that can serve to define a graduated excise tax schedule is the proportional tax on excess price:

$$t(p) = r(p - c)$$

In this general form the per unit tax becomes negative (i.e., a bounty is awarded) if the price falls below the fixed level, c. In practice the tax function is modified so that

$$t(p) = 0, \quad \text{for all } p < c$$

(In the subsequent analysis, attention will be given mainly to the modified version of the tax formula.)

This tax is equivalent to a combination of an ad valorem tax of rp per unit and a bounty of fixed amount, rc, per unit, and it becomes intuitively plausible to expect that such a tax could lower price, since the price-reducing effect of the bounty may well be stronger than the price-increasing effect of the ad valorem tax, particularly when the latter is slight. The tax has some of the characteristics of a price ceiling, in that a penalty is incurred if the price is raised or maintained above the level c. If the penalty is severe — for example, a tax rate of 100% applied to the excess of price above c — the effect of the tax on price is identical to that of a price ceiling.

A. *Limitations on Parameters*

There are two parameters, r and c, whose values must be specified in order to use this formula to devise a tax schedule. If r is positive, the formula defines a tax; if negative, a bounty. The value of r may exceed unity. The value of c will usually be lower than the pre-tax price, particularly if the modified version is adopted, unless the tax authorities are anticipating a price increase.[1] If c is zero, the tax is identical to the ad valorem tax. The value of c may be negative; if so, the tax rate, r, is applied to some amount larger than the price. In general, the combination of values for r and c will be such that the average rate of tax, given by

$$r(1 - c/p)$$

is less than 100%. Increases in price will raise the average tax rate, and vice versa.

B. *Tax Elasticity*

As noted in Chapter 2, the elasticity of the per unit tax with respect to price is given by

$$E_t(p) = \frac{p}{p - c}$$

The value of c thus determines the tax elasticity at any price. If c is negative, the elasticity is less than unity and the tax is regressive. If c is zero, the elasticity is unity and the tax is proportional. Similarly, for positive values of c (smaller than p), the elasticity is positive and greater than unity. As is true also of the power tax, the proportionality factor (in this case, r; for the power tax, k) does not affect the tax elasticity. Unlike the power tax, this tax does not have a constant elasticity; it varies according to the price. For a given positive value value of c, smaller than p, increases in price reduce the tax elasticity and at very high prices the elasticity approaches unity (and the tax formula approaches that of the ad valorem tax). If the price is only slightly above c, the elasticity will be very high and, it might be added, the average rate of tax will be very low.

---

[1]When c is equal to the pre-tax price, this tax function is similar in form to one proposed by M. F. Scott ("A Tax on Price Increases?" *Economic Journal*, LXXI, 350–66). Scott's tax differs in that some measure of price increase would serve to determine, not a per unit tax, but rather a tax rate to be applied to profits. Again if c is equal to the pre-tax price, the tax shifts the monopolist's demand and marginal revenue curves (net of tax) in exactly the same manner that the presence of several competitors has been judged to affect it, if the competitors match price cuts but fail to match price increases. See P. Sweezy, "Demand under Conditions of Oligopoly," *The Journal of Political Economy*, XLVII, 568–73, in particular, Figure 1.

After-tax Equilibrium: Tax on Excess Price

C. Examples

Examples of tax schedules derived by this formula are shown in Table 3 for various combinations of values of r and c. From these schedules it will be noted that, for a given value of c, changes in the value of r simply alter the per unit tax at any price by the proportionate change in r (compare taxes 2 and 3). Increases in the value of c, for a given value of r, reduce the per unit tax by removing part of the price from the tax base and lower the entire schedule by a constant amount (compare taxes 1 and 2). The ad valorem tax is also shown (tax 4), as well as the schedule resulting from a negative value of c (tax 5). The latter is seen to be a combination of 10% ad valorem tax and a $0.05 specific tax per unit.

TABLE 3. *Tax per Unit, at Various Prices, for Different Combinations of r and c: Proportional Tax on Excess Price*

Price	(1) $r = 0.10$ $c = \$0.50$	(2) $r = 0.10$ $c = \$1.00$	(3) $r = 0.20$ $c = \$1.00$	(4) $r = 0.10$ $c = \$0.00$	(5) $r = 0.10$ $c = -\$0.50$
$1.00	$0.05	$0.00	$0.00	$0.10	$0.15
1.10	.06	.01	.02	.11	.16
1.20	.07	.02	.04	.12	.17
1.30	.08	.03	.06	.13	.18
1.40	.09	.04	.08	.14	.19
1.50	.10	.05	.10	.15	.20
1.60	.11	.06	.12	.16	.21
1.70	.12	.07	.14	.17	.22
1.80	.13	.08	.16	.18	.23
1.90	.14	.09	.18	.19	.24
2.00	.15	.10	.20	.20	.25

D. Direction of Price Change

The elasticity of the proportional tax on excess price is now given by

$$E_t(p) = \frac{p(x)}{p(x) - c}$$

and the demand elasticity by[2]

[2] J. Robinson, *The Economics of Imperfect Competition* (London, 1950), p. 34.

$$E_x(p) = \frac{p(x)}{p(x) - MR}$$

where *MR* is the level of marginal revenue with respect to output increases, that is, the addition to total revenue produced by increasing output slightly. The ratio of the tax and demand elasticities (which will determine whether the tax raises or lowers marginal revenue) is then

$$\frac{E_t(p)}{E_x(p)} = -\frac{p(x) - MR}{p(x) - c}$$

It follows that whether marginal revenue is raised or lowered at any output by the tax depends upon the relative levels of marginal revenue and the parameter *c*. If *c* exceeds marginal revenue, the ratio of the elasticities is negative (and greater in absolute value than unity) and the marginal revenue at the pre-tax output is raised by the tax. Since, at the pre-tax output, marginal revenue and marginal cost are equal, if a tax of this form is to lower price and increase output, *c* must be given a value larger than marginal cost at the pre-tax output. Similar reasoning shows that, if *c* equals marginal cost at the pre-tax output, the price will not be changed by the tax; and that, if *c* is smaller than marginal cost at the pre-tax output, the price will rise as a result of the tax.

The general effect of the tax on marginal revenue and output is shown in Charts 15a and 15b. The marginal revenue curve is rotated around the point where marginal revenue and *c* are equal. [The amount of rotation is determined by the parameter *r* in the tax function. If (26) is positive, increasing *r* will increase $t[p(x)]$, which in turn will increase (26) and the before- and after-tax marginal revenue curves will now be further apart, at any output, than before.] It will be noted that, if variant (4a) of the proportional tax on excess price is charted, whereby the tax can never become a bounty, the after-tax marginal revenue curve is discontinuous. When price (or average revenue) falls below the level *c*, the per unit tax is still zero and does not become a bounty; the after-tax marginal revenue curve drops, at the output at which price equals *c*, abruptly to the before-tax marginal revenue curve. If a bounty is awarded, proportional to the amount by which price falls short of *c*, the after-tax marginal revenue curve continues as shown by the dotted line labeled (4b).

After-tax Equilibrium: Tax on Excess Price

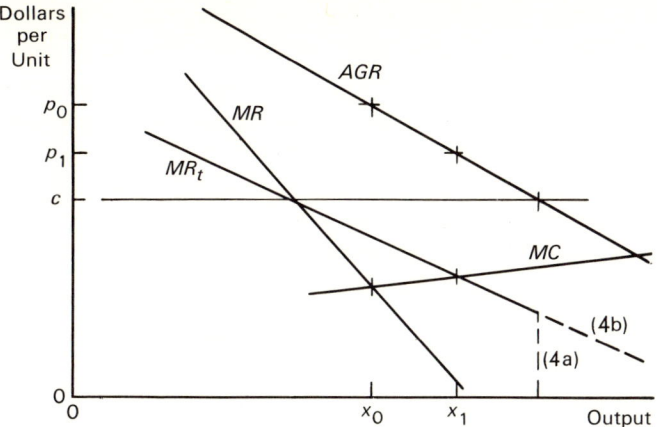

CHART 15a.
Effect on marginal revenue, output and price: proportional tax on excess price; c exceeds marginal cost at pre-tax output.

When c is set higher than the level of marginal revenue (or marginal cost, since the two are equal at the pre-tax output), marginal revenue is raised by the tax and output increases. Price must fall, as shown by the average revenue curve (Chart 15a).

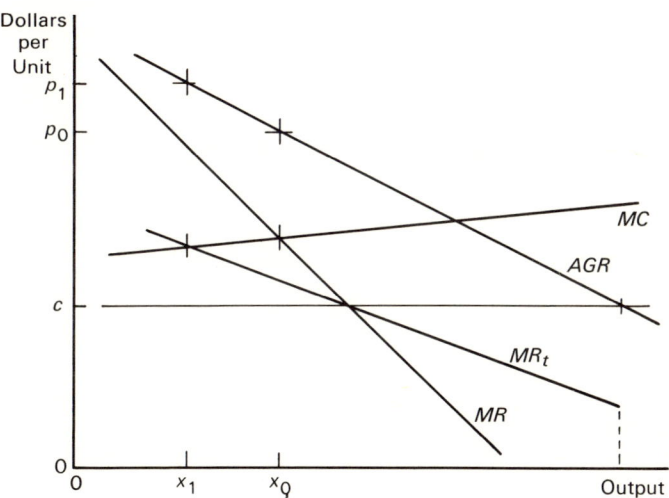

CHART 15b.
Effect on marginal revenue, output and price: proportional tax on excess price; c is smaller than marginal cost at pre-tax output.

If c is given a value smaller than marginal revenue at the pre-tax output, output will fall and price will rise (Chart 15b). It is clear that, if the value of c were equal to marginal revenue at the pre-tax output, marginal revenue would not have been changed by the tax and neither output nor price would have changed.

The direction of price change from this type of tax is not subject to the qualifications that applied to the power tax, for this tax does not distort the shape of the marginal revenue curve to the extreme extent that the power tax may distort it. Since the tax formula can be rewritten as

$$t[p(x)] = r \cdot p(x) - rc$$

the manner in which the tax shifts the marginal revenue curve is perhaps best shown in two stages: (1) that portion of the total shift that results from the first term, which is equivalent to an ad valorem tax at rate r; and (2) that portion that results from the second term, which is a bounty of amount rc per unit.

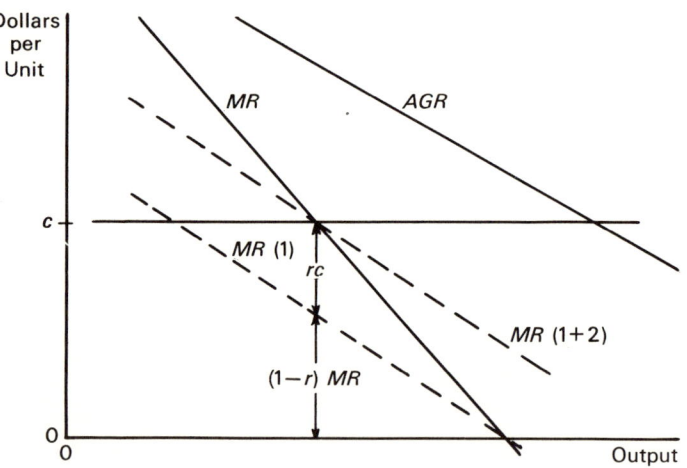

CHART 16a.
Proportional tax on excess price: effect on marginal revenue.

As shown in Chart 16a, an ad valorem tax rotates the marginal revenue curve counterclockwise around the point where marginal revenue equals zero. This may be seen by substituting the appropriate

After-tax Equilibrium: Tax on Excess Price

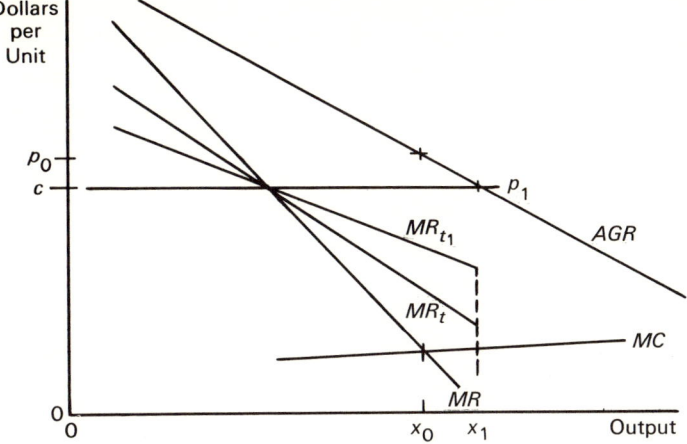

CHART 16b.
Increasing the weight of tax need not produce further price change.

functions in (24), namely,

$$t[p(x)] = r \cdot p(x)$$
$$t'[p(x)] = r$$

Expression (24), the marginal revenue after this change, is seen to be

$$(1-r)[x \cdot p'(x) + p(x)]$$

and marginal revenue is changed, at all outputs, by the proportion r. If marginal revenue is positive, it is reduced; if zero, it is unchanged; if negative, it is raised. This shift is shown by the curve labeled $MR(1)$ in Chart 16a. As long as r is not greater than unity, the marginal revenue curve cannot be given a positive slope by this shift, unless the pre-tax marginal revenue curve has a positive slope, which is unlikely.

The second portion of the shift results from the bounty of rc per unit, which raises marginal revenue by the amount of the bounty at all outputs.

The combined effect of both shifts is shown by the curve labeled $MR(1+2)$. Unless both the pre-tax marginal revenue curve and the marginal cost curves are very unusual in shape, there will be only a single after-tax equilibrium output and price, and the direction of price change from this kind of tax will be as stated above.

E. *Amount of Price Change*

The factors affecting the amount of price change resulting from any continuous and smooth excise tax were studied and summarized in Section B of Chapter 4. The conclusions given hold, of course, for the proportional tax on excess price in its most general form, that is, when a bounty is paid if price falls below the value of c. If there is no bounty at prices below c, the tax function becomes discontinuous at a price equal to c and a minor exception to one of the general propositions arises.

This exception refers to the effect of the average rate of tax on the amount of price change. The rule for any excise tax is as follows: the heavier the tax, the greater is the amount of price change, if any, as long as second-order conditions for a maximum continue to be fulfilled and "perverse" price effects do not occur. However, it is quite possible for a tax of the type being studied here to reduce price to the value of c, at which the per unit tax falls to zero and no tax revenue is collected. Chart 16b illustrates this possibility, where a relatively light tax has produced the after-tax marginal revenue curve, MR_t. A tax with the same value of c but a larger value of r would be heavier at any output lower than x_1 and would change marginal revenue as shown by the curve labeled $MR_{t'}$. It is clear that the added weight of tax produces no further change in price. There is, however, no upper limit to the amount of price increase (short of the price that reduces sales to zero) that a heavy tax can produce. If c had been smaller than marginal cost at the pre-tax output, the before- and after-tax (two) marginal revenue curves would have been equal at an output greater than the pre-tax output, and increasing r (thus making the MR_t curve flatter) would eventually reduce sales to zero, as the MR_t curve would have intercepted the MC curve on the y axis.

For the version of this tax that is usually levied, the rule becomes as follows: the heavier the tax (with the tax elasticity held constant), the greater is the price increase, or the greater is the price decrease until the price falls to the value of c.

The effect of the elasticity of any excise tax on the amount of price change (with the tax rate constant at some price) can, as noted previously, be stated rigorously only when the two taxes being compared are equal at the price prevailing after one of the taxes is levied. Without specifying some form of tax function, it is not possible to

After-tax Equilibrium: Tax on Excess Price

compare taxes that differ in elasticity but are equal at the pre-tax price. This kind of comparison of the amount of price change resulting from two power taxes can be made but was seen to be intricate and lacking in firm conclusions. Such is not entirely the case for the proportional tax on excess price. In regard to the amount of price change, it is important to note that price cannot fall below the value of c in tax function (4a).

Proofs will be given of the following propositions:

1. If two taxes of this type are equal at the pre-tax price but have different elasticities, and if both taxes will reduce price, the more elastic tax will produce the greater price reduction, unless the less elastic tax would reduce price by more than the maximum possible amount attainable from the more elastic tax.
2. If the conditions of proposition 1 are otherwise met, but both taxes will increase price, the relative amount of price change depends upon the weight of the two taxes: if both taxes are very light, at the pre-tax price, the more elastic tax will produce the smaller price increase; there is some heavier tax rate such that both taxes will produce the same price increase; and, if the tax rate is still higher, the more elastic tax will produce the greater price increase.[3]

Let the first of the pair of taxes being compared be

$$t_1[p(x)] = r[p(x) - c]$$

The second tax may be given a higher elasticity, and this can be done by increasing the value of c in the tax function; however, two questions remain. In what manner should the value of c be increased? How should the tax function be changed so that both taxes are equal at the pre-tax price?

The parameter c could be increased either by adding some quantity to it or by multiplying it by some factor greater than unity. There must, however, be some assurance that c will not exceed the pre-tax price; otherwise, the per unit tax would be zero and the tax would have no effect. This assurance is provided by adding to c

---

[3]Proposition 2 is more general than but otherwise identical to one given by Musgrave and Suits (*Quarterly Journal of Economics*, LXVII, 602, their proposition No. 6) concerning a comparison of the ad valorem and specific taxes.

some fraction of the amount by which c falls short of the pre-tax price. The second tax of the pair will be defined *provisionally* as

$$t_2[p(x)] = r[p(x) - \{c + k[p(x_0) - c]\}]$$

where k is some fraction between zero and unity. This tax function will *not* serve as the second member of the pair since the two taxes are not equal at the pre-tax price. To determine how tax 2 should be modified to provide such equality, this tax is evaluated at the pre-tax price, $p(x_0)$:

$$\begin{aligned} t_2[p(x_0)] &= r[p(x_0) - \{c + k[p(x_0) - c]\}] \\ &= r[p(x_0) - c - k \cdot p(x_0) + kc] \\ &= r[p(x_0)(1-k) - c(1-k)] \\ &= r(1-k)[p(x_0) - c] \end{aligned}$$

Therefore, at the pre-tax price, tax 2 is smaller than tax 1 by the factor k. To make both taxes equal at that price, it is sufficient to increase the parameter r in tax 2 by dividing it by $(1-k)$:

$$t_2[p(x)] = \frac{r}{1-k}[p(x) - c']$$

where

$$c' = c + k[p(x_0) - c]$$

The slopes or first derivatives, with respect to output, of both tax functions will be needed and are given by

$$t_1'[p(x)] \cdot p'(x) = r \cdot p'(x) \tag{42}$$

$$t_2'[p(x)] \cdot p'(x) = \frac{r}{1-k} \cdot p'(x) \tag{43}$$

If (42) and (43) are substituted in the expression for the after-tax marginal revenue (24), the results are

$$\begin{aligned} MR_{t_1} &= MR - \{xr \cdot p'(x) + r \cdot p(x) - rc\} \\ &= MR - r[MR - c] \end{aligned}$$

$$MR_{t_2} = MR - \left[\frac{r}{1-k} \cdot x \cdot p'(x) + \frac{r}{1-k} p(x) \right.$$

$$\left. + \frac{r}{1-k} \{c + k[p(x_0) - c]\} \right]$$

After-tax Equilibrium: Tax on Excess Price

$$= MR - \frac{r}{1-k}[MR - \{c + k[p(x_0) - c]\}]$$

where MR represents the before-tax marginal revenue function.

To determine at what output, if any, both after-tax marginal revenue functions are equal, MR_{t_2} is set equal to MR_{t_1}, with common terms canceled:

$$-\frac{r}{1-k}[MR - c - k \cdot p(x_0) + kc] = r(MR - c)$$

The value of r is irrelevant to the conditions at equality, since r can be removed without disturbing the equality, and with some rearrangement of terms:

$$\frac{MR}{1-k} - \frac{c(1-k)}{1-k} - \frac{k \cdot p(x_0)}{1-k} = MR - c$$

$$\frac{MR}{1-k} - \frac{k}{1-k}p(x_0) = MR$$

$$= \frac{1-k}{1-k}MR$$

$$MR - k \cdot p(x_0) = (1-k)MR$$

$$MR(1 - 1 + k) = k \cdot p(x_0)$$

$$k \cdot MR = k \cdot p(x_0)$$

$$MR = p(x_0)$$

Therefore, the two after-tax marginal revenue functions are equal at the output at which before-tax marginal revenue takes the same value as the pre-tax price, regardless of the weight of the taxes or of their elasticities.[4] If both taxes are the most general form (4b), their marginal revenue curves will be equal at only *one* output. If

---

[4]This result is also identical to that given by Musgrave and Suits for the specific and ad valorem taxes (*Quarterly Journal of Economics*, LXVII, 602).

Although $p(x_0)$ is identified above as the pre-tax price for the purpose of raising a question that is often encountered in practice, it has been treated in the analysis as *any* price at which the two taxes are equal, and the conclusion as stated is more restricted than necessary. More generally, if two excise taxes of the type at issue here are equal at any price and if the elasticities of the two taxes differ, their marginal revenue functions will be equal at the output at which pre-tax marginal revenue equals that price.

the taxes are the usual type (4a), their marginal revenue curves rejoin the before-tax marginal revenue curve at the outputs at which c and c' are equal to average revenue. The relations of the before- and after-tax marginal revenue curves are shown in Chart 17a. If

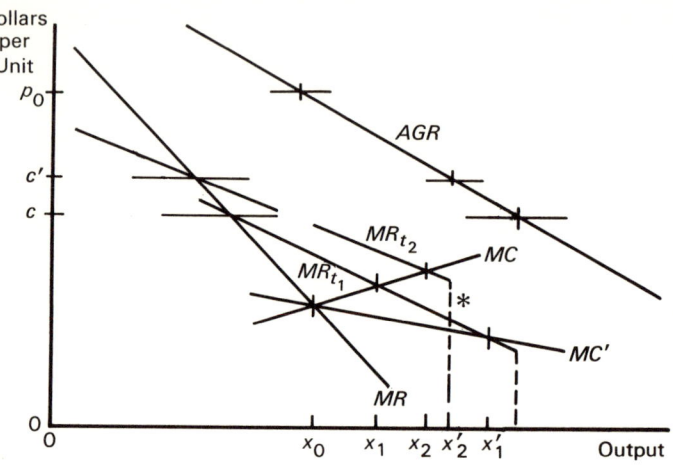

CHART 17a.
Effect of higher elasticity on amount of price change: taxes equal at pre-tax price and both taxes lower price.

marginal costs are below the values of c (and c') at the pre-tax output, as shown by MC, the more elastic tax, tax 2, would cause the greater increase in output and the greater drop in price. If, however, marginal costs are as indicated by MC', the more elastic tax would increase output only to x_2' whereas the less elastic tax would increase it to x_1'.

Since MR_{t_2} intersects MR at a level higher than c, and since MR_{t_2} and MR_{t_1} are equal at only one output (other than where MR_{t_2} becomes discontinuous), MR_{t_2} must lie above MR_{t_1} at the pre-tax output. Marginal cost must be less than c at the pre-tax output (in order for both taxes to lower price), and the more elastic tax will, as long as the marginal cost curve does not pass below the point marked with an asterisk (*), produce the greater output increase and the greater price reduction (proposition 1).

If c' and c had been smaller than marginal revenue at the pre-tax output, both taxes of the pair would have reduced output and raised price. Chart 17b shows three pairs of such taxes, A, B and C, with

After-tax Equilibrium: Tax on Excess Price

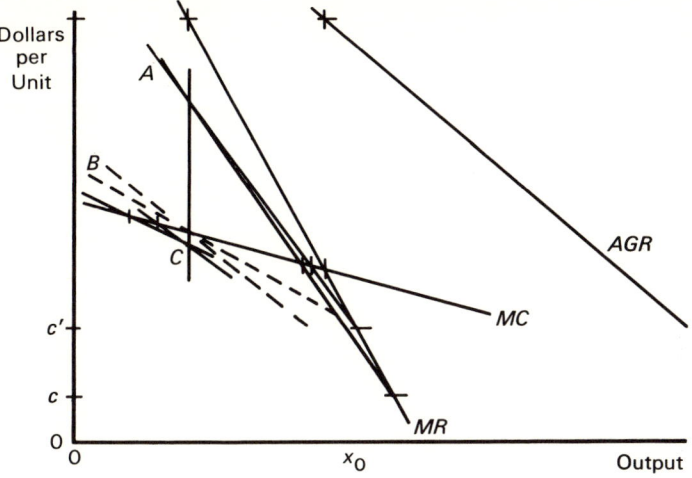

CHART 17b.
Effect of higher elasticity on amount of price change: pairs of taxes equal at pre-tax price and each pair raises price.

progressively larger values of r. Of the "light" pair the more elastic tax (that with the higher value for c) reduces output and raises price to a smaller extent than the less elastic tax; there is some heavier pair (pair B), such that both will lead to the same output reduction and price increase; and if the tax rate is still higher (pair C), the more elastic tax will produce the greater output decline and price increase (proposition 2).

Chapter 7. *After-tax Equilibrium: Bracketed Taxes*

Although both the power tax and the proportional tax on excess price define the per unit tax at each price, they do not show this tax explicitly. To facilitate the administration of an excise tax, it is not uncommon for the authorities to prepare a tax schedule that lists many conceivable prices and shows the per unit tax at each price. Tables 2 (p. 53) and 3 (p. 75) are examples of such tax schedules. In order to simplify the schedule (and perhaps for other purposes as well), the prices are often grouped into intervals. Within each price interval, the per unit tax may be a fixed amount or it may be stated as a fixed percentage of the price. (Other formulae may, of course, be used to calculate per unit taxes *within* a price interval, but this is rarely done.)

The fixed per unit tax or the fixed percentage tax generally varies from one price interval to another; otherwise, there is no point in distinguishing the intervals. Thus there is invariably a "step," up or down, in the per unit tax from a price near the upper end of a bracket to a price near the low end of the next higher bracket, and it is the existence of these steps that gives rise to the unusual price effects of bracketed taxes.

If a tax is defined in terms of price intervals, three distinct, but not independent, factors are pertinent to price change: (1) the size of the steps in the per unit tax from the end of an interval to the beginning of the next; (2) the tax formula employed to calculate per unit taxes within the interval; and (3) the tax formula employed to adjust the per unit taxes (at, say, the midpoint of an interval) from one interval to another.

If the steps are large and the brackets narrow, the steps will exert the dominant influence on price, regardless of the other factors.

If the brackets are wide and a single bracket includes most of the practicable range of price, the tax formula used within the bracket will determine the effect on price. If the brackets are narrow and the steps small, the formula that determines the general level of per unit taxes from one bracket to the next will have the predominant effect on price.

Since the steps in the per unit tax between brackets introduce discontinuities in the tax function, the elasticity of the tax is no longer defined at the prices at the ends of the intervals and a comparison of the tax and demand elasticities cannot be made. After-tax profit is not a continuous function of output, and the methods used in the previous sections are not appropriate for determining the effects of the step in the per unit tax on price.

A. *Upward Step*

The direction of the step effect on price depends upon the nature of the steps. If the tax is progressive over some range and, from the end of one price bracket to the beginning of the next, the per unit tax jumps upward (as in Charts 1, panel c, and 2, panel c), the existence of the step may exert a downward effect on price. This downward effect can be either of two types; (*a*) the price may fall, as a result of the tax, to the end of a price interval; or (*b*) if the within-bracket tax formula exerts an upward influence on price, the existence of a step at the upper end of the bracket may stop the price rise even though, if the bracket had no upper end, the price would have risen more.

If the tax is regressive over some range (i.e., if, from the end of one bracket to the beginning of the next, the per unit tax *declines*, as shown in Chart 1, panel d), the step may exert either an upward or a downward effect on price. The upward effect will occur whenever it is profitable to raise price (to get into the next, lower-tax bracket) to a greater extent than is called for by the within-bracket tax formula. The downward effect can occur when, in raising price in response to the within-bracket formula, the next, lower-tax bracket is reached *before* price has fully responded to the within-bracket formula.

The step effect will be examined first for the simplest type of tax, one with a low price bracket in which there is no tax and with a

After-tax Equilibrium: Bracketed Taxes

high price bracket in which a specific tax of t dollars per unit applies (as in Chart 2, panel b):

$$t(p) = 0, \quad \text{for all } p \leq p_1 \text{ (price bracket 1)}$$
$$t(p) = t, \quad \text{for all } p > p_1 \text{ (price bracket 2)} \qquad (44)$$

At a price just above p_1, the per unit tax jumps from zero to t. This tax will change the marginal revenue curve as shown in Chart 18a, where ABC represents the marginal revenue before tax; MC, the marginal cost curve; and x_0 and p_0, the pre-tax output and price. The after-tax marginal revenue curve is now discontinuous at output x_1, corresponding to price p_1, and consists of two branches—one shown by DHE and the other by BC. Since marginal revenue becomes "infinite" at output x_1,[1] there are now two outputs where marginal cost and marginal revenue are equal, namely, x_2 and x_1.

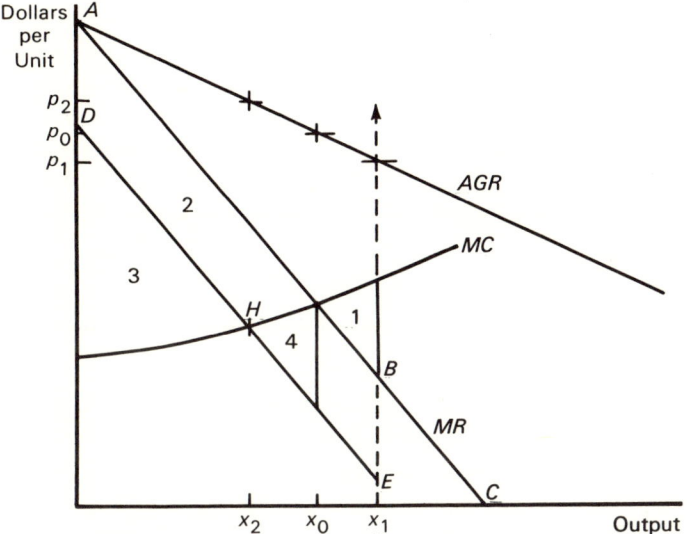

CHART 18a.
Effect on marginal revenue, output, and price of bracketed specific tax.

---

[1] An infinitesimal increase in output from below to above x_1 will result in an infinitesimal decrease in price from above p_1, where all units sold are taxed, to below p_1, where no units are taxed, and as the tax bill drops suddenly from some level to zero, net marginal revenue will be increased substantially. For a detailed treatment of discontinuities in tax functions, see P. Folliet, *Les tarifs d'impot* (Lausanne, 1947).

Output and price after the tax is imposed will be either x_1, p_1 (i.e., price falls just enough so that the lower tax—in this case, zero—in the next lower bracket applies), or x_2, p_2 (i.e., the after-tax price is exactly the same as if the specific tax t had applied at all prices). Although conceivably both of these price-output combinations could result in the same monopoly profit, generally one will be preferable to the other. The before-tax profit, tax bill, and the after-tax profit functions for this type of tax are shown in Chart 18b. As long as the taxable price range includes the pre-tax price, there will be two outputs at which a peak in profit is reached.

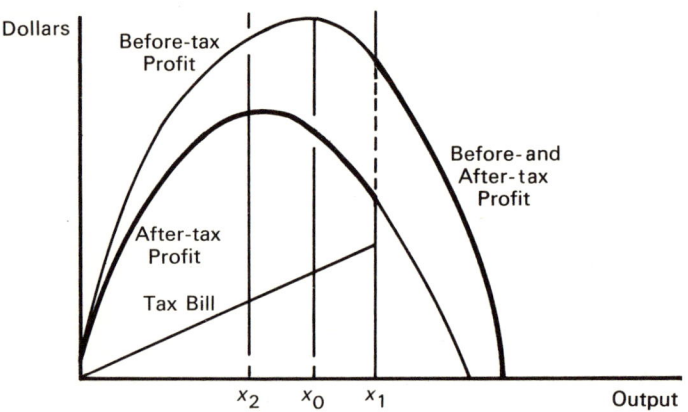

CHART 18b.
Before-tax profit, after-tax profit, and tax bill: bracketed specific tax.

Whether the step effect will reduce price to p_1 or the specific tax t will raise price to p_2 depends upon many factors, including two characteristics of the tax schedule; (1) the difference between the taxes in the low and the high bracket, and (2) the extent to which the end of a price bracket falls below the pre-tax price.

Various amounts of profit and loss (before- and after-tax) are shown as numbered areas in Chart 18a. For example, before-tax profit at output x_0 is the sum of areas 2 and 3, since over this range of output marginal revenue exceeds marginal cost. After-tax profit at output x_0 is area 3 *less* area 4 (at outputs between x_2 and x_0, marginal revenue is below marginal cost and increasing output over this range reduces profit). As long as some tax is levied at the

After-tax Equilibrium: Bracketed Taxes

pre-tax price and output, profit must be higher at output x_2 than at x_0, for the loss measured by area 4 can be avoided by reducing output to x_2, and the price must change as a result of the tax.

If the price falls to p_1 (and output increases to x_1), after-tax profit will be the sum of areas 2 and 3, less area 1. At output x_2 and price p_2 profit is represented by area 3. Whether the higher price p_2 or the lower price p_1 is more profitable after the tax depends upon the sizes of areas 1 and 2. If area 1 – the loss incurred by reducing price sufficiently to obtain the lower tax – is small compared to area 2, the price will fall. If reducing price to the next lower bracket decreases profit greatly compared to area 2, the price will rise.

While there are no a priori grounds for deductions concerning the sizes of areas 1 and 2, changes in the two characteristics of the tax just mentioned affect these areas differently and some general conclusions are possible.

1. The difference between the per unit taxes in the two brackets can be increased by raising the tax in bracket 2. This change will lower the *DE* portion of the after-tax marginal revenue curve (increasing the size of area 2) but will not affect the *BC* portion (and area 1 is unchanged). For pre-tax equilibrium conditions and a bracketed tax such that p_2 and p_1 produce equal after-tax profit, increasing the tax will make p_1, the lower price, preferable. Decreasing the tax in bracket 2 would make p_2 preferable. In other words, the greater the step in the per unit tax from one bracket to the next, the greater is the profit incentive to escape the heavier tax by decreasing price to p_1.

2. If the price at the end of the bracket, p_1, had been very much below the pre-tax price, output x_1 would have been much larger than the pre-tax output, and the cost to the firm, in terms of profit, of moving into the lower rate bracket (shown by area 1) would have been much larger. The size of area 2 would, however, not have been affected. Again, suppose that pre-tax conditions and a tax are such that after-tax prices p_1 and p_2 are equally profitable; if the tax is changed only by reducing the price that separates the two brackets, the higher price, p_2, is now preferred.

3. If the price rises as a result of this simple tax, the increase will be the same as if the within-bracket formula had applied to *all* prices, not merely those higher than p_1. If the price falls, because of the step effect, it will fall to the price at which a lower tax applies.

It may be noted that, as long as some tax applies at the pre-tax price, the price cannot remain unchanged by the tax.

Although the tax being examined here is a two-bracket one with no tax in the lower price bracket, the conclusions just given apply equally well to a tax levied in two brackets. The characteristic of a bracketed tax that leads to a downward price change is, not the level of the per unit tax that applies at the pre-tax price, but rather the reduction in the per unit tax that can be obtained by lowering price. The curve labeled BC in Chart 18a could represent marginal revenue as changed by the (lower) tax in the low price bracket. The relative sizes of areas 1 and 2 in the chart still determine which of the two after-tax prices, p_1 or p_2, is the more profitable.

If the within-bracket tax formula is the ad valorem tax instead of the specific tax, the analysis is not substantially changed. Chart 19a shows the effect on marginal revenue of a two-bracket tax with no tax in the lower price bracket and a fixed ad valorem rate in the higher bracket. The DE portion of the marginal revenue curve is no longer parallel to the pre-tax marginal revenue curve, but the meaning, in terms of profit or loss, of the various areas on the chart is the same as before. The *differential* tax rate (between the two brackets) and the nearness of the "critical" price to the pre-tax price still determine whether price will fall to the end of a bracket, or rise as a result of the within-bracket tax formula.

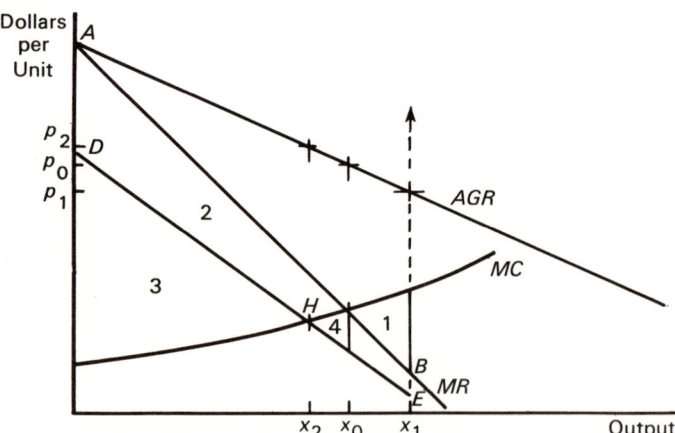

CHART 19a.
Effect on marginal revenue, output, and price of bracketed ad valorem tax.

After-tax Equilibrium: Bracketed Taxes

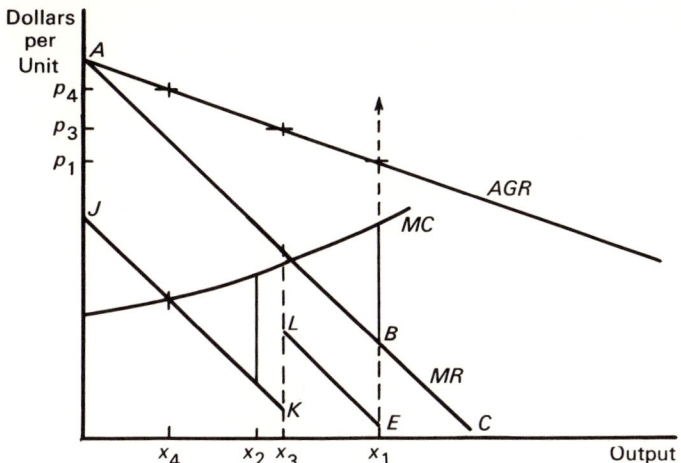

CHART 19b.
Effect on marginal revenue of several price brackets: specific tax.

The second way in which a "step up" in the tax may exert a downward influence on price is by preventing as large a price increase as would have occurred without the step. Suppose (contrary to the appearance of Chart 18a) that the two-bracketed tax described above would have increased price to p_2. If the tax schedule is revised (by adding a third bracket)

$$t(p) = 0, \quad \text{for } p \leq p_1$$
$$t(p) = t, \quad \text{for } p_1 < p \leq p_3$$
$$t(p) = t', \quad \text{for } p_3 < p, \quad \text{where } t' > t$$

a second discontinuity is introduced in the marginal revenue curve at output x_3, corresponding to price p_3. Chart 19b includes the new marginal revenue curve, which now consists of three disconnected portions: JK, LE, and BC. Since the end price, p_3, is lower than p_2 (in order that the third bracket affect price at all), there are again three prices to be considered: those corresponding to outputs x_2, x_3, and x_4. But output x_2 no longer maximizes profit, for profit can be increased by reducing output to x_4 (the argument is identical to that which ruled out x_0 as an optimum output under the two-bracket tax). Similarly, the comparison of x_3 and x_4, in terms of profitability, is made on exactly the same grounds as the previous comparison of x_1 and x_2, before the third bracket was added. There is no necessary reason why the best price-output combination under the three-bracket tax may not be p_3, x_3, in which case the second step in the per unit tax will have prevented the price from rising as much as it would otherwise have done.

As before, if the second step is large or if the end price, p_3, is not much below p_2, p_3 is likely to be the after-tax price. Otherwise, the price may rise, in response to the tax formula within the third bracket, to p_4.

B. *Downward Step*

At the beginning of Section A it was stated that, if the step in the per unit tax is downward—in contrast to the upward steps examined previously—the effect of the step could be to make the price higher or lower. Consider a tax similar to (44) but levied in the lower bracket and not in the upper one:

$$t(p) = t, \quad \text{for } p < p_1$$
$$t(p) = 0, \quad \text{for } p \geqslant p_1$$

Chart 20a shows one possibility, namely, that where the price at which the tax drops is substantially above the pre-tax price. The after-tax marginal revenue curve consists of section AB (where no tax applies) and section DEF, with a discontinuity at output x_1. The profits gained after tax at several prices and outputs are shown as areas between the marginal cost and the appropriate marginal revenue curves:

x_0, p_0 — area 1 plus 5 less 3
x_2, p_2 — area 1 plus 5
x_1, p_1 — area 1 plus 4

Price must change since the pre-tax price, p_0, will invariably yield a smaller profit than p_2. Whether price will rise somewhat to p_2 (as it would if the specific tax t had applied at all prices) or rise further to p_1 (at which price the lower tax, in this case zero, applies) depends upon the same features of the steps and brackets as before.

1. If the step is increased, area 5 will be reduced, area 4 will be increased, and it is more likely that price will rise all the way to p_1.
2. If the price at which the step occurs is only slightly above the other possible after-tax price, p_2, area 5 will be small compared to area 4, and price is more likely to rise to p_1.

After-tax Equilibrium: Bracketed Taxes

Chart 20b shows another possible effect of a downward step in the per unit tax. The price at which the tax declines, p_1, may be below the level to which price would have risen without the step. The after-tax marginal revenue curve is in two parts, AB and DF. Output x_2 would have been the optimum output if the tax had applied at all prices — as shown by the dotted extension of the DF portion of the after-tax marginal revenue curve toward the point G. At this output the lower tax applies and profit is the sum of areas 1 and 4; at output x_1 (the lower tax still applies) profit is the sum of areas 1, 4, and 2, which must be greater than the profit at x_2.

Therefore, if the price at which the per unit tax steps downward is higher than the pre-tax price but lower than the level to which price would have risen without the step, the price will rise only to the price at which the lower tax becomes effective.

C. *No Step Effect*

When the step in the per unit tax exerts any influence on price, the after-tax price must be at one end of a tax bracket. If this is *not* the case, the after-tax price must be the same as the price that the

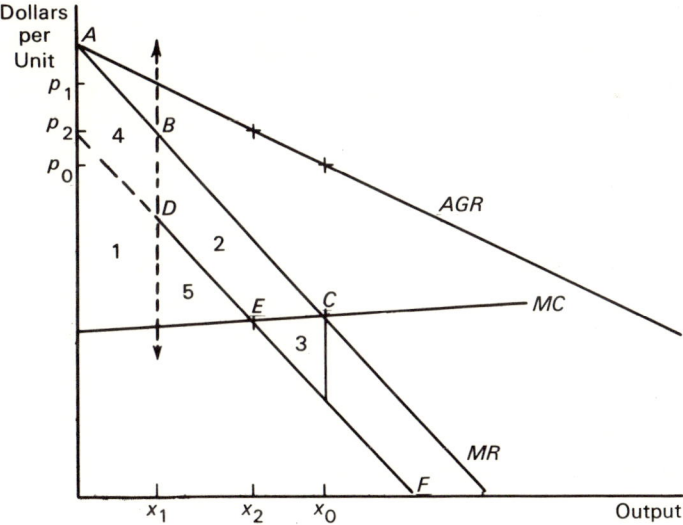

CHART 20a.
Effect of downward step in tax: price may rise farther than without step.

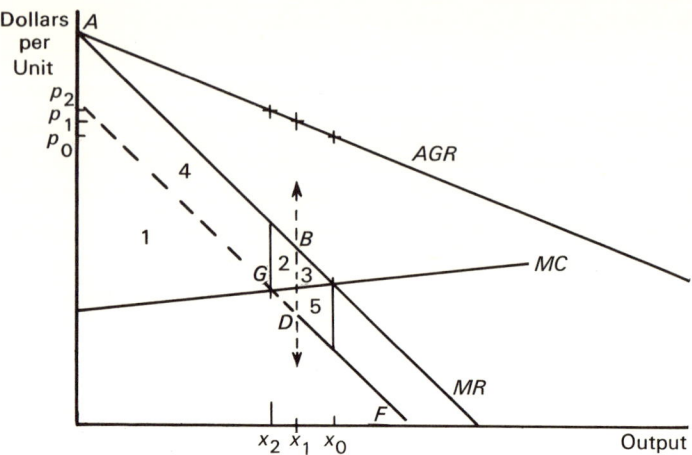

CHART 20b.
Effect of downward step in tax: price may rise less than without step.

within-bracket formula would have produced if it had applied to all prices. Consider a modification of the tax underlying Chart 18b. If the price at which the per unit tax steps up is lowered, the output at which the after-tax profit curve is discontinuous will be increased, and the right peak of profits will be lowered. If p_1 is sufficiently low (see statement 2, p. 91), profit will be maximized at output x_2 and price p_2. But it is clear that a specific tax of amount t without the exclusion of low price items from the tax would also have led to price p_2.

When a tax schedule is bracketed, the formula that specifies the level of tax from one bracket to another will partially determine the after-tax price in accordance with the conclusions given for continuous tax functions. The final price will then depend upon either the tax formula within each bracket or the steps between brackets.

D. *Gap in After-tax Prices*

Under any form of bracketed tax with steps upward between brackets, there is some range of price at the low end of each interval that cannot be profit-maximizing as long as the demand curve has a negative slope. For example, if a specific tax of $5 per unit is levied, provided the price is equal to or greater than $50, any price between

After-tax Equilibrium: Bracketed Taxes

$50 and $54.98 is not a possible after-tax price. Any price in this range yields a net revenue per unit that is smaller than the $49.99 that would be obtained if the price were set at $49.99. Since the negative slope of the demand curve assures that fewer units will be sold at prices above $50 than below $50, a lower price must produce greater profit than any price between $50.00 and $54.98.

A similar argument applies if there is a tax in the lower bracket (as long as there is an *upward* step to the next bracket), or if the tax is ad valorem and the tax rate rises from one bracket to the next.[2]

---

[2]The British Purchase Tax at one time consisted of many excises, some of which were equivalent to a two-bracket ad valorem tax with no tax in the low bracket. The resulting gap in the spectrum of prices (and of qualities) aroused complaints that led to a change in the tax schedule to the form of the proportional tax on excess price [J. F. Due, *Sales Taxation* (Urbana, 1957), 221–22]. The latter tax does not rule out any prices by simple arithmetic.

Chapter 8. *After-tax Equilibrium: Bounties*

The conditions that determine whether a tax will increase or reduce price (and output) have been described in the previous chapters in terms of the relative sizes of the tax and demand elasticities. These conditions must be reformulated slightly if, instead of a tax being levied, a bounty is awarded to the producer of a commodity or service. It will be seen that there are bounty (or subsidy) schemes that do not necessarily increase output and reduce price.

The analysis of the effects of bounties fits conveniently within the structure developed in Chapter 6. The per unit bounty is represented as a function of price and as a negative tax. If output is chosen as the independent variable, marginal revenue including the subsidy (with respect to output changes) will be lowered, raised, or left unchanged, depending upon whether the marginal subsidy, given by

$$t[p(x)]\left[1 - \frac{E_t(p)}{-E_x(p)}\right] \tag{27}$$

is positive, negative, or zero. [It will be recalled that, in the general expression for the after-tax marginal revenue function (24), the equivalent of the above expression is preceded by a minus sign. The expression for the marginal subsidy here is a slightly modified form of that for the marginal tax bill in Chapter 6, Expression (26).]

Since the bounty is a negative tax and the per unit tax was defined in (1) as a positive quantity, for all per unit bounties, $t(p)$ must be negative.

The sign of the *slope* of the bounty function must be ascertained with some care.
   1. If the per unit bounty is constant, regardless of price, the slope of the bounty function is zero.

2. If the per unit bounty increases as price increases, the slope of the bounty function is *negative* [since $t(p)$ is negative and p is positive].
3. If the per unit bounty decreases as price increases, the slope of the bounty function is positive.

The elasticity of the bounty function is given by

$$E_t(p) = \frac{p \cdot t'(p)}{t(p)} \qquad (6)$$

If the per unit bounty is constant, the bounty elasticity is zero; if the per unit bounty increases with price, the elasticity is positive since both $t(p)$ and $t'(p)$ are negative; if the bounty decreases as price increases, the elasticity is negative.

A bounty will leave output and price unchanged if marginal revenue at the pre-bounty price is unaffected by the bounty, that is, if the marginal subsidy, (27), is zero. The marginal subsidy will be zero if the per unit bounty elasticity is positive and equal to the demand elasticity, for then the term in brackets in (27) will be zero and this expression will also be zero. Just as a lump-sum tax was shown to be equivalent to a per unit tax with the tax elasticity equal to the demand elasticity (Chapter 4), a lump-sum bounty is also equivalent to a bounty with an elasticity equal to the elasticity of demand. Neither a tax nor a bounty of this form would have any effect on the optimum price and output. Also, a bounty of any form such that the bounty and demand elasticities are equal at the pre-bounty price would leave price and output unchanged.

Similarly, a bounty will increase output and reduce the price to buyers if marginal revenue is increased, that is, if (27) is negative. This will occur whenever the portion in brackets is positive, since t is now defined as negative. The bracketed portion of (27) remains positive as long as the per unit bounty elasticity is smaller than the negative of the demand elasticity. Therefore a wide variety of conceivable bounty arrangements will increase output: the bounty per unit may increase with price (although not too rapidly), remain constant, or even decline as price increases. Under each of these arrangements, output will increase and price will fall. That is to say, an ad valorem bounty (as long as the demand elasticity exceeds unity), a specific per unit bounty, and a regressive bounty (i.e., the

After-tax Equilibrium: Bounties

per unit bounty decreases as price increases) would each reduce price and increase output.

Finally, the converse of the proposition that some excise taxes will reduce price (Chapter 4) is that some bounties will lead to higher prices, with the bounty being paid in addition to the price. For price will rise and output will fall if (27) is positive. Since t is negative for a bounty, (27) will be positive if the bracketed portion is negative, that is, if the bounty elasticity is positive but greater than the demand elasticity. Thus if, roughly speaking, the per unit bounty increases rapidly as price rises (specifically if the bounty elasticity exceeds the demand elasticity), higher prices become very desirable and the price will rise.

An interesting combination of a tax and bounty was suggested by Joan Robinson as a possible measure for the control of monopoly.[1] A per unit bounty is awarded, of such amount that the monopolist's best reaction is to produce the output that would be forthcoming in a competitive industry.[2] The total amount of subsidy paid can then be recouped by a lump-sum tax that will not disturb the after-bounty price and output. A monopoly is converted into a "competitive" industry at no cost to the treasury other than administrative and enforcement expenses.

It may be noted that, in principle, there is some progressive excise tax that would also lead to the "competitive" price and output. If the monopolist is to remain in business, however, the tax bill would have to become zero at that point. If the tax bill is still positive, the firm would not be earning normal profits and its resources would shift to other industries.

---

[1] *Economics of Imperfect Competition*, p. 163. Mrs. Robinson attributed the device to E. A. G. Robinson, who originated it in an answer to an examination question.

[2] The amount of per unit subsidy needed to lead to this output is the difference between marginal costs and marginal revenue at the competitive output. For a detailed analysis of the proposal, see B. Higgins, "Fiscal Control of Monopoly," in *Readings in the Economics of Taxation*, ed. by R. A. Musgrave and C. S. Shoup (1959), pp. 312–21. This is a condensed version of a longer article by Higgins, "Post-war Tax Policy (Part I)," *Canadian Journal of Economics and Political Science*, IX, 408–28.

Chapter 9. *Other Market Structures*

Up to this point the analysis has pertained to a single-firm industry, that is, a firm faced by a demand curve that is negatively sloped and that does not shift as a result of other firms' reactions to price or output changes. Other sets of market conditions are worthy of some attention, if only to show the extent to which the scope of the conclusions reached so far can perhaps be broadened.

In this chapter four additional types of markets are examined briefly to determine the general statements that can be made about the price and output effects of excise taxes in each case. Section A deals with a converse of the monopolistic seller, namely, the monopsonistic buyer. In the remaining sections, pure competition, monopolistic competition, and oligopoly are discussed.

A. *Monopsony*

A monopsonist is defined as a sole buyer of a factor of production (or, more generally, any good or service) that is offered by a competitive industry. (In contrast, monopoly obtains when one firm offers the total output of an industry for sale to a group of buyers who act competitively.)

1. PRE-TAX EQUILIBRIUM

The price offered and the amount of the factor purchased by the monopsonist are determined by two functions or schedules: (*a*) the monopsonist's *demand* for the factor at each price—this demand is derived from the demand curve for the final product; and (*b*) the supply curve for the factor. But it is not the intersection of the demand and supply curves that determines price and purchases— that would be the case only if the purchases were made by a large number of competitive buyers, whose individual purchases were such a small portion of total demand that price would be unaffected by them; then the marginal cost of a unit of the factor would be equal to price. The monopsonist, however, purchases the entire supply, and his marginal cost is not equal to price; to purchase an added unit, he must raise the price of *all* units purchased.

These relations are shown in Chart 21a. The buyer's marginal cost curve is marginal to the sellers' supply curve. The monopsony purchases, x_m, are indicated by the intersection of the buyer's

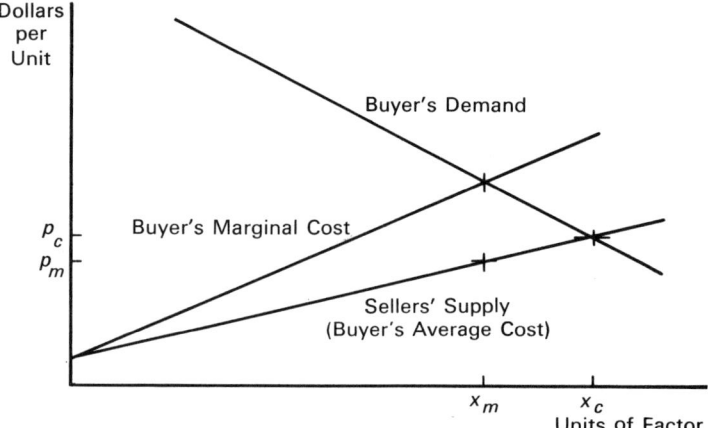

CHART 21a.
Monopsony equilibrium: price and purchases.

demand and marginal cost curves—since the marginal cost curve lies above the average cost curve, purchases must always be smaller than the amount that would be taken by a group of competing buyers with the same total demand.

The monopsony price, p_m, is the price required to call forth x_m units of the factor, that is, the price corresponding to x_m on the supply curve. This price will be below the price p_c that would result from competitive bidding for the factor.

In short, price and purchases are determined by the intersection of the buyer's demand and marginal cost curves. Just as a monopolist finds it to his advantage to restrict output and raise the price he receives, so a monopsonist gains by restricting purchases and lowering the price he pays.

Any change that raises (lowers) the marginal cost curve will reduce (increase) price and purchases, as long as the change does

Other Market Structures

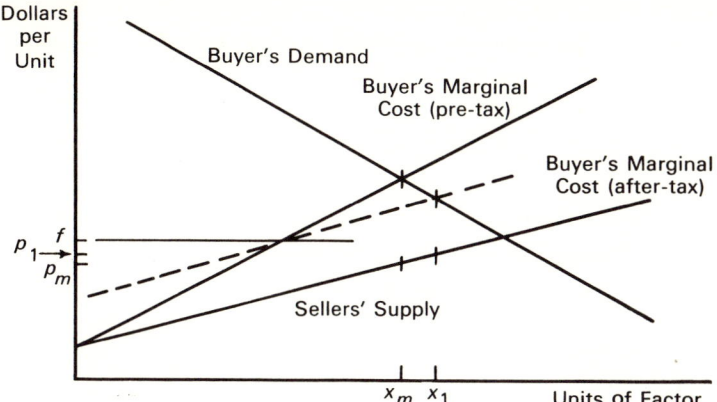

CHART 21b.
Effect of "tax on price deficiency" on monopsony price and purchases.

not shift the demand curve and as long as the marginal cost curve continues to intersect the demand curve from below (this requirement is, in effect, the second-order condition for equilibrium).

To show how an excise tax will shift the marginal cost curve, an algebraic expression for the marginal cost function is needed. Let the sellers' supply curve (and the buyer's average cost curve) be given by

$$p = p(x)$$

where p represents the price per unit, and x represents purchases per time period. It may be noted here that, since the factor is the output of a competitive industry, the supply curve will be upward sloping, that is,

$$p'(x) > 0$$

The buyer's total cost will be the product of the number of units and the per unit price, or

$$TC = xp(x)$$

His marginal cost curve, with respect to the volume of purchases, x, will be

$$MC = x \cdot p'(x) + p(x)$$

and since $p'(x)$ is positive, marginal cost will, if any units are purchased, always exceed average cost, $p(x)$.

2. AFTER-TAX EQUILIBRIUM

It remains to be shown how an excise tax will affect the marginal cost curve. The tax bill can be regarded as an addition to total costs, particularly since the per unit tax will be defined as a function of the buyer's cost per unit, that is,

$$t = t[p(x)]$$

Total costs including tax are now given by

$$TC = x \cdot p(x) + x \cdot t[p(x)]$$

and marginal costs by

$$MC = x \cdot p'(x) + p(x) + \{xt'[p(x)]p'(x) + t[p(x)]\} \quad (45)$$

The marginal tax bill is

$$MTB = x \cdot t'[p(x)]p'(x) + t[p(x)] \quad (46)$$

Marginal costs will be raised (lowered) by the tax if the marginal tax bill is positive (negative).

The characteristics of the tax and supply functions that will make the marginal tax bill positive or negative could be determined by manipulating the bracketed term of (45), but this has already been done in Chapter 6. A comparison of (46) and the bracketed portion of (24) shows that the marginal tax bill is analytically the same in both instances. The only difference is that in the monopsony case the marginal tax bill is added to marginal cost (previously, the tax bill was subtracted from marginal revenue).

According to the algebra in Chapter 6, the marginal tax bill will be positive or negative whenever

$$t[p(x)]\left[1 - \frac{E_t(p)}{-E_x(p)}\right]$$

is positive or negative. In other words, marginal cost including tax will be raised (lowered) if (27) is positive (negative).

One other difference between monopsony and monopoly must be noted. The elasticity of supply, $E_x(p)$, is positive (i.e., the curve is positively sloped), whereas the monopolist's demand elasticity is negative. The effects of various types of excise taxes on (27), hence on marginal cost and on monopsony price and output, may be listed as follows.[1]

---

[1] Bounties are not considered here — $t[p(x)]$ is always positive.

Other Market Structures

$E_t(p)$	Marginal Tax Bill	Price	Purchases
Positive	Positive	Falls	Fall
Zero	Positive	Falls	Fall
$= -E_x(p)$	Zero	No change	No change
$< -E_x(p)$	Negative	Rises	Rise

Thus an excise tax with an elasticity that is negative (i.e., a highly regressive tax) and larger in absolute value than the elasticity of supply will raise both monopsony price and purchases. A negative tax elasticity means that the per unit tax declines as price increases (see, e.g., tax 7, Table 2). Or, more generally, a tax with an elasticity smaller than "zero" may raise monopsony price and purchases.[2] Thus both the specific tax (elasticity equals zero) and the ad valorem tax (elasticity equals unity) will *lower* both the net price a monopsonist pays and the amount of the factor he will buy.

The power tax function can be devised to have a negative elasticity by choosing a negative value of n. Similarly, the proportional tax on excess price can be modified in form so that the elasticity is negative, if the tax rate is applied, not to the amount by which the price exceeds some level c, but to the amount by which price remains below some floor f. That is, the tax is levied on the amount of price deficiency. Let the per unit tax be defined by

$$t = r[f - p(x)]$$

where

$$f > p_m$$

and

$$t = 0, \quad \text{for} \quad p > f$$

The elasticity of this tax with respect to price is given by

$$E_t(p) = \frac{t'(p) \cdot p}{t}$$

$$= \frac{-r \cdot p}{r(f - p)}$$

$$= -\frac{p}{f - p}$$

---

[2]The corresponding rule for monopoly is as follows: a tax with an elasticity larger than unity may lower monopoly price and increase output.

Since both f and p are positive and $f > p$, the tax elasticity will be negative. At a low level of purchases (and price), the (negative) elasticity will be very near zero and the marginal cost curve will be raised above the pre-tax marginal cost curve; at some high level of purchases (and price) the tax elasticity will become larger, neglecting the negative sign, than the supply elasticity and the marginal cost curve will be lowered by the tax. The overall effect of the tax on marginal cost is shown in Chart 21b (compare with Chart 15a, where the effect of the tax on excess price is shown). The tax raises price from p_m to p_1 and increases purchases from x_m to x_1.

Just as there is some tax on excess price that will lower monopoly price to the level c, as long as c is above marginal cost (see Chart 16b), there is some tax that will raise monopsony price to the level f, as long as f is set below marginal cost at the pre-tax level of purchases. Any increase in monopsony price will, of course, bring this price closer to the corresponding "competitive" level.

B. *Pure Competition*

The theoretical effects of excise taxes, under conditions of pure competition, have been examined in great detail by many students of tax incidence.[3] These investigations have generally been limited to the specific tax and the ad valorem tax; the purpose of this section is to answer the question, "Do other forms of excise tax lead to price or output changes that differ in any substantial way from those resulting from the more common types of tax?" It can be shown easily that the answer is "no." Few important issues will be by-passed in restricting the analysis to long-run effects.

1. PRE-TAX EQUILIBRIUM

To summarize briefly, a purely competitive industry is one consisting of a large number of firms each of which produces a relatively small amount of an identical product. At each price there is some total supply of product that will, in the long-run, be offered for sale, and all pairs of prices and outputs constitute the industry supply curve.

---

[3] J. F. Due, *The Theory of Incidence of Sales Taxation* (New York, 1942), Chapter II, presents a comprehensive account that includes a discussion of the process of adjustment to the tax over time.

Other Market Structures

The total demand for the product at each price consists of the sum of the demands of individual buyers, none of whom purchases a sufficiently large amount to affect the total appreciably by his appearance on or withdrawal from the market. The total demand curve, showing the amounts that would be taken at all prices, is negatively sloped, indicating either that at high prices each consumer purchases smaller amounts than at low prices or that at high prices some consumers purchase no units at all.

The long-run equilibrium price is the price at which consumers are willing to buy the amount that suppliers are willing to offer. In other words, the intersection of the long-run demand and supply schedules determines the equilibrium price and output (the possibility that there are several points of intersection is ignored). It is essential, for equilibrium to exist, that the demand function intersect the supply function from above.

At the equilibrium output and price, average revenue and marginal revenue (to the individual firm) are equal; average cost and marginal cost are equal; and average revenue (or price) is equal to both average and marginal cost. Since average costs are just covered by price, no firm is making profits higher than the level necessary to induce it to remain in the industry.

2. AFTER-TAX EQUILIBRIUM

In these circumstances, *any* excise tax — whether the per unit tax is proportional to price, progressive, or regressive — must lower output and raise price. The after-tax demand curve, that is, the average net revenue curve, is given by

$$p_n = p(x) - t[p(x)]$$

As long as $t[p(x)]$ is positive, the net demand curve is lowered by the tax at all outputs (by varying amounts depending upon the type of tax). It is the intersection of the supply curve and the net demand curve that determines the smaller after-tax output (x_t in Chart 22), but the price that this reduced output will command in the market is shown by the pre-tax demand curve (p_t in Chart 22). (The net demand curve in the chart is based on a per unit tax function that increases as price rises.)

The increase in price from the tax does not come about from price changes by individual firms—no firm has any control over price[4]. The tax does, however, reduce the net price to the firm, and output must be decreased to bring marginal cost down to the level of this lower net price. The general output reduction will raise the market

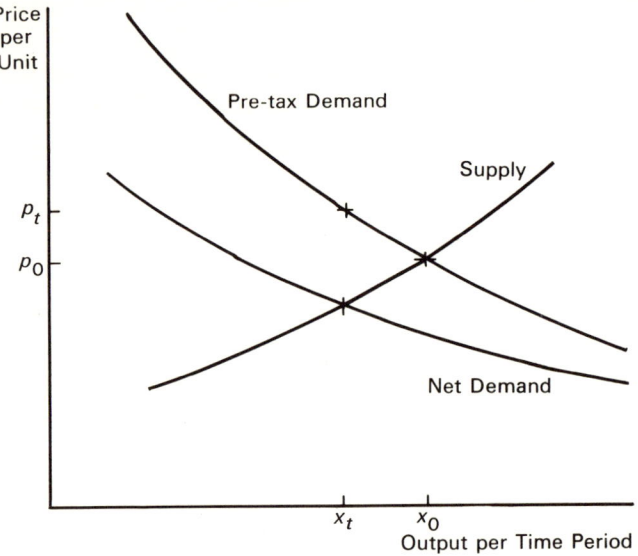

CHART 22.
Effect of any excise tax on price and output: pure competition.

price somewhat; an added increase results, with the passage of time, as firms—no longer able to cover average costs plus the tax—leave the industry, reducing total output further until price rises enough to cover the average costs, plus tax, of the remaining firms.[5]

A distinctive element in the mechanism of tax-induced price change is the departure of unprofitable firms from the industry; the firms that remain do not *decide* to raise price—they *discover* that price is increasing.

---

[4]The number of firms in a purely competitive industry must be so large that the output decisions of any one firm have no effect on the market price. The demand curve facing each firm, before tax, is horizontal; at a price higher than the market price, no output could be sold at all; at the market price or any lower price, the firm could sell as much as desired.
[5]Due, *Incidence of Sales Taxation*, pp. 17–22.

Other Market Structures

C. Monopolistic Competition

The structure of the markets considered above can be described as one of extremes: a sole seller (or buyer) dealing with a large group of competitors, and a large group of competing sellers (of identical products) dealing with a large group of competing buyers. One intermediate structure that will be examined here is monopolistic competition. "This designation is used... to refer to markets where there are many small sellers, and where their products are differentiated. In effect, it refers to competition within large groups of close—but not perfect—substitute products."[6] The number of studies of excise taxes in this context is very small.[7]

The purposes of this section are: to illustrate the pre-tax equilibrium in only enough detail for subsequent use; to show the possibility that, if entry is blocked and firms do earn excess profit, there is some (progressive) excise tax that may not change price and output or that may increase output and reduce price; and to demonstrate that, even though entry to the industry is sufficiently free to eliminate all excess profits, a progressive excise tax may lower price. It must be admitted, however, that the existence of many possible interrelationships among firms precludes definitive conclusions.

1. PRE-TAX EQUILIBRIUM

The nature of the pre-tax equilibrium for the individual firm is not substantially different from that for the pure monopolist. The firm, to maximize profit, must operate at the output such that marginal revenue equals marginal cost (Chapter 3).

However, the demand curve facing each of many firms is not the same as the industry demand curve. Since the product of each firm differs in some way from those of other firms, in a sense there is no

---

[6] J. S. Bain, *Price Theory* (New York, 1952), p. 350. Much of the theoretical groundwork of monopolistic competition is due to E. H. Chamberlin, *The Theory of Monopolistic Competition* (6th ed.; Cambridge, 1950) and J. Robinson, *Economics of Imperfect Competition*.

[7] The major work is that of Due, *Incidence of Sales Taxation* (his Chapter IV, on the specific tax, is reprinted in R. A. Musgrave and C. S. Shoup, *Readings in the Economics of Taxation*); Otto von Mering presents a very short section on tax incidence under monopolistic competition (which was apparently prepared without knowledge of Due's work), *The Shifting and Incidence of Taxation* (Philadelphia, 1942), pp. 71–77. Musgrave, in *Theory of Public Finance*, also mentions the subject briefly.

industry demand curve. Furthermore, at least two demand (or average revenue) curves face each firm.

One shows the amounts that the firm could sell at each price, provided the other firms did not change price, output, type of product, amount of selling effort, etc. This demand curve may be referred as the *ceteris paribus* demand. The fact that the firm's product has some unique characteristics assures that this demand curve will not be horizontal, as under pure competition with identical products; it will be negatively sloped but will be more elastic than it would if there were no close substitutes. The level and shape of this *ceteris paribus* demand curve depend, however, on the policies of other firms. Since the number of firms in the "industry" is large, the profit-maximizing adjustments of any one firm will go unnoticed by the others and will have no effect on their policies.

The second demand curve facing the firm shows the amounts it could sell at all prices, provided that all firms change prices jointly in some specific manner. Joint price changes may occur if, for example, cost conditions are altered for all firms, or if an excise tax is imposed.

The pre-tax equilibrium for each firm is shown in Chart 23a. The average revenue (or *ceteris paribus* demand) curve for a firm is labeled AR—similar curves for other firms may have different shapes or levels—and the curve marginal to it, MR. With average costs, AC, and marginal costs, MC, as shown, the best output for

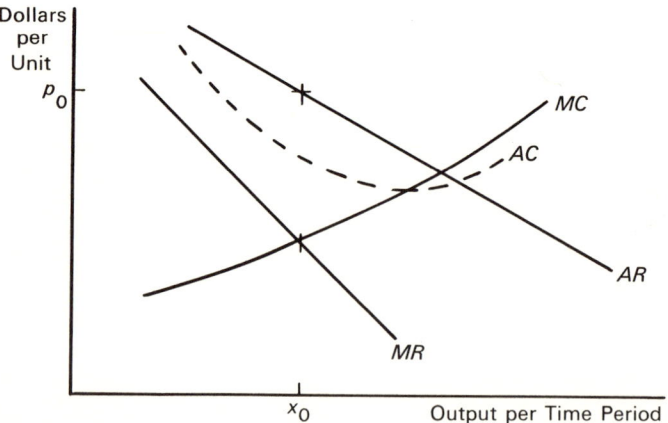

CHART 23a.
Pre-tax equilibrium: monopolistic competition, excess profit.

Other Market Structures

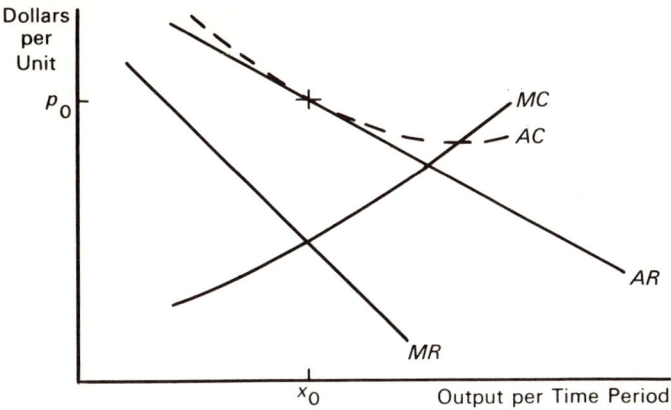

CHART 23b.
Pre-tax equilibrium: monopolistic competition, no excess profit.

this firm is x_0, at price p_0, and the firm is earning an excess profit, as price is higher than average cost (which includes the profit necessary to keep the firm in the industry) at output x_0. Other firms may also be obtaining an excess profit if entry into the industry is blocked.

On the other hand, if entry is free, firms will be attracted by the excess profit and the appearance on the market of the products of the new entrants will lower the average revenue curves of the previous members. Ideally, entry will continue until all excess profit has disappeared; each firm finds that its average revenue curve has fallen to an extent that average costs are nowhere below average revenue, as shown in Chart 23b.

One of the features of equilibrium that has been emphasized[8] is that no firm is operating at the point of lowest average costs, particularly when excess profits are zero or small. Since the average cost curve is tangent to a negatively sloped demand curve, the lowest average cost point must be at some output greater than x_0. Thus "excess capacity" or the ability to produce at lower than actual costs is a characteristic of each firm in this type of industry.

2. AFTER-TAX EQUILIBRIUM

An excise tax will shift the marginal revenue curves (with respect to output) of each firm in the manner shown in Chapter 6: if the tax

[8]Chamberlin, *Monopolistic Competition*, pp. 104–6.

elasticity exceeds the demand elasticity at x_0, marginal revenue at x_0 will be raised; if the two elasticities are equal, marginal revenue will be unchanged; if the tax elasticity is smaller than the demand elasticity, marginal revenue will fall.[9]

a. If all firms earn excess profit, there is some tax that will leave all prices unchanged, provided one of two unlikely assumptions is made. It may be supposed either that (i) the elasticity of demand for each firm, at its optimum price and output, is the same for all firms; or (ii) the marginal costs of each firm, at equilibrium, are all equal.

On the first assumption, a progressive excise tax with an elasticity equal to the common demand elasticity will not provide any incentive for any firm to change price or output. Each firm finds its level of marginal revenue at x_0 unchanged; x_0 and p_0 still provide maximum profit, even though profit is reduced by the tax. The structure of prices and the total output would remain the same as before the tax.

On the second assumption, a proportional tax on excess price, with the parameter c set equal to the common marginal cost, would similarly have no effect on prices.[10]

It is, of course, much more likely that the demand elasticities and marginal costs of the firms are not the same. In this case it may be of interest to show the possible effects of a highly progressive tax.

Given that the firms' demand elasticities differ, consider a progressive tax with an elasticity greater than the demand elasticity of any firm (e.g., a power tax with large n).[11] Each firm finds that after-tax profit can be increased by *lowering* price and increasing output. If all firms are earning normal after-tax profits, and *if there were no other changes*, all prices would be lowered by the tax.

But the general price reduction will lower the average revenue curves of each firm. The decline in the *ceteris paribus* demand of the firm will, in turn, affect its marginal revenue curve. At this point an added difficulty is encountered. J. Robinson has shown that a decrease in demand *may* lower marginal revenue, but it may also

---

[9] Through this section it will be assumed that the tax does not change the pattern of product differentiation in the industry.

[10] In both cases it is necessary that the tax be sufficiently small so that no firm is earning less than normal profit after the tax is imposed. Otherwise some firms would leave the industry, which would shift the pre-tax demand curve of the remaining firms.

[11] It should be pointed out that, if the elasticity of a tax is large, at prices just below the pre-tax price the per unit tax is very small, and at prices just above the pre-tax price the per unit tax may be very large (e.g., tax 6, Table 2).

Other Market Structures

leave it unchanged or increase it.[12] If marginal revenue for each firm is reduced by the drop in average revenue, the output of each firm will fall and price will rise from the initial after-tax levels; no general comparison between the pre-tax and after-tax equilibria is possible, although it is not inconceivable that prices will be lower and output higher than before the tax.

If marginal revenue of each firm is unchanged by the widespread price reduction that follows the imposition of the tax, the secondary adjustments lead to a further decline in price. For the initial price reduction lowered the average revenue curve of each firm, which will in turn lower price more. This process would end, on the assumptions made, only when all excess profits have disappeared; it would end more quickly if marginal revenue began to shift downward as the average revenue curves fell. At the after-tax equilibrium, all firms will have larger output at lower prices. Since the after-tax average revenue curve for each firm is below the pre-tax curve, excess profits will be reduced by the tax.

Should it happen that each firm's marginal revenue was *raised* by the initial price decline, there would be a similar tendency toward still higher output and still lower prices.

b. If there is freedom of entry, firms will enter the industry until excess profits have been reduced to zero, as in Chart 23b (for present purposes it is assumed that no firm can maintain a position of excess profit). Due has shown that, in this situation, a specific tax or an ad valorem tax will increase price.[13] The reason that price rises is partly the same as under pure competition: marginal revenue is reduced by the tax, so price is increased; each firm's output is reduced below the level at which price just covers average cost; normal profits are no longer earned; and some firms leave the industry, raising the after-tax average revenue curves of those remaining to a point of tangency with the average cost curve.

To show the effect of a progressive excise tax, it is necessary to make one of the two assumptions given on p. 114. Consider, then, a progressive excise tax that will not shift the marginal revenue curve (at x_0) of any firm. There is, therefore, no inducement to change

---

[12]*Economics of Imperfect Competition*, Chapter 4. In problems of this kind, Due assumes that the shift in marginal revenue is in the same direction as the shift in demand (*Incidence of Sales Taxation*, pp. 52–53).

[13]*Incidence of Sales Taxation*, pp. 52–53, 96–97.

output or price. But it is clear that no firm is earning normal profits (the after-tax average revenue curve will be everywhere below the average cost curve). Some firms will now leave the industry, raising the average revenue curves (both before- and after-tax) of the remaining firms. The ambiguous relation between a change in demand and the resulting change in marginal revenue again causes difficulties: if marginal revenue is unchanged, no firm will wish to change output, but enough firms will have to leave the industry to raise the after-tax average revenue curve to tangency with the average cost curve. Prices are higher by the amount of the tax; the number of firms is smaller; and, since each firm is producing the pre-tax amount, x_0, total output is smaller.

If the marginal revenue curve is shifted upward by the rise in pre-tax average revenue (accompanying the exodus of firms), the remaining firms will find it advantageous to increase output. The after-tax prices may be higher or lower than the pre-tax level, depending upon many factors, the net effect of which is unclear. Total output may also be greater or smaller than that before tax, but, since each of the remaining firms has increased output, average costs are nearer the least average cost point, a result that Due noted in connection with the ad valorem tax.[14]

D. *Oligopoly*

Remaining to be discussed in this chapter is one very common type of industrial structure — oligopoly, which is characterized by a small number of firms. The number of firms must be small enough and each firm's volume must be a large enough share of total output so that the price and output policy of any one firm has a perceptible effect on the profits of the other firms. Within this classification there are many possible subgroups, depending upon (*a*) the conditions of entry into the industry, which may range from easy to very difficult; (*b*) the ability of the firms to maintain effective price collusion; and (*c*) the extent of product differentiation. Models of price determination have been developed for some combinations of these joint possibilities, especially for those that can be defined precisely. For other combinations the "theory of oligopoly price" is generally

---

[14] Due, *Incidence of Sales Taxation*, p. 97.

stated in terms of the strength of the separate factors influencing price rather than in terms of a cleanly drawn price model.

It is, therefore, to be expected that there are not many studies of excise tax effects on the price or price structure in industries of few firms. The only writer who has discussed this problem in any detail is Due, who treats only the specific tax.[15] He shows that such a tax must raise price, whether entry is impeded and excess profit is earned in the industry or entry is free and price has been forced down to a level equal to average cost. He mentions also the possibility that the imposition of an excise tax, when no excess profit is earned before the tax, could initiate a price "war," as firms struggle to avoid losses by cutting prices to gain volume. "It is conceivable that the low levels [of price] may remain over a considerable period of time."[16]

There are several sets of conditions under which the determination of oligopoly price can be described in terms that permit the analysis of the effects of an excise tax. These conditions and the prices that result may be described as follows: (1) collusion is perfect, and the price is, in effect, the one that a pure monopolist (who owned all the firms in the industry) would adopt; (2) collusion is absent (entry into the industry is easy), but products are differentiated—price falls to a level equal to average cost; and (3) collusion is perfect and products are nearly homogeneous, but entry is costly—outside firms will be attracted if profits are "very high" but will not enter the industry if profits are only "slightly" above the normal level; price will fall somewhere between the corresponding monopoly price and the "competitive" price.

1. There are several ways by which a group of oligopolists (or duopolists) can maintain a price at or near the monopoly level. Collusion is an absolute necessity; each firm in the industry must regard its own interest (profits) as a *share* of the industry profit and in no way attempt to increase its profit at the expense of others. "The ... most extreme version of perfect collusion is found in what has been designated as the *perfect cartel.* In such a cartel, the price and output of the industry, and of each of the separate member firms, are determined solely by a central administrative agency in just such

---

[15]*Incidence of Sales Taxation*, Chapter IV.
[16]*Incidence of Sales Taxation*, p. 57.

a way as to maximize the joint profit of the member firms.[17] The decisions of the central agency may, in some countries but not in the United States, be legally binding on the members.

The collaboration of the firms in the industry may arise and persist, however, through less formal arrangements. If price changes are exactly and immediately matched, the monopoly price results. Also, if firms correctly anticipate that each of their rivals will insist on maintaining its share of the market, a near-monopoly price will result.[18] Furthermore, "... collusion need not be explicit and formal in the sense of rivals meeting, agreeing on outputs and price, and similar conspiratorial actions.... [The firms] must realize that their policies effect one another and they may develop a common price policy without express collaboration...."[19]

For any of these formal or informal arrangements to be successful, it is necessary that entry to the industry be effectively blocked. Otherwise, the excess profits of the members will attract outsiders, increasing the number of shares to be "distributed" without adding anything to total profit.

In any of the above instances, an excise tax would have exactly the same effects on price as in a pure monopoly (it is assumed that there is little or no product differentiation), and these effects have already been described in Chapters 4 to 7. A tax will raise or lower price, depending upon the relative sizes of the tax and industry demand elasticities.

2. When entry into the industry is open or the existing members make no attempts to forestall entry, new firms will enter until no firm can earn an excess profit. (Or, at least, new firms enter up to the point that the entry of one more firm would make all firms unprofitable. With two firms in the industry, both may earn excess profits; with three, all may be unprofitable. This possibility is left out of account.) If products are differentiated, price will fall until it just equals average cost. The pre-tax equilibrium is shown, in effect, in Chart 23b.[20]

The imposition of an excise tax will change price in the same directions indicated for monopolistic competition with no excess

[17] J. S. Bain, *Price Theory*, p. 284.
[18] G. J. Stigler, "Notes on the Theory of Duopoly," *Journal of Political Economy*, XLVIII, 528–31.
[19] G. J. Stigler, *The Theory of Price* (rev. ed.; New York, 1952), p. 229.
[20] See also Bain, *Price Theory*, pp. 289–90.

Other Market Structures
119

profit (Section C-2b). A specific or ad valorem tax must raise price and reduce output; a progressive tax may reduce price or leave it unchanged.

3. The third set of circumstances for oligopoly pricing includes the concept of "limit price," developed by Bain.[21] It is assumed that collusion is perfect or nearly so and that entry into the industry is not completely blocked, nor is it completely free. There are, in effect, costs involved in entering the industry (over and above the costs of *being* in the industry). The existence of these entry costs means that the established firms can earn some profit above the normal level without attracting rivals. The price which will produce the greatest profit short of that which will attract rivals is designated p_L, the limit price (this price is lower than the monopoly price, p_M, and the profit earned at p_L is less than that which could be earned at p_M if entry were blocked).

The established firms may believe that long-run profits are maximized by charging the monopoly price and earning large profits that will gradually be reduced as other firms enter. On the other hand, they may believe that long-run profits will be maximized by setting price at the level which forestalls entry and hence earn a smaller profit over a longer period.

If the limit price is adopted, an excise tax may either increase or reduce price through two effects: (*a*) the tax changes the limit price, p_L; and (*b*) it changes the monopoly price, p_M.

The imposition of *any* tax must *raise* the limit price. Rivals are presumably attracted by after-tax profit (the tax, being levied on one industry, does not affect any of the other alternatives of potential rivals). The after-tax profit at the limit price is reduced by the tax, and the firms in the industry are now free to raise price. Price can rise until after-tax profits are just below the entry level but will not rise above the after-tax monopoly price.

The tax may also change the monopoly price: a specific or ad valorem tax will raise it; a progressive tax may leave it unchanged or lower it. If the monopoly price is raised by the tax, the after-tax price (the new, higher limit price) will be above the pre-tax level. Price will rise, if possible, by just the amount necessary to raise after-tax profit to the pre-tax level! No other principle of pricing

---

[21]*Price Theory*, pp. 213–18, 290–92. See also J. S. Bain. "Pricing in Monopoly and Oligopoly," *American Economic Review*, XXXIX, 448–64.

known to the writer that is consistent with profit maximization leads to this unusual conclusion. The excess profit of a firm may not by reduced at all by a tax. Under other market structures that permit excess profit, an excise tax invariably reduces such profit.

There is some progressive tax that will lower the monopoly price to a level below the limit price. If this happens, price will fall as a result of the tax. After-tax profit is then smaller than the level that would attract rivals, and the firms in the industry are free to exploit their joint "after-tax" monopoly without fear that others will enter.

It should be added that the concept of a limit price applies equally well to the pricing problem of a single monopolist.[22] The effects of a tax on the price set by a monopolist who is preventing entry by deliberately holding the price down are not specifically examined in this study, but they would not differ from those just given for a collusive industry.

---

[22] The threat of entry changes the monopolist's demand and marginal revenue curves in precisely the same manner as would a proportional tax on excess price with a value of c (in the tax function) set equal to the limit price and a high value given to r. See Bain, *Price Theory*, pp. 213–18, especially figure 28.

Chapter 10. *Summary of Part II*

The scattered conclusions of this part are summarized here, without all the qualifications that may apply.

1. It is not true that, apart from special cost and demand conditions, all excise taxes must increase monopoly price. The characteristic of the tax that determines the direction of price change is the elasticity of the per unit tax function with respect to price.

   a. The direction of price change resulting from the levy of any continuous excise tax function depends upon the relative sizes of the tax and demand elasticities at the pre-tax price:

      i. if the tax elasticity exceeds the demand elasticity, price will fall;

      ii. if the tax elasticity equals the demand elasticity, price will not change.

      iii. if the tax elasticity is smaller then the demand elasticity, price will rise.

   b. The amount of price change, if any, depends upon the weight of the tax, the slope of the marginal cost function, and the tax elasticity:

      i. the heavier the per unit tax, the greater is the amount of price change, whether price is increased or decreased by the tax;

      ii. if marginal costs are decreasing, the amount of price change from the tax will be greater than it would be if marginal costs were increasing;

      iii. if two taxes with unequal elasticities are equal in weight at the price after the less elastic tax is levied, the more elastic tax will lead to a lower price than the less elastic tax.

2. A wide variety of tax schedules, including the specific tax and the ad valorem tax, can be generated by a simple power function.

a. One parameter of this function, the exponent of price, determines the tax elasticity, which in turn determines whether the tax will raise or lower price.
   b. If two power taxes with unequal elasticities are equal at the pre-tax price and both change price in the same direction, the likelihood that the more elastic tax will produce the larger price decline (or smaller price increase) is greater if:
      i. marginal costs are increasing;
      ii. both taxes are light.
3. A second general tax function can be defined by applying the tax rate, not to the entire price as an ad valorem tax, but to the portion of the price above a fixed level, c.
   a. The elasticity of this tax at each price is determined by the parameter c.
      i. if, at the pre-tax price, c exceeds marginal revenue (or marginal cost), price will fall;
      ii. if c is less than marginal cost at the pre-tax price, price will rise;
      iii. if c equals marginal cost at the pre-tax price, price will not change.
   b. If two taxes of this form are levied, with unequal elasticities such that both taxes lower price, the more elastic tax will produce the greater price decline. If two such taxes raise price, the likelihood that the more elastic tax will produce the smaller price increase is greater if the weight of the taxes is low.
4. If the tax function is discontinuous, there will be sudden steps in the tax as price is changed very slightly.
   a. If the steps are upward and have any effect on price, the price will be lower than without the steps.
   b. If the steps are downward and affect price, the price will be higher or lower than otherwise, depending upon the location and sizes of the steps.
   c. The existence of steps in the per unit tax means that some prices near the steps are unprofitable, regardless of cost and demand conditions.
5. Just as some forms of an excise tax will not raise price, some forms of a bounty will not lower price. Corresponding to the above criterion of price change for any tax is the following:

Summary of Part II

    i. a per unit bounty will raise price and lower output if the elasticity of the per unit bounty exceeds the demand elasticity;
    ii. if the bounty elasticity equals the demand elasticity, price will not change;
    iii. if the bounty elasticity is smaller than the demand elasticity, price will rise.

6. Another facet of the general manner in which a tax affects a marginal revenue function pertains to pricing in a market with a single buyer. In such a market, the volume of purchases and the price are below the levels that would be reached by a group of competitive buyers. The direction of price changes (and of change in purchases) resulting from an excise tax depends upon the elasticity of the tax:

    i. if the tax elasticity is zero or positive, both price and volume of purchases will fall;
    ii. if the tax elasticity is negative (i.e., a highly regressive tax) and equal in absolute value to the (positive) elasticity of supply, price and purchases will not change;
    iii. if the tax elasticity is negative and greater in absolute value than the (positive) elasticity of supply, both price and volume of purchases will rise.

7. In a purely competitive industry, any excise tax, regardless of the type, must raise price and reduce output.

8. Under monopolistic competition, it appears possible to devise a tax that is sufficiently progressive to reduce prices.

9. In an industry of few sellers, there are circumstances under which a progressive excise tax will lower price.

Part III. *Effects of Excise Taxes on Selling Effort*

In Part III the optimum adjustments to an excise tax are examined in a context that includes not only price and output reactions but also changes in the amount of selling effort exerted by the firm. The results of these chapters will be found to extend and modify, but not conflict with, the conclusions obtained in Part II, where only price and output changes were considered.

Chapter 11. *Pre-tax Equilibrium: Price, Output, and Selling Effort*

Selling effort is defined to include all the activities that raise the demand curve for the product without changing the variable costs of production. Many different forms of advertising fall within this classification; also included are the provision and maintenance of selling facilities, the staffing and administration of sales departments, and so on.

It may be helpful at this point to glance forward briefly to Part IV, in order to note the differences and similarities between two closely related concepts: selling effort and product quality. In Chapter 20 product quality is defined in terms of the characteristics of the product itself. An improvement in quality is taken to mean any change in the nature of the product, for example, in the materials, workmanship, design, or packaging, that raises the demand curve for the product and increases variable production costs.[1]

---

[1] The distinction made here between selling effort and product quality is close but not identical to that made by Chamberlin between selling effort and product differentiation. He would include in selling effort advertising a product by printing the seller's name on the package (which would increase variable production costs and, if effective, also increase demand and therefore fall within the meaning of product quality, as here defined). "Selling costs are defined as costs incurred in order to alter the position or shape of the demand curve for a product" (Chamberlin, *Monopolistic Competition*, p. 117). He also apparently includes the cost of quality changes in selling costs. The distinction made here is dictated by the method of analysis and seems reasonable in view of the fact that the present study is aimed at the effects of taxes and not at the economic effects of selling effort or product differentiation per se. The present definition of selling costs is identical to that adopted by R. Dorfman and P. O. Steiner: "... advertising [is] any expenditure which influences the shape or position of a firm's demand curve and which enters the firm's cost function as a fixed cost, i.e., a cost which does not vary with the quantity of output" ("Optimal Advertising and Optimal Quality," *American Economic Review*, XLIV, 826–36).

The effects of excise taxes on advertising expenditures and other selling effort appear to have received little attention from economists. In the first major study of tax incidence to appear after the publication of Chamberlin's work, Due attempts to take non-price variables into account to determine how their existence influences the price effects of a tax. Yet his attempts fall short of completeness for he puts the question in the form, "How does the possibility that selling outlays can be varied affect the amount of price change from a tax?" rather than asking, "How does the tax affect the optimum selling outlays?"[2] If there is interdependence among price, output, and selling outlays, the first question cannot be answered until the second one is.

The volume of advertising expenditures has been suggested as a base for taxation,[3] on the presumption that such a tax would reduce selling outlays. In Appendix III the effect of a tax based on advertising outlays is shown.

To keep the analysis as simple as possible, the effects of excise taxes on selling effort and on product quality will be examined separately. This procedure neglects the interaction between product quality and advertising, which will not be treated here.

The firm's choices regarding selling outlays affect not only the demand for its product but also the costs of operation. It is assumed that one combination of choices produces greater profit than any other combination, and the conditions for maximizing profit are now studied with respect to several variables, not merely output.[4]

The product price or average revenue function now includes two independent variables, output per time period and advertising

---

[2]"The existence of advertising expenditures... provides a possible outlet for absorption of the tax, under certain pricing and advertising policies. But in general selling activities apparently do not introduce significant changes in the theory of incidence" (Due, *Incidence of Sales Taxation*, p. 61).

[3]W. H. Nicholls, "The Tobacco Case of 1946," *American Economic Review*, XXXIX, 294.

[4]The extension of the analysis to two independent variables does more than add a new symbol to the equations. Not only is the number of conditions necessary to assure a maximum position increased; in addition, a simple but widely used argument is no longer appropriate. If output (or price) is the only parameter subject to variation by the firm, it is true that any change (e.g., a tax) that reduces the marginal gain from output increases will lead to reduced output. If *both* output and selling costs are variable, it is not true that a change which reduces the marginal gain from, say, selling costs will *necessarily* lead to lower selling costs. This point will be discussed further in Chapter 12.

Pre-tax Equilibrium: Price, Output, Selling Effort

expenditures (or selling costs) per time period:

$$p = p(x, s)$$

A given amount might be spent for advertising in a wide variety of ways with differing degrees of effectiveness, but if profits are to be maximized, the optimum level of selling outlays must be expended in the best possible manner. It is assumed that the firm can and does optimize the effectiveness of any advertising outlay it chooses and that it remains free to adjust the advertising budget to changes in other conditions.

The total costs are a function of output and selling costs:

$$c = c(x, s)$$

This formulation of the cost function is more general than is necessary for present purposes. It would be sufficient to represent total costs by two terms, that is, as a function of output *only*, plus the volume of selling costs themselves. The reason for retaining the more general cost function is that the analysis can then be applied almost unchanged in later pages to the study of tax-induced changes in product quality.

The per unit tax is still to be regarded as a function of price, which is in turn a function of output and selling costs, so that the per unit tax is a function of a function of output and selling costs:

$$t = t[p(x, s)]$$

Increases, say, in selling costs can affect the per unit tax, at a given output, by raising the price at which that output can be sold. Before the tax is levied, total profit is given by

$$\pi = x \cdot p(x, s) - c(x, s) \tag{47}$$

and will be a maximum when the partial derivatives, first with respect to output variation and second with respect to selling cost variation, are both equal to zero:

$$\pi^x = x \cdot p^x(x, s) + p(x, s) - c^x(x, s) = 0 \tag{48}$$

or

$$x \cdot p^x(x, s) + p(x, s) = c^x(x, s) \tag{49}$$

The left-hand side of (49) represents the marginal *revenue* with respect to output and price variation at a constant level of selling cost, and the right-hand side the marginal *cost* of output and price variation only.[5]

Profit will not be maximized unless these two quantities are equal. The second-order conditions require in addition that, as output is increased toward the optimum, marginal revenue be greater than marginal cost, that is, $\pi^{xx} < 0$.

For any *given* level of s, there is some output that will satisfy equality (49). To determine which level of selling costs maximizes profit, the partial derivative with respect to selling costs of the profit function (47) must also equal zero:

$$\pi^s = x \cdot p^s(x,s) - c^s(x,s) = 0 \tag{50}$$

or

$$x \cdot p^s(x,s) = c^s(x,s) = 1 \tag{51}$$

The left-hand side of (51) represents the marginal revenue from selling cost only. This marginal revenue is the product of two factors: the fixed level of output at which selling costs are imagined to vary and the increase in price per unit resulting from a small rise, say $1, in selling costs. This product is, then, the increase in total receipts resulting from a $1 increase in selling costs. For some level of selling costs other than zero to be optimum, the effect of selling costs must be to increase the price at which a given output can be sold, that is,

$$p^s(x,s) > 0$$

The right-hand side of (51) is simply the marginal cost of increasing selling costs by one unit at a constant output. Since selling costs do not change variable production cost, the marginal cost of an added dollar of selling outlay is $1.[6] Equation (51) will hold only when the

---

[5]Since output, price, and selling costs are interrelated by the demand function, it is not appropriate, within a context of profit maximization, to consider variation of only one of these variables at constant levels of the other two. The equality shown in (49) is imagined to occur through changes in output, at a fixed level of selling costs, while the price changes, because of output change, as indicated by the demand function. If the demand function had been written with output rather than price as the dependent variable, the same sort of marginal revenue-marginal cost equalization would occur by changes in price, at a fixed level of selling costs, while output would change because of the price change, again as indicated by the demand function.

Partial derivatives of a variable, say x, with respect to another variable, s, are shown as x^s. This notation is equivalent to $\partial x/\partial s$.

[6]Price will, of course, vary with selling costs (see footnote 5). If output were the dependent variable, the marginal cost of selling outlay variation would not be simply $1 as above. At a fixed price, increases in selling costs increase output; therefore the marginal cost of increasing the selling outlay consists not only of the added selling outlay but also the added cost of the extra units produced.

Pre-tax Equilibrium: Price, Output, Selling Effort

marginal revenue from selling cost variation is equal to the marginal cost of such variation. In addition, as selling costs are increased toward the optimum level, the marginal revenue must be greater than $1, that is, $\pi^{ss} < 0$. When profit is maximized with respect to *two* independent variables, another second-order condition is necessary, for the profit "surface" now has three dimensions: dollars of profit, units of output, and dollars of selling costs. Even if the slope of the profit surface with respect to output (at a fixed level of selling costs) is zero—equation (48)—and the slope of the profit surface with respect to selling costs (at a fixed level of output) is zero—equation (50)—profit may not be maximized. The satisfaction of these two equations does not rule out the possibility that some combination of output and selling cost changes could increase profit, even though separate changes in these variables would not. This possibility *is ruled out* by the condition[7]

$$\pi^{xx} \cdot \pi^{ss} > (\pi^{sx})^2 \tag{52}$$

This second-order condition is given a geometric interpretation in Appendix II.

Only when (*a*) marginal revenue from output variation equals the marginal cost of output variation, *and* (*b*) marginal revenue from selling cost variation equals the marginal cost of selling cost variation, will optimum levels of both output, x_0, and selling cost, s_0, have been found. For this combination there is some price p_0 at which the output x_0 can just be sold.[8]

---

[7] Allen *Mathematical Analysis*, pp. 354–55.

[8] These results are the same as those presented by Dorfman and Steiner, *American Economic Review*, XLIV, 828: "A firm which can influence the demand for its product by advertising will, in order to maximize its profits, choose the advertising budget and price such that the increase in gross revenue resulting from a one dollar increase in advertising expenditure is equal to the ordinary elasticity of demand for the firm's product." This condition is identical in content, though not in form, to the second of the two profit-maximizing conditions given above, which states that at equilibrium a $1 increase in advertising must increase the price of all units sold just enough to raise gross revenue by $1, or

$$x \frac{\partial p}{\partial s} = 1$$

Dorfman and Steiner's statement of the condition is

$$p \frac{\partial x}{\partial s} = E_x(p)$$

$$= \frac{\partial x}{\partial p} \cdot \frac{p}{x} \quad \text{or} \quad = \frac{\partial x}{\partial s} \cdot \frac{\partial s}{\partial p} \cdot \frac{p}{x}$$

Consider the following example. Let the average revenue function be[9]

$$p = 100 - x + s^{1/2} \tag{53}$$

For simplicity, production costs are neglected so that the total cost function is

$$c = s$$

Profit is total receipts less total costs, or

$$\pi = x(100 - x + s^{1/2}) - s$$

or

$$\pi = 100x - x^2 + xs^{1/2} - s \tag{54}$$

The two partial derivatives of the profit function are set equal to zero:

(I) $\quad \pi^x: \quad 100 - 2x + s^{1/2} = 0 \tag{55}$

The left-hand side of (55) is the marginal revenue from output variation, and the right-hand side is the marginal cost, with respect to output, which is equal to zero in this example.

(II) $\quad \pi^s: \quad \tfrac{1}{2}xs^{-1/2} - 1 = 0$

$$\frac{x}{2\sqrt{s}} = 1 \tag{56}$$

[8](continued)

On canceling common terms and rearranging, it is seen that the two conditions are equivalent:

$$1 = \frac{\partial s}{\partial p} \cdot \frac{1}{x} \quad \text{or} \quad x\frac{\partial p}{\partial s} = 1$$

[9]In view of the fact that this function shows the effect of selling costs on price to be the same at low and high levels of output, this model of price, output, and selling cost interrelationships may appear to be too primitive even for purposes of illustration. The model does, however, have the reasonable feature that higher levels of selling cost are required to maximize profit at high outputs than at low outputs.

The selection of the *dollar cost* of selling effort as a variable, rather than some measure of a specific type of selling effort, is partly a matter of convenience (there is no necessity to refer to any particular type of selling effort; the possibility of discontinuities does not arise explicitly) and partly intentional. The purpose of this part is to determine the effect of excise taxes on the dollar volume of selling outlays and not on the level of any one type of selling effort. It is not inconceivable, given interdependence among types of selling effort, that a tax which reduces the dollar volume of all advertising done by a firm may increase the use of one or more specific kinds of advertising. Another reason, then, for dealing with selling outlays as a whole is to avoid the necessity of taking such interdependence into account without making the assumption that only one type of selling effort is available to the firm.

Pre-tax Equilibrium: Price, Output, Selling Effort

The left-hand side of (56) is the marginal revenue from selling cost variation, at each output, and the structure of the fraction shows (1) that the return from an added dollar of selling cost declines as the selling outlay increases (which is an essential condition for equilibrium with respect to selling costs), and (2) that at high outputs the best level of selling cost is high, and vice versa.

If (56) is solved for x in terms of s,

$$x = 2\sqrt{s}$$

and this value substituted in (55) and solved for s,

$$\sqrt{s_0} = 33\tfrac{1}{3} \qquad s_0 = \$11111\tfrac{1}{9}$$
$$x_0 = 66\tfrac{2}{3} \text{ units}$$
$$p_0 = \$66\tfrac{2}{3} \text{ per unit}$$

This combination of values satisfies *all* conditions for a maximum of profit:

1. The second derivative of profit with respect to output, that is, the next derivative of (55), is negative:

$$\pi^{xx} = -2$$

2. The second derivative of profit with respect to selling outlays, that is, the next derivative of (56), is negative for admissible (positive) values of x and s:

$$\pi^{ss} = -\frac{x}{4s^{3/2}}$$

3. The product of the two second-order derivatives is greater than the square of the second-order "cross" derivative:

$$\pi^{xx} \cdot \pi^{ss} > (\pi^{sx})^2$$

$$\pi^{sx} = \frac{1}{2\sqrt{s}}$$

$$-2\left(-\frac{x}{4s^{3/2}}\right) > \left(\frac{1}{2\sqrt{s}}\right)^2$$

$$\frac{x}{2s^{3/2}} > \frac{1}{4s}$$

$$\frac{x}{\sqrt{s}} > \frac{1}{2}$$

Substituting the equilibrium values of x and s yields

$$\frac{66\frac{2}{3}}{33\frac{1}{3}} > \frac{1}{2}$$

and the condition holds.

It may be noticed that, if the firm were prohibited from advertising, (55) would have been

$$\pi^x: \quad 100 - 2x = 0$$

and

$$s_0 = 0$$

$$x_0 = 50 \text{ units}$$

$$p_0 = \$50 \text{ per unit}$$

The effect of advertising in this model is to increase price, output, and, of course, total expenditures on the product.[10] The increase in expenditures $[(\$66\frac{2}{3} \cdot 66\frac{2}{3}) - (\$50 \cdot 50) = \$1943.56]$ is greater than selling costs ($\$1111\frac{1}{9}$); advertising has increased profit by $832.44

The pre-tax equilibrium may be illustrated as in Chart 24. In this chart the closed curves are contours of the profit surface, that is, each curve consists of all points representing values of s and x that are solutions to the equation

$$\pi = k$$

or

$$100x - x^2 + xs^{1/2} - s = k$$

for different values of k, as indicated on the chart. All output and selling cost combinations shown by the points on one of these contours will yield the same profit. (Thus the contours are similar to indifference curves, iso-product curves, transformation curves, etc.)

The line labeled W-E shows the path of one "ridge" of the profit surface, dropped to the s-x plane. This ridge is identified as follows: adopting a fixed output and increasing selling costs (i.e., proceeding north from a point on the x-axis) increases profit up to a maximum,

---

[10] For a proof that advertising, to be profitable, need not increase output and may reduce it, see P. A. Samuelson, *Foundations of Economic Analysis*, (Cambridge, 1948), pp. 41–42.

Pre-tax Equilibrium: Price, Output, Selling Effort 135

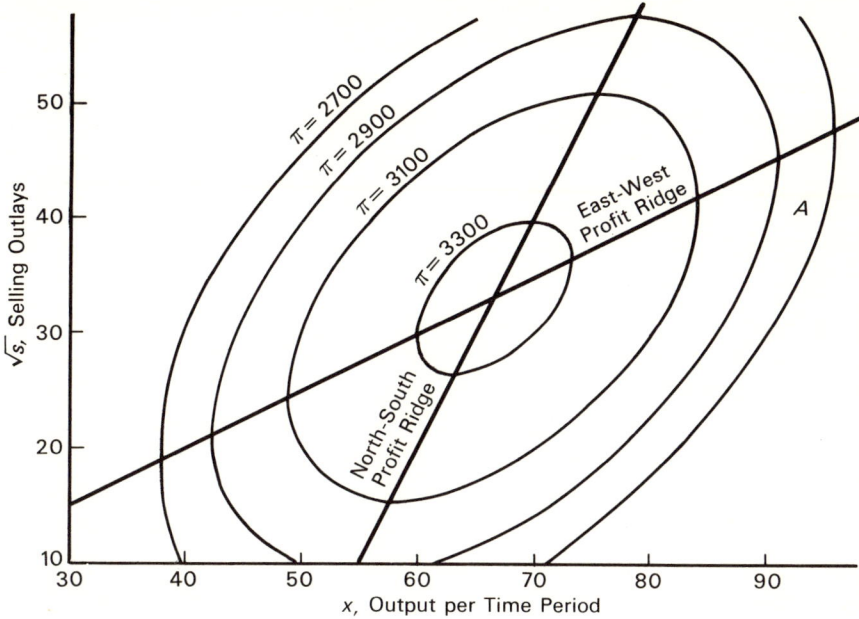

CHART 24.
Contours of profit surface and ridge lines: specific demand and cost functions.

then further additions to selling costs *reduce* profit. The levels of selling costs that maximize profit for each output are shown by the W-E ridge line. [The equation of this line on the s-x plane is simply the first derivative of the profit function, with respect to selling costs, that is equation (56), set equal to zero.] It will be noted that, along the W-E ridge line, the profit contours are always vertical with respect to the x-axis.

Similarly, the line labeled N-S represents the path (on the s-x plane) of another ridge of the profit surface. This ridge is found by adopting a fixed level of selling costs and increasing output from zero (i.e., moving east from a point on the s-axis). At first profit increases — as shown by the increasing level of the profit contours — then reaches a maximum, and subsequently declines. The level of output that maximizes profit, for a given amount of selling costs, is one point on the N-S ridge line path. The equation of the N-S ridge line is the first derivative of the profit function, with respect to output, that is, equation (55), set equal to zero. Along the N-S ridge line, the profit contours are horizontal to the x axis. (A square root scale is used for selling costs on the chart simply to make the ridge lines linear.)

The equilibrium values of selling cost and output are indicated by the intersection of the two ridge lines. This is nothing more than translating into geometry the requirement that, for maximization, both partial derivatives of the profit function must be equal to zero. (Each ridge line shows the values of s and x where *one* of the partial derivatives equals zero.) The second-order conditions assure that both ridges are, in fact, ridges and not "gullies," and that the point of intersection is a true peak, rather than a peculiar type of surface such that proceeding from the intersection point in some direction other than N, E, W, or S would increase profit. At the intersection of the two ridge lines, an output of $66\frac{2}{3}$ units per time period and selling costs of $\$1111\frac{1}{9}$ are indicated. (These two values and the demand function imply a price of $\$66\frac{2}{3}$ per unit.)

Chart 24 gives no clues as to what might be happening to price as various combinations of output and selling costs are selected. "Constant" price lines could be shown on this chart, but to avoid undue complexity these are shown instead on Chart 25, together with the W-E and N-S ridge lines. The main restrictions on the constant price lines are as follows: (1) at a fixed level of selling costs, as output is increased, price must decline; and (2) the price lines must have a positive slope in the s-x plane. The first restriction is simply the negative slope of the ordinary demand curve; the second may not be obvious.

Consider the demand function:

$$p = p(x, s)$$

The constant price lines represent the implicit function

$$p(x, s) = k$$

for various values of k. The slope of this function (with respect to the x axis) is given by[11]

$$-\frac{p^x(x, s)}{p^s(x, s)} \qquad (57)$$

---

[11] Allen, *Mathematical Analysis*, p. 341.

Pre-tax Equilibrium: Price, Output, Selling Effort

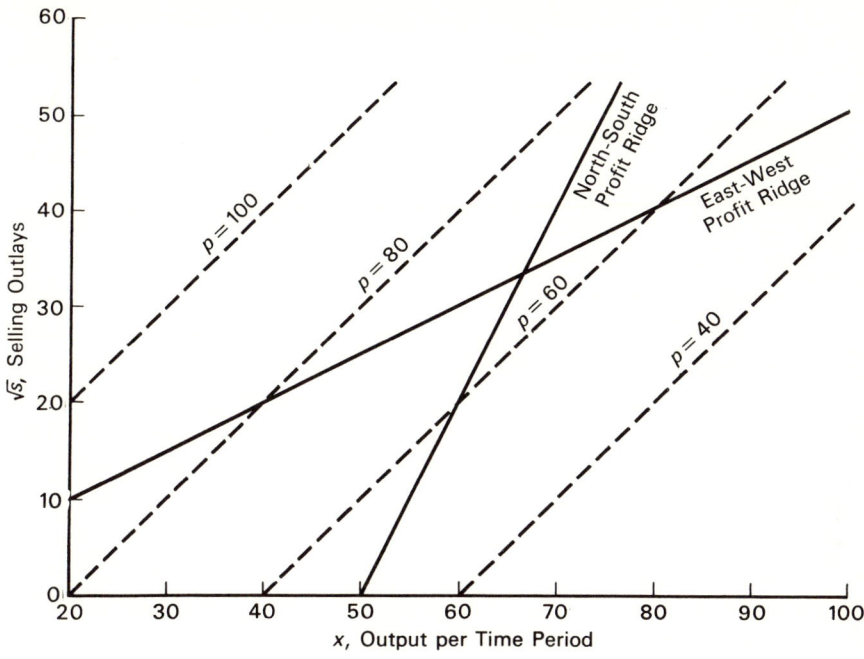

CHART 25.
Constant price lines and ridge lines: same functions as chart 24.

But the numerator of (57) is the slope of the demand curve at a fixed level of selling costs (i.e., the amount that the price of all units change if an additional unit is offered for sale) and is negative. The denominator of (57) is the amount by which price changes as selling costs are increased by $1, at a fixed output, and is usually positive. Thus the slope of each constant price line is positive, meaning that, if an increased output is to be sold without changing price (i.e., moving along a constant price line to a higher output), selling outlays must be increased. Movements over the surface in any direction between N and W inclusive must represent implicit price increases; movements in other directions may represent either increases or decreases, depending upon the direction chosen and the slope of the price lines. The price associated with each price line is indicated on Chart 25. "Constant" output lines are, of course, verticals erected from the arbitrarily selected output; constant selling outlay lines are horizontal.

The analytical and graphic approach used here bears a close resemblance to that developed by F. H. Hahn.[12] This graphic device is not introduced for purposes of illustration only; it will be used in a more substantive manner. The analytical methods of Chapter 4 (comparison of before- and after-tax marginal revenue functions; concluding that, if a tax lowers marginal revenue with respect to price, price will fall; etc.) are, with the introduction of a second independent variable, no longer adequate. It will be shown that, given the weak restrictions usually placed on the relation of price and output, and given the effect that advertising, to be profitable, must have on price or output, the hypothesis of profit maximization provides few conclusions concerning the direction of the effect of an excise tax on the optimum level of selling costs. Therefore, only qualified conclusions can generally be obtained. The graphic procedure outlined above will assist in determining what form of qualification would be informative, or, in other words, what kind of empirical research is needed to shed light on the effects of taxes on selling costs. These effects will be studied primarily by noting how a tax affects the two ridge lines of the profit surface.

For example, if a tax did not shift either the N-S or the W-E ridge line, it would have no effect on selling outlays, price, or output (it will be shown that there is no such excise tax); and if a tax did not shift the N-S ridge line but did lower the W-E ridge, it could be concluded that the tax would lower selling costs (whether output would fall or rise would depend upon the slope of the N-S ridge line).

---

[12]Hahn identifies two ridge lines of the profit surface and shows that the equilibrium position is determined by their intersection ("The Theory of Selling Costs," *Economic Journal*, LXIX, pp. 293–312).

Chapter 12. *After-tax Equilibrium: General Statement*

A. *Description of Equilibrium*

The after-tax equilibrium is not difficult to describe—one need only add to the equation representing profit, expression (47), a product term representing the tax bill and rewrite the partial derivatives of profit with respect to output and selling outlays.

Thus, the after-tax profit function will be [cf. (47)]

$$\pi = x \cdot p(x, s) - x \cdot t[p(x, s)] - c(x, s)$$

The first-order partial derivative with respect to output will be

$$\pi^x = x \cdot p^x(x,s) + p(x,s)$$
$$- \{x \cdot t^p[p(x,s)] \cdot p^x(x,s) + t\} - c^x(x,s)$$

where the terms in brackets represent the marginal tax bill, with respect to output. The characteristics of the demand, cost, and tax functions that would make this marginal tax bill zero, positive, or negative have already been discussed in Chapter 4. In any event, at the after-tax equilibrium after-tax marginal revenue must be equal to marginal cost (both with respect to output).

The first-order partial derivative of profit with respect to selling outlay will be

$$\pi^s = x \cdot p^s(x,s) - \{x \cdot t^p[p(x,s)] p^s(x,s)\} - c^s(x,s)$$

or

$$\pi^s = x \cdot p^s(x,s) \{1 - t^p[p(x,s)]\} - c^s(x,s) \qquad (58)$$

Again, after-tax marginal revenue with respect to selling outlays must be equal to the marginal cost of selling outlays.

The slope of the tax function, that is, $t^p[p(x,s)]$, the rate of change in the per unit tax as price changes, emerges as the important characteristic of the tax. That the *slope* of the tax function should become the critical feature in this context is easily seen. Expression (58) represents the approximate gain in profit to be obtained by a small increase in selling costs *as output is held constant* (in which case price must be allowed to vary). At a constant output the total tax bill will change only if the price change (accompanying the selling outlay variation) leads to a change in the per unit tax, that is, only if the slope of the tax function is not zero.

Therefore, if the slope of the tax function *is* zero (as it is for a specific tax), the before- and after-tax marginal revenue functions with respect to selling outlays will be the same. [Compare (50) and (58).] If the slope of the tax function is positive (e.g., ad valorem tax or tax on excess price), the marginal revenue function with respect to selling costs will be reduced. If the tax is highly regressive (i.e., the per unit tax declines as price rises and the slope of the tax function is negative), marginal revenue from selling outlay will be increased.[1]

Although the above statements concerning the after-tax equilibrium are true, unfortunately they do not provide a firm basis for conclusions concerning the direction of change in the optimum level of selling costs that may result from the imposition of an excise tax. Even though a tax reduces the marginal revenue curve for selling outlays, the optimum level of selling outlays after the tax is levied may be higher, lower, or the same as that prevailing previously. The price and output changes that generally result from the tax will usually *shift* the marginal revenue curve for selling outlays, even though the tax itself may not.[2]

The manner in which price or output changes shift the marginal revenue function for selling outlays (such changes cannot affect the marginal *cost* of selling outlays) is thus a major factor in determining

---

[1]The above mathematical descriptions of before- and after-tax equilibrium could equally well have been expressed in terms of price and advertising expenditures as independent variables rather than output and advertising expenditures. The resulting marginal revenue functions would have been different, particularly the function for selling expenditures, but the conclusions of the analysis would not have been changed.

[2]"...with more than one variable input [parameter of action], the position of the marginal revenue productivity curve of any one input [parameter] depends upon the quantity of other inputs employed [i.e., upon the levels of the other parameters]" [K. E. Boulding, *Economic Analysis* (rev. ed.; New York, 1948), 701–2].

After-tax Equilibrium: General Statement

the direction of change in selling costs after a tax is imposed. In the example given above, the marginal *revenue* (from which marginal costs must be deducted to yield the marginal gain) from an increase in selling outlay was seen to be [see (56)]

$$\frac{x}{2\sqrt{s}}$$

Decreases in output at a constant level of selling outlays reduce marginal revenue, and vice versa.

In general terms, the marginal revenue from selling outlays is given by

$$x \cdot p^s(x,s) \qquad (59)$$

Whether the change in marginal revenue, as output changes, is positive, zero, or negative depends upon the form of the demand function. More specifically, it depends upon the sign of the derivative of (59) with respect to output, or

$$x \cdot p^{sx}(x,s) + p^s(x,s)$$

No information on the sign of this derivative is available from the maximization conditions, since in the only condition in which it appears–as π^{sx} (in 52)–it is squared and thus could be of either sign. Accordingly, some of the different possibilities will be discussed below.

B. *Types of Demand Functions*

For present purposes it will be useful to classify demand functions into three categories, depending upon the direction in which an output increase shifts the marginal revenue of selling outlays. Another way of describing the same classification is by the *slope* of the W-E ridge in the neighborhood of the pre-tax equilibrium.

1. The "best" level of selling costs may increase as output increases. In this context the "best" level of selling costs means the level that maximizes profit for a *fixed* level of output. To clarify this, suppose the firm to select some arbitrary output, x_1, and then, by choosing several pairs of values of selling cost and price (such that the demand function is satisfied), to determine the pair, say s_1 and p_1, that produces the most profit. This procedure is assumed to be repeated for each of several higher outputs, x_2, x_3, x_4, and so on,

142   *Effects of Excise Taxes on Selling Effort*

yielding pairs of values for selling costs and price: s_2 and p_2, s_3 and p_3, etc. The values $s_1, s_2, s_3, \ldots$ may be increasing. They represent points on the W-E ridge of the profit surface. A demand function of this type underlies the example given in Chapter 11 and shown in Charts 24 and 25. It will be noted that the W-E ridge has a positive slope. In Appendix II it is shown that, if the W-E ridge has a positive slope at the pre-tax equilibrium, the N-S ridge must also have a positive slope at that point. The effect of advertising is to increase output; price may be higher, lower, or unchanged.

2. The best level of selling costs may be independent of output. That is, in terms of the above experiment, $s_1 = s_2 = s_3 = \ldots$, and whatever output the firm arbitrarily adopts, the *same* level of selling costs will yield the best profit. A demand function of this type leads to a profit surface like that shown in Chart 26. If the W-E ridge line is horizontal at the pre-tax equilibrium, the N-S ridge line must be

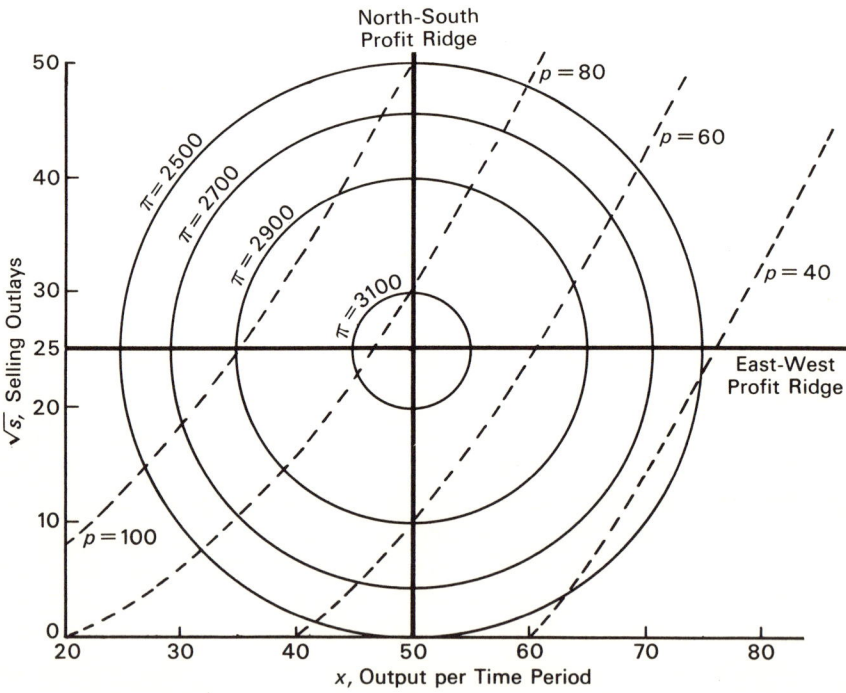

CHART 26.
Contours of profit surface, ridge lines, and constant price lines: demand function type ii.

After-tax Equilibrium: General Statement

vertical there (see Appendix II). The effect of advertising here is to increase price; output is unaffected.

3. The best level of selling costs may be lower at a high output than at a low output. In this case the W-E ridge line will be sloping downward toward the x axis, as in Chart 27, and the N-S ridge line must also have a negative slope at the pre-tax equilibrium (Appendix II).

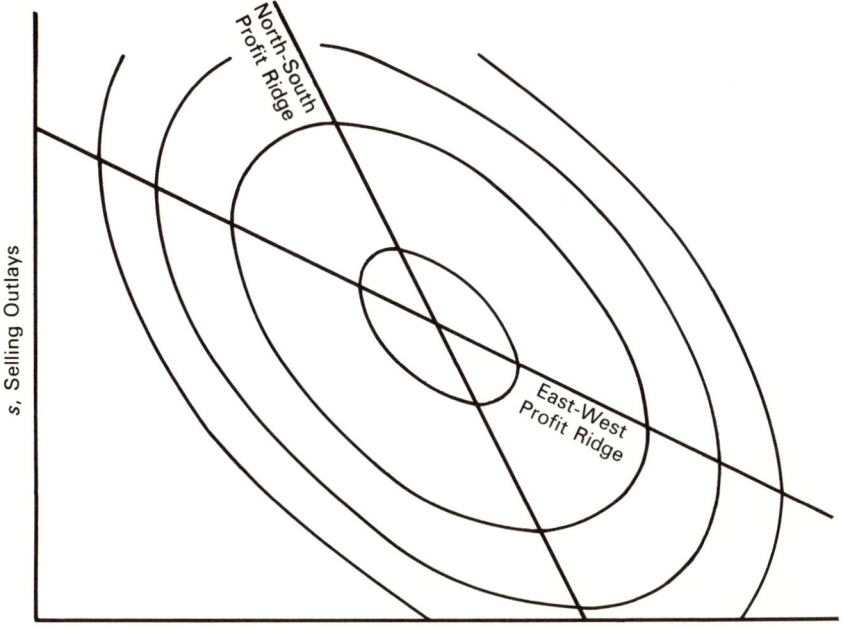

CHART 27.
Contours of profit surface and ridge lines: demand function type iii.

Demand functions of these three types will be referred to subsequently as demand type i, ii, and iii, respectively.

4. The above classification of demand functions is not inconsistent with the basic properties that a demand function must have, either on economic grounds or from the assumption that a profit maximum exists. A demand function may be any of the above three types, even though (*a*) the relation between price and output, at any fixed level of selling outlays, is inverse; (*b*) at some output there are diminishing returns to added dollars of selling outlays.

5. A different way of classifying demand functions is according to the way that the marginal profitability of selling costs is affected by *price* changes, rather than by output changes. The best level of selling costs (i.e., the level at which their marginal profitability at a constant price is zero) may, as price rises, (*a*) increase, (*b*) remain unchanged, (*c*) decline.

It should be emphasized that these two classifications of demand functions are not identical. It might appear at first glance that, if the best level of selling costs is independent of output, it should also be independent of price. This is not true; it can be shown (see Appendix IV) that demand type i may be of any type — 1, 2, or 3 — in the present classification, that type ii must be type 1 (not type 2); and type iii must be type 1.

The various possible forms of demand functions may be categorized according to both principles, giving the following table (the letter "f" placed in a cell represents the possibility of a demand function satisfying both conditions):

Relation between s_0 and Output	*Relation between s_0 and Price*		
	Rising (1)	*Independent (2)*	*Falling (3)*
Rising (i)	f	f	f
Independent (ii)	f	...	...
Falling (iii)	f	...	...

Demand functions will be classified in the sequel according to the relation between the best level of selling costs and output.

Chapter 13. *After-tax Equilibrium: Specific Tax*

The effect of a specific tax on selling outlays is easier to specify than that of any other excise tax, for two reasons: one, the shift in the N-S ridge line induced by the tax can be determined unequivocally; second, the tax does not shift the W-E ridge line at all.

A. *Tax-Induced Shift in N-S Ridge Line*

The equation of the N-S ridge line before the tax is levied is given by

$$x \cdot p^x(x,s) + p(x,s) - c^x(x,s) = 0$$

and the after-tax ridge line by

$$x \cdot p^x(x,s) + p(x,s) - \{xt^p[p(x,s)]p^x(x,s) + t\} - c^x(x,s) = 0$$

The results of p. 40 can be applied directly to this point. It was shown there that a tax will reduce marginal revenue with respect to output (when changes in variables other than price and output were assumed not to occur) and hence lead to a reduction in output, provided the elasticity of the tax is smaller numerically than the elasticity of demand. Since the elasticity of the specific tax is zero (even if advertising changes the demand elasticity, it should never be carried to the point where the elasticity of demand is zero), this means in the present context that, *at each level of selling costs*, the optimum output is less, that is, the N-S ridge line (which shows the output at which marginal revenue equals marginal cost for output changes) is shifted to the left. The *amount* of shift depends upon, among other things, the ratio of the tax and demand elasticities, but the *direction* of the shift does not. The amount of shift, at each level of selling costs also depends upon the weight of the tax, for it was shown in Chapter 4 that the heavier the tax (for a fixed tax elasticity) the greater is the effect on marginal revenue and thus on price and output.

Therefore, a specific tax will shift the N-S ridge line to the left at each level of selling costs, and the heavier the tax, the greater the shift.

B. *Tax-Induced Shift in W-E Ridge Line*

The equation of the before-tax W-E ridge line is given by

$$x \cdot p^s(x,s) - 1 = 0$$

and the after-tax ridge by

$$x \cdot p^s(x,s) \{1 - t^p[p(x,s)]\} - 1 = 0 \tag{60}$$

The specific per unit tax function has a slope, with respect to price, of zero, that is, if

$$t[p(x,s)] = k$$

then

$$t^p[p(x,s)] = 0$$

Therefore the specific tax leaves the W-E ridge line unchanged.

C. *Net Effect*

When selling outlays, as well as price and output, can be varied in reaction to a specific tax, one conclusion can be drawn without qualification: output will fall. For if the N-S ridge line is everywhere shifted to the left, that is, toward a lower output, the new intersection of both ridge lines must be at a lower output.

The effect of the change on selling costs depends entirely upon the slope of the W-E ridge between the before- and after-tax positions:
1. If the best level of selling costs is lower at low than at high outputs (demand type i) as in Chart 24, selling costs will decline as a result of the tax.
2. If the best level of selling costs is independent of output, as in Chart 26, selling costs will not change.
3. If the best level of selling costs is higher at low than at high outputs, as in Chart 27, selling costs will rise.

After-tax Equilibrium: Specific Tax 147

These results hold regardless of the weight of the tax, of cost conditions, or of demand conditions.

These conclusions may be illustrated as in Chart 28. Each of the three panels in the chart shows the effect of a specific tax, given one type of demand function (according to the slope of the W-E ridge line). The ridge lines of the gross or before-tax profit surface are shown as solid lines; those of the net profit (after-tax) surface, as dotted lines. It will be recalled than an equilibrium position is indicated at the intersection of the two ridge lines. In each instance,

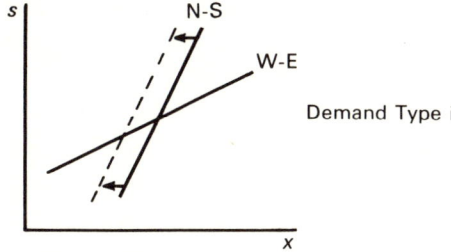

Demand Type i

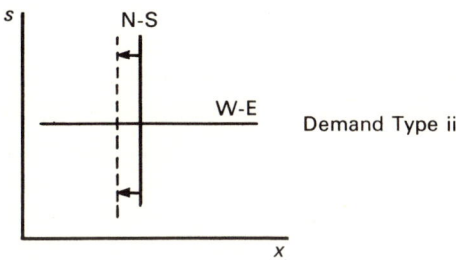

Demand Type ii

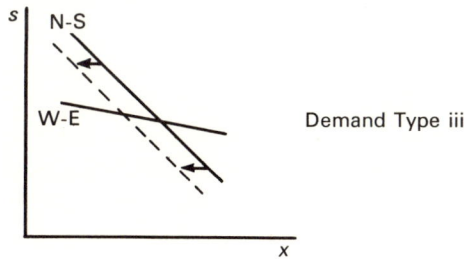

Demand Type iii

CHART 28.
Effects of specific tax on selling outlays and output: three types of demand functions.

output is lower than before. Whether selling costs (and price) are higher, lower, or unchanged depends upon the type of demand function.

The fact that the direction of tax-induced change in the optimum level of selling outlays depends upon the form of the demand function is not peculiar to the specific tax. In specifying the change in selling costs that results from *any* excise, some classification of demand functions (either the classification used here or a related one) will generally be necessary and will always be made. Hence, even though all conditions for profit maximization are satisfied, it is not possible to predict how most types of excise tax will affect selling costs (or product quality) without additional knowledge about the demand and cost functions.

Since the specific tax does not affect the W-E ridge line, the after-tax level of selling outlays is no different from that which the firm would voluntarily select if, without the tax, a dictator were to require the firm to market the after-tax output. In this sense the specific tax may be said to have had *no* effect at all on selling outlays; advertising changed in response to the tax-induced change in output exactly as though it had been optimally adjusted to *any* arbitrary output level.

In both the second and the third cases, it is clear that price must rise as a result of the tax (the after-tax position is either to the left or to the left and above the pre-tax position: in either case, price must be higher). If the W-E ridge line is positively sloped, there is doubt about the change in price; depending upon the relative slopes of the W-E ridge and the price lines, price may be higher, lower, or the same as before the specific tax is levied. This uncertainty contrasts sharply with the clear prediction that follows if selling outlays are not taken into account.

It also follows, from the previous statements about the extent of the shift in the N-S ridge lines, that the heavier the tax, the greater is the change in selling costs, if any, as long as the slope of the W-E ridge line does not change sign. That is, if lowered output is reducing the best level of selling costs (W-E ridge is positively sloped), increasing the weight of the tax will lower output and also selling outlays further. If the optimum level of selling outlays is independent of output, no specific tax, however heavy, can lead to a change in selling outlays (as in Chart 26, where a shift of the N-S ridge line of

After-tax Equilibrium: Specific Tax

any amount will not change selling outlays). A similar argument applies if the best level of selling costs is declining with output. The arguments of this paragraph rest on the assumption that the slope of the W-E ridge line does not change *sign* at outputs below the pre-tax output. The validity of the assumption will not be vigorously defended here; nature may not make "jumps," but she is undoubtedly capable of graceful curves.

A somewhat more rigorous statement of this conclusion is as follows: as long as the best level of selling costs is not independent of output, there are two different specific taxes such that the heavier tax will produce a greater change in selling outlays than the lighter one.

Chart 28—and subsequent charts of the same nature for other types of tax—can be used to illustrate some of the conclusions of Part II. If selling outlays must be held constant, the only movement that the firm can make from the pre-tax equilibrium in response to a tax must be on the horizontal line representing one level of selling outlays. Within this limitation the best adjustment to a tax is to move horizontally to the after-tax N-S ridge line. Thus, in all three panels of Chart 28, it is clear that, if selling costs are not changed, a specific tax will reduce output and increase price.

These results may be illustrated by a specific example. Consider the demand and cost functions given above. With this demand function, it was shown that the best level of selling costs increases with output and that the slope of the W-E ridge is always positive (as in Chart 24). Thus a specific tax will reduce selling costs and a heavier tax will lead to a larger reduction.

If a tax of $1 per unit is levied, the after-tax profit function will be given by the before-tax profit function (54) less a tax bill of $1 times the number of units sold:

$$\pi = 100x - x^2 + xs^{1/2} - s - x$$

or

$$\pi = 99x - x^2 + xs^{1/2} - s \tag{61}$$

The partial derivatives of (61) with respect to output and selling costs are

$$\pi^x = 99 - 2x + s^{1/2} \tag{62}$$

$$\pi^s = \frac{x}{2\sqrt{s}} - 1 \tag{63}$$

150   *Effects of Excise Taxes on Selling Effort*

If these derivatives are set equal to zero and the equations solved for x and s, the results are as follows:

After-tax Values	Pre-tax Values
$x = 66$ units	$x = 66\frac{2}{3}$ units
$s = \$1089$ ($\sqrt{s} = 33$)	$s = \$1111\frac{1}{9}$ ($\sqrt{s} = 33\frac{1}{3}$)
$p = \$67$ per unit	$p = \$66\frac{2}{3}$ per unit

The tax has lowered output (as it must, regardless of the form of the demand function), lowered selling costs (because the W-E ridge of the profit surface is turned toward lower selling costs at lower outputs, as in Chart 28, top panel, and the tax did not shift this ridge line) and increased price.

It may be noted that the after-tax equilibrium is not what it would have been if selling costs could not have been changed (or that the after-tax equilibrium differs from what would have been predicted if selling costs had been ignored). If selling costs are kept at the pre-tax level, (62) becomes

$$\pi^x = 99 - 2x + 33\frac{1}{3}$$
$$\pi^x = 132\frac{1}{3} - 2x \tag{64}$$

If (64) is set equal to zero and solved for x, the results are

$$x = 66\frac{1}{6} \text{ units}$$
$$p = \$67\frac{1}{6} \text{ per unit}$$

In this instance, if selling costs cannot be adjusted, the output decline resulting from the tax is smaller (and the price increase is greater) than would otherwise be the case.

If the tax is $\$6\frac{2}{3}$ per unit instead of $\$1$, (62) and (63) become, respectively,

$$\pi^x = 93\frac{1}{3} - 2x + s^{1/2}$$
$$\pi^s = \frac{x}{2\sqrt{s}} - 1$$

Setting these derivatives equal to zero and solving yields

$$x = 62\frac{2}{9} \text{ units}$$
$$s = \$968 \ (\sqrt{s} = 31\frac{1}{9})$$
$$p = \$68\frac{8}{9} \text{ per unit}$$

After-tax Equilibrium: Specific Tax

The heavier tax has reduced output and selling costs further and has led to a greater increase in price; the shift to the left of the N-S ridge line is more marked than under the lighter tax (cf. Chart 28, top panel).

A second example is presented here to confirm, in one instance, that a specific tax will not necessarily affect the level of selling costs. Let the demand function be

$$p = 100 - x + \frac{50s^{1/2}}{x}$$

This demand function differs from the previous one in that the effect of advertising on price depends upon the level of output — specifically, at a low output a given increase in selling costs has a greater absolute effect on price than at a high output. This may be seen by substituting some values in the demand function. At an output of 10 units per time period and *no* selling outlays, price will be $90 per unit; increasing selling outlays to $16 would raise the price at which 10 units could be sold from $90 each to $110 for a price increase of $20. At an output of 20 units and *no* selling outlays, price would be $80; again increasing selling outlays to $16 would raise price from $80 to $90 for an increase of only $10.

This result obtains for two reasons: (1) the term in the demand function that includes selling outlays is *added* to the other terms, so that at a fixed output a given increase, say, in selling outlays *adds* so much to the price; (2) the term that includes selling outlays also includes output in the denominator — thus at a low output the amount that a selling outlay increment *adds* to price is greater than at a large output.

However, the W-E ridge line of the profit surface will be horizontal, as in Chart 26 (this is shown below).

If costs other than advertising are ignored, the cost function is

$$c = s$$

Total profit will be

$$\pi = x\left(100 - x + \frac{50s^{1/2}}{x}\right) - s$$
$$= 100x - x^2 + 50s^{1/2} - s \tag{65}$$

The derivatives of (65) are

$$\pi^x = 100 - 2x$$
$$\pi^s = \frac{25}{\sqrt{s}} - 1$$

The equations of the ridge lines in the s-x plane are given by

N-S ridge: $100 - 2x = 0$ or $x = 50$

W-F ridge: $\frac{25}{\sqrt{s}} - 1 = 0$ or, $\sqrt{s} = 25$

Thus the N-S ridge line is vertical at an output of 50 units and the W-E ridge is horizontal at a level of selling outlays equal to $625. If the partial derivatives are equated to zero, the pre-tax equilibrium is found to be

$x = 50$ units
$s = \$625$ ($\sqrt{s} = 25$)
$p = \$75$ per unit

The imposition of a tax of $1 per unit changes the profit function to

$$\pi = 100x - x^2 + 50s^{1/2} - s - \$1 \cdot x$$

or

$$\pi = 99x - x^2 + 50s^{1/2} - s \qquad (66)$$

The derivatives of (66) are

$$\pi^x = 99 - 2x$$
$$\pi^s = \frac{25}{\sqrt{s}} - 1$$

Equating these to zero yields the after-tax values:

$x = 49.5$ units
$s = \$625$ ($\sqrt{s} = 25$)
$p = \$75.25$ per unit

The effects of the tax are to reduce output, leave selling outlays unchanged, and raise price (Chart 28, center panel). Since selling outlays did not change, the after-tax price and output are the same as would be given by the conventional one-variable analysis, provided the demand function were written with selling costs fixed at $625 per time period:

$$p = 100 - x + \frac{50 \cdot \sqrt{\$625}}{x}$$

Chapter 14. *After-tax Equilibrium: Ad Valorem Tax*

The ad valorem tax will be discussed here in its simplest form, the per unit tax amounting to some fraction, r, of the price (inclusive of tax):

$$t[p(x,s)] = r \cdot p(x,s)$$

The analysis follows closely the pattern of the previous chapter on the specific tax, but the results will be rather different.

A. *Tax-Induced Shift in N-S Ridge Line.*

It follows from Chapter 6 that the N-S ridge line of the profit surface will be shifted to the left, at all levels of selling cost, if the demand elasticity at points on the ridge line is greater than the tax elasticity. The elasticity of the ad valorem tax was shown to be always equal to unity; the demand elasticity will be unity if marginal production costs with respect to *output* changes are zero and will be higher than unity in all other cases.

Therefore (1) if marginal costs are zero, an ad valorem tax will not shift the N-S ridge line at all; (2) if marginal costs are not zero, the N-S ridge line will be shifted everywhere (i.e., at all levels of selling costs) to the left, that is to say, toward lower outputs.

It also follows, from Chapter 4, that the heavier the ad valorem tax, the greater will be the shift, if any, in the N-S ridge line. Since the effect on price and output at each level of selling costs of an ad valorem tax is the same as the effect of a related change in the level of marginal cost, the lower marginal cost is, the smaller will be the shift in the N-S ridge line.[1]

---

[1] C. S. Shoup, *Shifting and Incidence Theory: Taxes on Monopoly* (New York, 1950), p. 25, and Cournot, *Principes mathématiques*, Chapter VI, reprinted in Musgrave and Shoup, *Economics of Taxation*, p. 252.

B. Tax-Induced Shift in W-E Ridge Line

The general expression for the after-tax W-E ridge line (60) includes one characteristic of the tax function, the slope, which is equal to the parameter r. Therefore, if r is not equal to zero, the W-E ridge line will be shifted by the tax. Furthermore, the shift will be toward lower selling costs at all outputs. That the tax must lower the W-E ridge line can be seen from the following argument. From any selling cost and output combination on the W-E ridge line, before a tax is levied, changes in selling cost (and price) at a constant output will reduce profit; however, following the argument developed in Section A-3 of Chapter 3 "small" changes in selling costs would lead to "very small" reductions in profit. If the firm maintains selling outlays, output, and price at pre-tax levels *after* the tax is imposed, it will be earning the same level of gross profit before taxes are deducted. But the tax bill will reduce the profits net of tax. If now the firm experiments with selling cost (and price) adjustments, at a constant output, it will make the following discoveries.

1. A small *increase* in selling costs (and in price, since this adjustment is represented on a chart of the gross profit surface by moving above the W-E ridge) at a constant output will reduce gross profit slightly.

The rise in price, which must accompany the selling cost increase if demand is to be just satisfied, will increase the tax per unit, since the slope of the tax function is positive.

The increase in the per unit tax at a constant output must increase the tax bill. Neither increase will be "very small"; it will be of the same order of magnitude as the increase in price and selling outlays.

The sensible increase in the tax bill when combined with the slight decrease in gross profit means that the profit net of tax has been reduced. Therefore the point on the W-E ridge line, from which the adjustments began, is no longer on a ridge line of the net profit surface; movements upward reduce net profit substantially.

2. A small *decrease* in selling costs (and price) at a constant output will also reduce gross profit slightly. The order of magnitude of the reduction in gross profit will be much smaller than the order of magnitude of the decrease in selling outlays.

The *decrease* in price, which must accompany the reduction in selling outlays if the same output is to be sold, will reduce the per unit tax.

After-tax Equilibrium: Ad Valorem Tax

The reduction in the per unit tax at a constant output must lower the tax bill substantially.

The combination of a substantial reduction in the tax bill and a slight reduction in gross profit means that net profit is increased. Therefore movements downward from the before-tax W-E ridge line increase profit (up to a point, of course, since eventually gross profit will begin to decline rapidly), and the W-E ridge line on the net profit (net of tax) surface lies below the W-E ridge line on the gross profit surface.

Since this argument holds at *any* fixed output, the after-tax W-E ridge line is *everywhere* lower than the before-tax ridge.

C. *Net Effect of Both Shifts*

Since the shift of the N-S ridge line depends upon the level of marginal production cost, the effects of an ad valorem tax can be conveniently discussed under two headings: (1) marginal costs are zero, and (2) marginal costs are positive.

1. Marginal production costs are zero. In the traditional analysis, in which selling outlays are not taken into account, an ad valorem tax will not change either price or output if there are no marginal costs. But since the marginal revenue from selling outlays has been reduced at all outputs (i.e., the W-E ridge line is lower), if selling outlays can be adjusted in response to the tax, they *must* fall (left-hand panels, Chart 29), whatever type the demand function happens to be. (A comparison with the specific tax is apparent; a specific tax may or may not lower selling outlays.)

The decline in selling outlays means that either output or price or both must change, if demand is to be satisfied. If Cournot's fictitious proprietor of a mineral spring[2] has to incur advertising expenses to maintain the demand for mineral water, an ad valorem tax will not leave both price and output unchanged. Whether the movements of price and output are up or down depends upon the type of demand function. The left-hand panels in Chart 29 show the following:

(*a*) If the demand is type i (best level of selling costs rising with output), output will fall, and price will rise, fall, or remain the same.

---

[2]Cournot, *Principes mathématiques*, Chapter V.

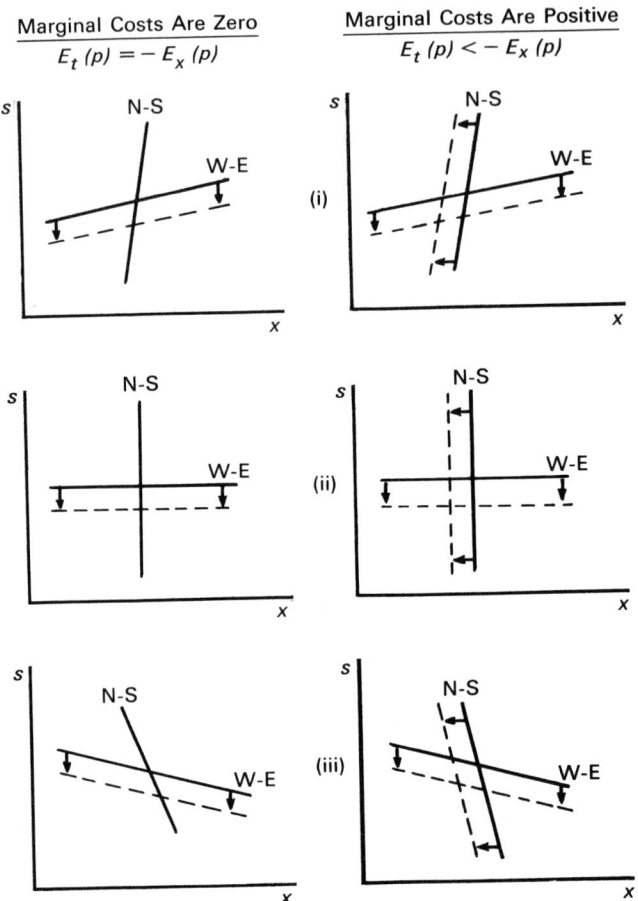

CHART 29.
Effect of advalorem tax on selling outlays and output: three types of demand functions and two marginal cost conditions. (Left-hand panels, $MC = 0$; right-hand panels, $MC \neq 0$).

(b) If the demand is type ii (best level of selling costs independent of output), output will remain the same, and price will fall.

(c) If the demand is type iii (best level of selling costs lower at higher outputs), output will rise, and price will fall.

2. Marginal production costs are positive. When marginal costs are not zero, the elasticity of demand at the pre-tax equilibrium will be greater than unity and, as noted above, the N-S ridge line will be shifted—at all levels of selling costs—to the left. The W-E ridge is

After-tax Equilibrium: Ad Valorem Tax

shifted downward, as before. Both shifts, for the three types of demand functions, are shown in the right-hand panels of Chart 29. The effects of an ad valorem tax when marginal costs are positive are not substantially different from those produced when marginal costs are zero; however, it is no longer *certain* that selling outlays will be reduced by the tax. For if the profit surface is shaped so that the best level of selling costs is *lower* at *high* outputs, and if the shift in the N-S ridge is "large" compared to that in the W-E ridge, the after-tax level of selling costs may be the same as the pre-tax level or higher. An ad valorem tax, then, may increase selling outlays *if* the demand conditions are such that raising these outlays reduces the optimum output. Whether this situation tends to hold generally or is a rare exception is a matter of fact, and no conjectures will be offered here.

The negative slope of the W-E (and N-S) ridge is a necessary but not a sufficient condition that an ad valorem tax increase selling outlays. The shift in the N-S ridge line must be sufficient to bring the intersection with the *lowered* W-E ridge to a level of selling costs higher than the pre-tax level. In view of this added requirement, there is a strong presumption, at least, that an ad valorem tax will generally reduce advertising expenditures. (If it does not have this effect, it must reduce output and increase price.)

The difference between the left- and right-hand sets of charts in Chart 29 is attributable to the existence of marginal production costs. To the extent that, in a given situation, marginal costs are a small proportion of price, the effect of the tax is likely to be shown on the left-hand side of the chart; if marginal costs are a large proportion of price, the situation is probably illustrated in one of the right-hand panels.

Another presumption (not a conclusion) follows from the foregoing. Even though selling outlays, as well as price and output, can be adjusted in response to a tax, an ad valorem tax will generally reduce output. The exception, an increase in output, will occur if the best level of selling outlays is lower at high outputs (the slope of the W-E ridge is negative) and if (1) marginal costs are zero, or (2) marginal costs are positive, but the shift in the N-S ridge to the left is small compared to the downward shift of the W-E ridge line.

Still another proposition, generally but not always true, is that the heavier the tax, the greater is the *decline* in selling costs. If marginal costs are zero, the proposition holds; for the heavier the tax, the greater are the slope of the tax function and the shift downward of the W-E ridge line. If marginal costs are not zero, but the demand function is type i or ii, the same result is obtained. The proposition will not hold if all of three conditions exist: (1) marginal costs are not zero and (2) the W-E ridge is downward sloping (as in the lower right panel of Chart 29) and (3) the shift in the N-S ridge is large compared to that in the W-E ridge. That is, if the tax *raises* selling outlays, a heavier tax will tend to raise them more.

The conclusions concerning the effects of an ad valorem tax may be compared to those reached by Hahn:

1. "Hence, the optimum price and selling cost for any level of output is reduced."[3] This is the equivalent to the statement that the ad valorem tax must everywhere lower the W-E ridge of the profit surface.

2. "The ... effect will normally tend to raise price ..."[4] This contrasts to the above implication that the tax may or may not raise price; in particular, if marginal costs are low compared to price, price may fall, remain unchanged, or rise.

3. Hahn does not say explicitly that the tax will reduce both selling outlays and output, but this result is implied several times. He does not consider the possibility that output will rise or remain unchanged.

Hahn does not study any other type of excise tax; however, the ad valorem tax is compared to a tax based on the volume of selling outlays. His findings concerning the latter tax are discussed in Appendix III.

Boulding also develops a partial diagramatic solution to the price-output-selling outlay equilibrium and briefly examines the effect of a tax. "A variable tax will reduce ... output ..."[5] (It is not clear from the context exactly what Boulding means by a "variable" tax. While he contrasts it with a lump-sum tax, the forms of variable tax are quite numerous, and, as will be seen below, some of them will increase output.) For the functions underlying his diagrams, it appears that the tax would also reduce selling outlays and

---

[3] Hahn, *Economic Journal*, LXIX, 307.
[4] *Economic Journal*, LXIX, 307.
[5] Boulding, *Economic Analysis*, p. 727.

After-tax Equilibrium: Ad Valorem Tax

increase price. He adds, "A case is even conceivable in which a tax causes the monopolist to reduce his price."[6]

Some of these effects can be illustrated by examples. For the same demand (type i) and cost functions presented above, the before-tax profit function is

$$\pi = 100x - x^2 + xs^{1/2} - s \tag{54}$$

If a 10% ad valorem tax is levied, total receipts will be reduced by 10%, so the after-tax profit function will be

$$\pi = 90x - 0.9x^2 + 0.9xs^{1/2} - s$$

with partial derivatives

$$\pi^x = 90 - 1.8x + 0.9s^{1/2} \tag{67}$$

$$\pi^s = \frac{0.45x}{\sqrt{s}} - 1 \tag{68}$$

If the partial derivative of profit (67) is set equal to zero and both sides of the equations are multiplied by 10/9, the equation is still satisfied by the same values of x and s, but reads

$$\pi^x = 100 - 2x + s^{1/2} = 0$$

which is the same as the equation of the pre-tax N-S ridge line. Since marginal costs are zero, the tax does not change this ridge line at all.

However, the tax has shifted the W-E ridge line, since the partial derivative of profit with respect to selling costs (68) is *not* the same as the before-tax derivative, expression (56). If both partial derivatives are equated to zero and solved for x and s, the results are as follows:

After-tax Equilibrium
$x = 64.5$ units
$s = \$841$ ($\sqrt{s} = 29$)
$p = \$64.5$ per unit

Pre-tax Equilibrium
$x = 66\frac{2}{3}$ units
$s = \$1111\frac{1}{9}$ ($\sqrt{s} = 33\frac{1}{3}$)
$p = \$66\frac{2}{3}$ per unit

The tax has reduced selling costs and also output (as it must for this type of demand function) and has lowered price (cf. upper left panel, Chart 29). If selling costs had been kept at the pre-tax level,

[6]*Economic Analysis*, p. 728.

this tax would not have changed either output or price. On the other hand, if output had been kept at the pre-tax level, selling outlays would have declined (but by a slightly smaller amount); thus the reduction in selling expenditures is not simply attributable to a tax-induced change in output and an adjustment of selling outlays to the new output level.

A heavier tax (20%) would have changed the partial derivatives of profit to

$$\pi^x = 80x - 0.8x^2 + 0.8xs^{1/2}$$
$$\pi^s = \frac{0.4x}{\sqrt{s}} - 1$$

If these are solved for x and s the results are as follows:

After-tax Equilibrium (20% ad valorem tax)
$x = 62.5$ units
$s = \$625$ ($\sqrt{s} = 25$)
$p = \$62.50$ per unit

The heavier tax has caused a larger decline in both selling outlays and output, as expected. Since the light tax reduced price (and the slope of price lines does not change sign: Chart 25), the heavier tax has reduced price further.

The juxtaposition of two of the previous findings: (1) if the slope of the tax function is zero, the N-S ridge line will be shifted, and (2) if the slope of the tax function is not zero, the W-E ridge line is shifted, shows why there is no excise tax that will leave price, output, and selling costs unchanged under the circumstances treated here. The specific tax that may not change selling outlays *must* change output and price; the ad valorem tax that may not change output *must* change selling costs and price; and so on.

In view of the possibility that the thick layer of qualifications and conditions attached to the conclusions thus far may be obscuring whatever advance has been made, it may be well to interrupt the sequence of steps and proofs for a few comments of a somewhat less stringent nature. It is hoped that all possible results have been obtained from the assumptions with which the analysis began; if, indeed, this much has been achieved, some benefit may be gained by the diversion of others from attempts to prove the unprovable,

After-tax Equilibrium: Ad Valorem Tax

for example, to find simple statements concerning the effects of taxes. Furthermore, the necessity for qualifications in the answers to important questions points the way directly to significant research — empirical studies can replace the qualifications, or a reformulation of theoretical concepts may lead to less equivocal conclusions. In addition, it is interesting to observe the linkage between two apparently different questions: "What is the effect of advertising on output?" and "What is the effect on advertising of the specific excise tax?" A single set of data describing the price-output-selling outlay relationship will provide exact answers to both questions. Finally, although it may be difficult to state precisely the effect on advertising of one excise tax, it is possible to make clear-cut comparisons (on some grounds) between two different taxes. Thus, whenever it has been decided that some commodity will be taxed (for whatever purpose), the results obtained here may provide some assistance in determining what *type* of tax to levy. For example, it will be shown that, of a specific tax and an ad valorem tax that would lead to the same after-tax output, the ad valorem tax will cause the greater decline (or perhaps the smaller increase) in selling costs.

Chapter 15. *After-tax Equilibrium: Progressive Tax*

Unlike Chapters 13 and 14, in which particular tax functions were treated, this chapter will cover progressive taxes as a class of tax functions. There seems to be little point to a separate treatment of every possible type of progressive tax.

A. *Tax-Induced Shift in N-S Ridge Line*

The overall effect of a progressive tax on the N-S ridge line of the profit surface raises an issue that was not important in the discussion of specific and ad valorem taxes. Following the results of Chapter 6, it is true that, if the elasticity of a tax is equal to the pre-tax demand elasticity, the tax will not shift the N-S ridge line at the pre-tax level of selling outlays. It is not true, however, that this ridge will be unaffected by such a tax throughout its range, for two possible reasons. First, price will vary from one point on the N-S ridge to another (unless the N-S ridge coincides with a price line); if the tax function is such that the elasticity varies with price, the elasticity of the tax will not be the same at all points on this ridge.[1] Second, it is generally true that the elasticity of *demand* will vary along the N-S ridge.

In one special case the elasticity of demand *must* be constant for all points on the N-S ridge. If marginal costs are zero, the optimum price and output, at *any* level of selling costs, must be such that the elasticity of demand equals unity.[2] Therefore a tax

---

[1]The elasticity of the proportional tax on excess price is equal to $p/(p-c)$; thus, at different prices, the tax elasticity is different. The power tax function, on the other hand, does have a constant elasticity—equal to the parameter n—at all prices.

[2]If price and output are adjusted to maximize profit, the elasticity of demand must be $p/(p-MC)$. If marginal costs are zero, that elasticity is unity.

with a constant elasticity of unity, that is, an ad valorem tax, will not affect the N-S ridge line at all.

As a rule, though, it must be expected that the elasticity of demand is not constant along this ridge. Then, even though the tax and demand elasticities are equal at the pre-tax equilibrium, they may not be equal at other points on the ridge. Or, if the tax and demand elasticities are *not* equal at the pre-tax equilibrium, they may be equal at other ridge points. The only unqualified statements concerning the effect of a progressive tax on the N-S ridge line are the following:

1. If the tax and demand elasticities are equal at the pre-tax equilibrium, the ridge will not be shifted at the pre-tax level of selling costs; at other levels of selling costs, the ridge may be shifted either to the right or to the left.
2. If the tax elasticity exceeds the demand elasticity at the pre-tax equilibrium, the N-S ridge will be shifted to the right; at levels of selling costs other than the pre-tax level, the ridge may not be shifted or may be moved to the left or, of course, to the right.
3. If at the pre-tax point the tax elasticity is smaller than the demand elasticity, the ridge will be shifted to the left; at other levels of selling outlays, the ridge may not be shifted or may be moved to the right or, of course, to the left.

This issue does not arise when marginal costs are zero (for reasons given above), and it is not important in studying the ad valorem tax when marginal costs are positive.[3] If it were known, for example, that the demand elasticity were smaller at the optimum than at the zero level of advertising expenditure, the charts could be drawn to take this information into account. However, since there seems to be no firm basis for expecting advertising to change the demand elasticity in any specific way, and since the introduction of more detail into the analysis seems likely to yield a very low return, it will be assumed that a tax which shifts the N-S ridge line in one direction at the pre-tax level of selling outlays will shift the ridge

---

[3] The sketches in the right-hand panels of Chart 29 involve a certain amount of graphic license in that the tax appears to shift the N-S ridge lines by the same *amount* at all levels of selling outlays. These shifts should be interpreted as being in the *direction* shown, but, since the demand elasticity may vary along the pre-tax N-S ridge line, the amount of shift would usually be different at different levels of selling outlays.

After-tax Equilibrium: Progressive Tax

in that same direction throughout the relevant range of selling outlays.

It will be noted that this assumption is not very strong; if a tax shifts the N-S ridge to the left, say, at the pre-tax point, the N-S ridge *must* be shifted to the left for values of selling outlay "slightly" above and "slightly" below the pre-tax level, as long as the demand, cost, and tax functions are continuous. Moreover, none of the conclusions of this section is intended to rest upon this assumption — it is made to justify the illustrations, not to provide further results.

This assumption provides that the N-S ridge line, at all points within the relevant range, will be shifted, if at all, in only one direction.

 a. If the tax and demand elasticities are equal, the N-S ridge will not be shifted at all.
 b. If the tax elasticity is smaller than the demand elasticity, the N-S ridge will be shifted to the left, that is, toward lower output and higher price.
 c. If the tax elasticity exceeds the demand elasticity, the N-S ridge will be shifted to the right, toward higher output and lower price.

B. *Tax-Induced Shift in the W-E Ridge Line*

The manner in which a progressive excise tax shifts the W-E ridge line is similar to that produced by an ad valorem tax: if the slope of the tax function is positive at all outputs, the W-E ridge line will be everywhere lowered by the tax. Since progressive excise taxes have been defined as those with an elasticity greater than unity (Chapter 2), and since a tax function with a positive elasticity must have a positive slope,[4] any progressive tax will have a positive slope.

However, unlike the ad valorem tax, which has a slope equal to the tax rate, r, regardless of price, the slope of a progressive tax may vary at different prices (the proportional tax on excess price, with a constant slope, is an exception). All that this implies, for the

---

[4]The tax elasticity is defined as

$$E_t(p) = t'(p)\frac{p}{t}$$

If $E_t(p)$ is positive, $t'(p)$ must be, since both p and t are positive.

present problem, is that the *amount* of lowering of the W-E ridge by a progressive tax may not be the same at all outputs. However, the W-E ridge line will be *lowered* at all outputs by any progressive tax.

C. *Net Effect of Both Shifts*

In the previous discussion of the ad valorem tax, it was convenient to classify possible situations according to whether marginal production costs were zero or positive. The same type of classification, although slightly expanded, may prove useful here.
1. The elasticity of the progressive tax is equal, at the pre-tax equilibrium, to the demand elasticity.
2. The tax elasticity is smaller than the demand elasticity.
3. The tax elasticity exceeds the demand elasticity.

1. If the tax and demand elasticities are equal before the tax is levied, the simplifying assumptions just made assure that the effects of the tax (insofar as they are considered here) are not substantially different from those of an ad valorem tax when marginal production costs are zero. For if marginal costs are zero, the pre-tax demand elasticity must be unity and hence equal to the elasticity of the ad valorem tax. In either case—ad valorem tax with zero marginal cost, or progressive tax with an elasticity equal to the demand elasticity—the N-S ridge line is not shifted by the tax at the pre-tax level of selling costs. In the latter case the N-S ridge line is, by assumption, not shifted at any other level of selling costs. Also, in either case, the W-E ridge line is lowered at all outputs by the tax. Therefore the left-hand panels of Chart 29, although labeled to illustrate the imposition of an ad valorem tax when marginal costs are zero, represent equally well the effects of a progressive tax whose elasticity equals the pre-tax demand elasticity. Furthermore, the effects of the taxes in both cases described would be identical, to the extent that these effects are being examined, and the conclusions given above concerning the effects of an ad valorem tax when marginal costs are zero apply also to any progressive tax whose elasticity equals the demand elasticity.

In short, the optimum level of selling outlays *must* fall; the optimum output may decline, remain unchanged, or increase—if output does not change or increases, price will fall; if output declines, price may fall, rise, or remain unchanged (upper left panel, Chart 29).

After-tax Equilibrium: Progressive Tax

2. Another possibility to be considered is that the tax elasticity (say, 2) may be smaller than the demand elasticity (say, 3). This situation does not differ in any essential way from that depicted in the right-hand panels of Chart 29 for the ad valorem tax when marginal costs are positive. For if marginal costs are positive, the demand elasticity must be greater than unity and thus greater than the elasticity of the ad valorem tax.

The effects of the ad valorem tax in the more realistic realm of positive marginal costs apply without further reservations to any progressive tax with an elasticity *smaller* than the demand elasticity. There is a strong presumption that both selling outlays and output will decline.

3. When consideration is given to the possibility that the tax elasticity may exceed the demand elasticity, the discussion is extended to new ground. In this instance the N-S ridge of the profit surface will be shifted to the *right*, while the W-E ridge is lowered, according to the arguments of pp. 154–155. This combination of changes is shown, for each of the three types of demand functions, in Chart 30.

If the demand is either type ii or iii, it is clear that selling outlays must decline, output must rise, and price must fall. Should the demand function be type i, it is no longer certain that all of these effects will occur, but there is some presumption that they will. Only a large shift of the W-E ridge and a small shift of the N-S ridge could lead to a lower output (although selling outlays would still decline); conversely, a small shift of the W-E ridge combined with a large shift of the N-S ridge could lead to higher selling outlays, in which case, however, output must increase.

It will be observed from Chart 30 that a progressive tax whose elasticity exceeds the demand elasticity will generally tend to increase output and reduce price (these results are certain if selling outlays cannot be adjusted to the tax). These tendencies are accompanied by a general—but not certain—downward effect on selling outlays. The reduction in selling outlays also means that the price and output changes resulting from the tax may, depending upon the form of the demand function, be the same as or greater or less than the changes that would have occurred if selling outlays could not be varied.

Some of the results for a tax with an elasticity exceeding the demand elasticity may be verified in specific instances. Consider

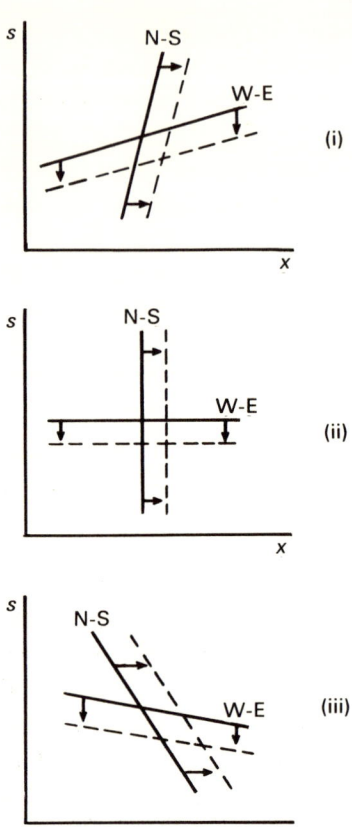

CHART 30.
Effects of progressive tax $(E_t(p) > -E_x(p))$ on selling outlays and output: three types of demand functions.

the demand and cost functions presented above. This demand function implies a profit surface with ridge lines that are positively sloped (as in Chart 24). Since marginal costs are assumed to be zero, the pre-tax elasticity of demand must be unity. Thus the effects of any tax with an elasticity greater than unity will be shown approximately by the top panel of Chart 30.

Let the per unit tax be determined by the function

$$t = 0.0015p^2$$

This tax has an elasticity equal to the exponent of the price variable — in this case, 2.

After-tax Equilibrium: Progressive Tax

Since p is an expression (53) in x and s and is squared in the tax function, the mathematical manipulations will be much simplified if the average revenue function

$$p = 100 - x + s^{1/2} \qquad (53)$$

is solved for x in terms of price and selling outlay:

$$x = 100 - p + s^{1/2}$$

The after-tax profit function

$$\pi = px - tx - s$$

becomes

$$\pi = p(100-p+s^{1/2}) - 0.0015p^2(100-p+s^{1/2}) - s$$
$$= 100p - 1.15p^2 + 0.0015p^3 + ps^{1/2} - 0.0015p^2s^{1/2} - s \qquad (69)$$

The partial derivatives of (69) with respect to price and selling outlays are

$$\pi^p = 100 - 2.3p + 0.0045p^2 + s^{1/2} - 0.0030ps^{1/2} \qquad (70)$$

$$\pi^s = \frac{p}{2\sqrt{s}} - \frac{0.00075p^2}{\sqrt{s}} - 1 \qquad (71)$$

If both derivatives are equated to zero and s is eliminated, the following cubic equation results:

$$9p^3 + 9000p^2 - 7{,}200{,}000p + 400{,}000{,}000 = 0$$

The relevant root of this equation is substituted for p in (70) or (71) to give the after-tax level of selling outlays. These two values and the demand function determine the after-tax output.

After-tax Equilibrium	Pre-tax Equilibrium
$x = 67.1$ units	$x = 66\frac{2}{3}$ units
$p = \$60.39$ per unit	$p = \$66\frac{2}{3}$ per unit
$s = \$754$	$s = \$1111\frac{1}{9}$

Output has increased slightly, price has fallen; and selling outlays have declined markedly. None of these changes—or even their directions—could have been predicted with certainty. Other changes could have occurred if different demand functions of the same type and different cost and tax functions had been selected.

Even so, some conclusions concerning combinations of changes are possible. As long as the demand function is type i and the tax elasticity exceeds the demand elasticity, (1) if the tax does not change selling outlays, it must reduce price and increase output (according to the top panel of Chart 30 and the results of Chapter 5); (2) if the tax does not change output—the output change in the example above was slight—it must reduce selling outlays and price. For another example, the demand function of type ii used above will be employed:

$$p = 100 - x + \frac{50s^{1/2}}{x}$$

Let the per unit tax be given by

$$t = 0 \cdot 10 \, (p - \$37.50)$$

The tax elasticity was shown in Chapter 2 to be

$$E_t(p) = \frac{p}{p-c}$$

At the pre-tax price of \$75, the elasticity is

$$E_t(p) = \frac{\$75}{\$75 - \$37.50} = +2$$

Since marginal production costs are zero, the demand elasticity is unity and the effects of the tax are illustrated in the center panel of Chart 30.

The after-tax profit function will be

$$\pi = x\left(100 - x + \frac{50s^{1/2}}{x}\right) - 0.10x\left(100 - x + \frac{50s^{1/2}}{x} - 37.50\right) - s$$

$$= 93.75x - 0.9x^2 + 45\sqrt{s} - s \tag{72}$$

The partial derivatives of (72) are

$$\pi^x = 93.75 - 1.8x$$

$$\pi^s = \frac{45}{2\sqrt{s}} - 1$$

The before- and after-tax values are as follows

After-tax Equilibrium: Progressive Tax

After-tax Equilibrium	Pre-tax Equilibrium
$x = 52$ units	$x = 50$ units
$p = \$69.60$ per unit	$p = \$75$ per unit
$s = \$506.25$	$s = \$625$

If the demand function is type ii, output must rise and price and selling outlays must fall as a result of the tax.

Chapter 16. *After-tax Equilibrium: Highly Regressive Tax*

The order in which the previous taxes were discussed began with the more familiar and proceeded to the less familiar. Up to this point the order has also been from the less elastic to the more elastic tax. The next type of tax to be examined is not common — in fact, no actual example has been discovered — but its rank according to elasticity is not at the upper range of the scale; rather, it belongs at the low range of elasticity. For discussion purposes, the term "highly regressive" means that the per unit tax *declines* as price increases; for one example of such a tax schedule, see tax 7 of Table 2.

Since the context is still one of taxes, rather than bounties, the per unit tax is positive; if the per unit tax declines at higher prices, the slope of the tax function (with respect to price) is negative. The tax elasticity, given by

$$E_t(p) = t'(p)\frac{p}{t}$$

must then be negative and clearly smaller than the demand elasticity.

A. *Tax-Induced Shift in N-S Ridge Line*

The shift of the N-S ridge line by the tax will be determined by the manner in which marginal revenue with respect to output, at a given level of selling costs, is changed by the tax. The reduction in the kind of marginal revenue referred to is given in expression 27 of Chapter 6:

$$t(p)\left[1 - \frac{E_t(p)}{-E_x(p)}\right]$$

Since $E_x(p)$ is always negative, and $t(p)$ is positive for a *tax*, if the tax elasticity is negative, the whole expression is positive. This means that, at each level of selling costs, marginal revenue with respect to output must be reduced. Therefore the N-S ridge line is moved toward lower outputs, that is, to the left. This same direction of shift occurs as a result of the specific tax and also the ad valorem tax when the demand elasticity is greater than unity.

B. *Tax-Induced Shift in W-E Ridge Line*

The effect of the tax on the W-E ridge line may be noted in the following manner. The general argument which showed that a tax function with a *positive* slope must lower the W-E ridge can be retraced, making the appropriate changes in the text for a tax function with a *negative* slope. The major change is, of course, that a price (and a selling outlay) *increase*, at a constant output, *reduces* the per unit tax and hence lowers the tax bill. The effect will be to *raise* the W-E ridge, at all outputs, above the pre-tax level.

C. *Net Effect of Both Shifts*

The leftward shift of the N-S ridge line and the upward shift of the W-E ridge line are shown, for each of the three types of demand functions, in Chart 31.

For demand types ii and iii, it is clear that each of the following changes must result from the tax: a decline in output, an increase in selling outlays, and an increase in prices.

If the demand function is type i, the same changes seem likely but a large shift in one ridge line combined with a small shift in the other could lead either to (1) a decline in output, no change or a decline in selling costs, and an increase or an indefinite change in price; or (2) no change or an increase in output, an increase in selling costs, and an increase or an indefinite change in price.

It is apparent that, unless the exception just described is in fact not an exception but rather the most common situation, a highly regressive tax will make higher selling outlays profitable.

An example of a highly regressive tax can be constructed as a variation of the "proportional tax on excess price":

$$t(p) = -r(p-c)$$

After-tax Equilibrium: Highly Regressive Tax

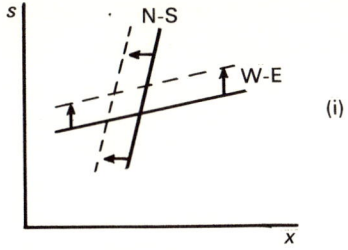

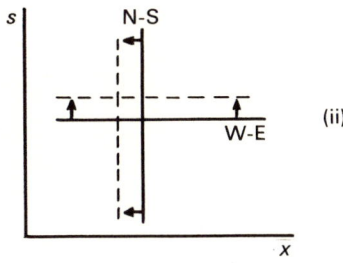

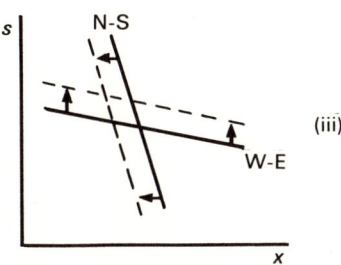

CHART 31.
Effect of highly regressive tax $[E_t(p) < 0]$ on selling outlays and output: three types of demand functions.

where c is some fixed value *larger* than the pre-tax price, instead of the smaller value in the more usual case. Since the term $(p-c)$ is now negative, the entire tax expression must be preceded by a minus sign in order for the expression to be positive.

The slope of this tax function is the value of r, which in this instance is negative; the tax elasticity, given by

$$E_t(p) = \frac{p}{p-c}$$

is negative, since $(p-c)$ is negative.

The power tax function

$$t(p) = kp^n$$

can also be made highly regressive if the value assigned to the parameter n is negative, in which case both the tax elasticity (equal to n) and the slope of the tax function (equal to nkp^{n-1}) are negative.

For a specific example, consider the demand function (of type i) and the cost function introduced above. Let the per unit tax function be

$$t(p) = -0.10(p - \$100)$$

At the pre-tax price, $\$66\frac{2}{3}$ per unit, the per unit tax is $\$3\frac{1}{3}$ and increases in price will reduce this tax.

The profit function is now

$$\pi = x(\$100 - x + s^{1/2}) - 0.10x(\$100 - x + s^{1/2} - \$100) - s$$

or

$$\pi = 100x - 1.1x^2 + 1.1xs^{1/2} - s \tag{73}$$

The partial derivatives of (73) are

$$\pi^x = 100 - 2.2x + 1.1s^{1/2}$$

$$\pi^s = \frac{0.55x}{\sqrt{s}} - 1$$

Setting both partial derivatives equal to zero yields the following:

After-tax Equilibrium	Pre-tax Equilibrium
$x = 62.7$ units	$x = 66\frac{2}{3}$ units
$s = \$1189 (\sqrt{s} = 34.49)$	$s = \$1111\frac{1}{9}(\sqrt{s} = 33\frac{1}{3})$
$p = \$71.79$ per unit	$p = \$66\frac{2}{3}$ per unit

The tax has reduced output and raised price, as expected from the results of Chapter 4; however, selling outlays have been increased by the tax.

Chapter 17. *Some Comparisons between "Equal" Taxes*

In this chapter an attempt will be made to compare different forms of tax functions in the search for conclusions that carry fewer qualifications and possible exceptions than those presented above. Although the comparisons will be based in part on one type of demand function, the conclusions will hold for any type. In Section A taxes will be compared on the basis of after-tax output. In Section B they will be compared on the basis of the amount of tax at the pre-tax price.

A. *Taxes That Lead to the Same After-tax Output*

Although the after-tax output is determined by a wide variety of demand, cost, and tax characteristics, there are generally several different tax functions that, given certain demand and cost conditions, will lead to the same output. It is the purpose here to compare the effects on selling outlays and price of taxes that have equal effects on output. In the simpler analysis (Part II), where the only variables studied are price and output, a comparison of this type is trivial, since two taxes that lead to the same output must lead to the same price. When selling outlays are also variable, many combinations of changes are possible.

The following theorem will be proved: *If two tax functions, with different slopes with respect to price, produce the same change in output, the tax with the greater slope must lead both to lower selling outlays and to a lower price than the tax with the lesser slope.*

For example, the specific tax has a slope of zero and an ad valorem tax has a (greater) slope equal to the tax rate, r. According to the theorem, if a specific and an ad valorem tax both lead to the same after-tax output, the ad valorem tax will lead to lower after-tax selling outlays and to lower after-tax price than will the specific tax.

The same kind of comparison can be made between a highly regressive and a specific tax, an ad valorem and a progressive tax, two progressive taxes, a tax and a bounty, etc.

The theorm is proven by noting first that, by hypothesis, the after-tax positions (i.e., the intersections of the after-tax N-S and W-E ridge lines) must fall at the same output—that is to say, each intersection must fall on the vertical line representing the after-tax output. The crux of the matter then becomes: which tax has the lower W-E ridge line at this output? This question is answered by the argument above, which shows that a positively sloped tax *must* lower the W-E ridge line, and by examination of the equation for the W-E ridge

$$x \cdot p^s(x,s)\{1 - t^p[p(x,s)]\} - 1 = 0 \tag{60}$$

Now, at a given output, all terms of this equation except t^p have some value that is unaffected by the tax. But if, as shown above, a positive value of t^p lowers the W-E ridge, a greater positive value must lower it further.

Therefore, of the two tax functions, $t_1(p)$ and $t_2(p)$, that lead to the same after-tax output, if $t_1'(p) > t_2'(p)$, after-tax selling outlays will be lower under tax 1 than tax 2.

The second part of the theorem, concerning price changes, follows directly from the fact that the intersection of the N-S and W-E ridge lines for each tax must fall on the same vertical line (at the after-tax output), and from the fact that movements to the south over the profit surface represent declines in price. Therefore, of the two taxes being compared, the tax that leads to lower selling outlays must also lead to lower price.

The theorem holds whether both of the pair of taxes being compared reduce output, raise it, or leave it unchanged, as long as they have the same effect on output.

B. *Taxes That Are Equal at the Pre-tax Price*

The analytical structure utilized to describe the equilibrium among selling outlays, output, and price does not permit the direct

Some Comparisons between "Equal" Taxes

comparison of taxes that are equal at the pre-tax price. This is true because, as a variable, price does not appear explicitly in either the analysis or the graphs. The way out of this difficulty is to rebuild the structure with selling outlays and price (rather than output) as independent variables. This will be done in summary fashion, following the main outlines of Chapters 11 and 12.

The demand function is now written as

$$x = x(p, s)$$

The cost function becomes

$$c = c[x(p,s)] + s$$

That is, each combination of price and selling outlays will determine some output. The total costs of each combination will be the sum of selling outlays and costs of producing the ensuing output.

The pre-tax profit function is

$$\pi = p \cdot x(p,s) - c[x(p,s)] - s \tag{74}$$

If this equation is set equal to k and "solved" for pairs of values of p and s, the pairs of values would represent one contour of the profit surface. The solution of (74) set equal to other constants would yield other contours.

The partial derivatives of (74) are

$$\pi^p = p \cdot x^p(p,s) + x(p,s) - c^x[x(p,s)]x^p(p,s) \tag{75}$$

$$\pi^s = p \cdot x^s(p,s) - c^x[x(p,s)]x^s(p,s) - 1 \tag{76}$$

Equation (75) represents the marginal *net* profit with respect to price at a fixed level of selling outlays; this net profit consists of the difference between marginal revenue with respect to price and marginal cost with respect to price. The marginal cost of a price change in turn consists of the product of the marginal production cost *with respect to output* and the marginal demand, that is, the change in the number of units demanded per unit change in price.

Equation (76) represents the marginal *net* profit with respect to selling outlays, at a fixed price. This net profit is the difference between the marginal *income* per unit increase in selling costs (or price times the increase in demand per unit increase in s) and the marginal *outgo*. The latter can be seen as two flows, one representing the increased production cost — as added advertising increases output — and the other the added advertising expenditures.

In order to maximize profit, both of these margins must jointly be brought to zero, that is, (75) and (76) must be equated to zero and solved, to yield the optimum values of p and s. In addition, the usual second-order conditions must be satisfied.

The implicit relations

$$\pi^p = 0$$

and

$$\pi^s = 0$$

constitute the equations in the s-p plane of the N-S and W-E ridge lines, respectively.

An argument analogous to that in Appendix II shows that (1) if the W-E ridge line is horizontal at the pre-tax equilibrium, the N-S ridge must be vertical; (2) if the W-E ridge slopes upward at p_0, the N-S ridge must also slope upward at p_0; (3) if the W-E ridge slopes downward at p_0, the N-S ridge must also slope downward at p_0.

A chart of the profit contours and the ridge lines could also include "constant output" lines. These, like the constant price lines of Chart 25, would be positively sloped, since, in order to sell the same output at a higher price, selling outlays must be increased.

So far, little has been added to the material of Chapter 11. Sharper contrasts will arise when the after-tax equilibrium is stated.

If now a per unit tax function is introduced, the profit equation (74) becomes:

$$\pi = p \cdot x(p,s) - t(p) x(p,s) - c[x(p,s)] - s$$

with partial derivatives

$$\pi^p = p \cdot x^p(p,s) + x(p,s)$$
$$- [t(p) \cdot x^p(p,s) + t'(p) \cdot x(p,s)] -$$
$$- c^x[x(p,s)] x^p(p,s) \qquad (77)$$

$$\pi^s = p \cdot x^s(p,s) - t(p) \cdot x^s(p,s) - c^x[x(p,s)] x^s(p,s) - 1 \qquad (78)$$

The effect of the tax on the marginal profitability of *price* change, as shown in (77), depends, as before, on the ratio of the tax and demand elasticities. If the tax elasticity exceeds the demand elasticity, the marginal profitability of a price increase is reduced by the tax.

Some Comparisons between "Equal" Taxes

The effect of the tax on the marginal profitability of selling outlays can be shown by comparing the before- and after-tax expressions:

Before-tax: $\quad \pi^s = x^s(p,s) \cdot p - c^x[x(p,s)]x^s(p,s) - 1 \quad$ (76)

After-tax: $\quad \pi^s = x^s(p,s)[p - t(p)] - c^x[x(p,s)]x^s(p,s) - 1 \quad$ (78)

The only difference between these two expressions is the term $t(p)$. Thus it is not, as before, the *slope* of the per unit tax function that affects the marginal profitability of selling outlays; it is the *level* of the per unit tax.

It is important to note that, if two different tax functions yield equal per unit taxes *at some price*, p_1, the after-tax W-E ridge lines for the two taxes would intersect (or touch) at this price, p_1. The equation of the after-tax W-E ridge in the *s-p* plane is (78) equated to zero; if $t_1(p_1) = t_2(p_1)$, the after-tax equations would take identical values at price p_1. This relation will be utilized below.

It is not difficult to see why the marginal profitability of selling outlays is apparently affected differently by a tax according to the method of analysis: there are really two different concepts of "marginal profitability." One, already treated in detail, is the marginal profitability of increased selling outlays (and increased price) *at a constant output*. The before- and after-tax marginal profitabilities differ only as the tax bill varies. If output is held constant, the tax bill can vary *only* if the per unit tax varies (through price changes). Thus the before- and after-tax marginal profitabilities differ only by a term describing how the per unit tax varies with price, namely, the *slope* of the tax function.

The second, the concept involved here, is the marginal profitability of increased selling outlays (and output) *at a fixed price*. As above, the before- and after-tax marginal profitabilities differ only if the tax bill is affected by selling outlay (and output) variation. Since price determines the per unit tax and is held constant, the per unit tax is also held constant. The tax bill will vary directly as output varies, and the marginal profitability of selling is affected only by the level of the per unit tax.

Detailed analysis would show that the W-E ridge of the profit surface is *lowered* by an amount proportional to the per unit tax at each price. (The N-S ridge line would be moved to the right or left, according to the tax and demand elasticities at the pre-tax price.) A whole new series of charts could be drawn, illustrating the effects of different types of taxes. The alternative classification of demand functions prescribed in Chapter 12 would be utilized in such illustrations. Such charts show that those previous conclusions which held regardless of the type of demand function still hold and that, where qualifications were needed before, they are still needed. Conclusions that pertain to a specific type of demand function may not carry over, since the two classifications of demand functions are different.

The groundwork is now complete for showing, insofar as possible, the relative effects on selling outlays of two taxes that are equal at the pre-tax price. In each panel of Chart 32, certain features of a

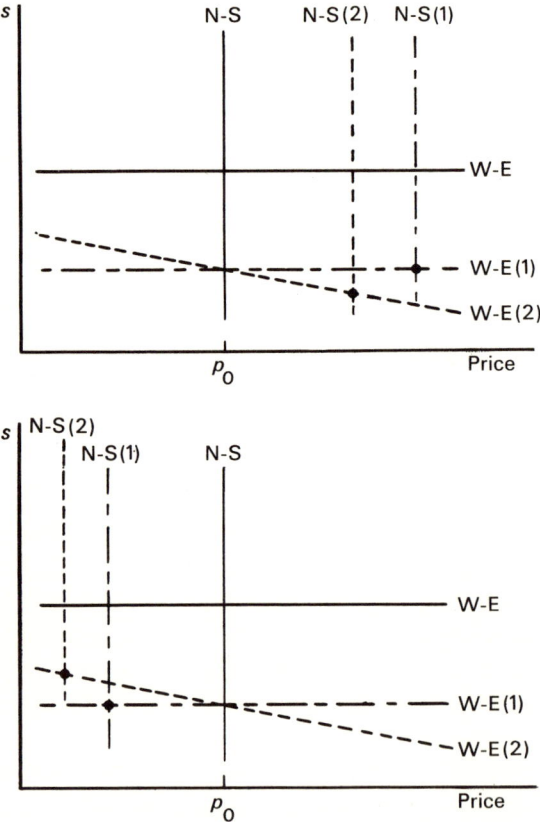

CHART 32.
Relative effects of taxes equal at pre-tax price: upper panel—both taxes increase price. Lower panel—both taxes reduce price.

Some Comparisons between "Equal" Taxes

profit surface are shown: the pre-tax N-S and W-E ridge lines and two sets of after-tax ridge lines, one set for each of two different taxes, $t_1(p)$ and $t_2(p)$. (It is to be noted that the variable measured along the horizontal axis is price per unit and not output.) The demand function underlying the chart is type 2, that is, the best level of selling costs remains the same at all *prices*. This choice will not affect the comparisons to be made.

In the top panel the effects of the two taxes (with different elasticities at the pre-tax price), both of which increase price, are shown. The two after-tax N-S ridge lines are to the right of the pre-tax ridge. The effect of each tax on the W-E ridge will depend upon the amount of each tax at different levels of price. As shown above, the after-tax W-E ridge lines must touch or intersect at the price at which the two per unit taxes are equal — in this case, at the pre-tax price, p_0.

It remains to be shown how the two after-tax W-E ridge lines differ at prices other than the pre-tax price. Let tax 1 have a smaller elasticity than tax 2:

$$E_{t_1}(p_0) < E_{t_2}(p_0)$$

or

$$\left[t_1'(p_0) \cdot \frac{p_0}{t_1(p_0)}\right] < \left[t_2'(p_0) \cdot \frac{p_0}{t_2(p_0)}\right]$$

Given $t_1(p_0) = t_2(p_0)$, that is, the two tax functions are equal at p_0, then

$$t_1'(p_0) < t_2'(p_0)$$

The slope of tax function 1 is smaller at p_0 than that of tax function 2 — that is to say, per unit tax 2 is increasing faster at p_0 than per unit tax 1. If both tax functions are continuous, the above inequality must hold at prices some distance from p_0 (for the types of continuous tax functions discussed in Part II, the inequality would hold at all prices). The relative sizes of the two per unit taxes at various prices would be:

Price	Relative Sizes
Greater than p_0	$t_1(p) < t_2(p)$
Equal to p_0	$t_1(p_0) = t_2(p_0)$
Smaller than p_0	$t_1(p) > t_2(p)$

For example, compare taxes 3 and 5, Table 2. Both taxes are equal at a price of $2.00; tax 3 has the smaller elasticity; at prices above $2.00, tax 3 is smaller than tax 5; at prices below $2.00, tax 3 is greater than tax 5.

Since the shift of the W-E ridge line, at each price, by a tax is proportional to the per unit tax at each price, it follows that at prices above p_0 the W-E ridge line for tax 2 must be below that for tax 1, at prices below p_0 the W-E ridge for tax 2 must be above that for tax 1, and at the pre-tax price the two after-tax W-E ridge lines must intersect.

If both taxes increase price, the after-tax equilibrium positions are indicated in the upper panel of Chart 32, and could represent the effects of, say, a specific tax (tax 1) and an ad valorem tax (tax 2). It is clear that, under the conditions implicit in the chart, the ad valorem tax (the more elastic one) must reduce selling outlays more than the specific tax.

It is not possible, however, to generalize this particular result without qualification, for three reasons. First, even though at prices above p_0 the W-E ridge for the more elastic tax is always below that for the less elastic tax, it does not follow that *all* points of the ridge line W-E(2) are below *all* points of the ridge line W-E(1). Second, there is no assurance that the two taxes will change price in the same direction. Third, there is no assurance that both taxes will reduce selling outlays.

These difficulties will be evaded if a rigorous conclusion is not drawn.

1. If any two excise taxes are equal at the pre-tax price and both taxes increase price, there is a tendency for selling outlays to be lower under the more elastic of the two taxes.[1]

A somewhat more rigorous, but less general, statement is as follows:

2. If any two excise taxes are equal at the pre-tax price and both taxes increase price *by about the same amount*, there is a *strong* tendency for selling outlays to be lower under the more elastic of the two taxes.

---

[1] Compare, for example, the $143 reduction in selling outlays per time period brought about by a $6⅔ specific tax (Chapter 13) and the $270 reduction after a 10% ad valorem tax is imposed (Chapter 14). Both taxes are equal at the pre-tax price ($66⅔), and the ad valorem is more elastic than the specific tax.

Some Comparisons between "Equal" Taxes

Finally, if both taxes lead to the same after-tax price, the uncertainties disappear. For it has already been shown that at any price above p_0 (including the after-tax price) W-E(2) must lie below W-E(1). None of the results of Chapter 4 rules out the possibility of two taxes with different elasticities causing the same price change.

3. If any two excise taxes are equal at the pre-tax price and both taxes increase price *by the same amount*, selling outlays will be lower under the more elastic of the two taxes.

None of the foregoing is inconsistent with the possibility that both taxes (contrary to the appearance of the chart) increase selling outlays. It may be added that, since downward movements over the *s-p* plane represent output decreases, the more elastic will also *tend* to lead to a lower output than the less elastic tax.

If both taxes reduce price, as in the lower panel of Chart 32, it is clear that the relative effects just stated are exactly reversed. At prices below p_0, the W-E ridge for the more elastic tax, W-E(2), must be above W-E(1) and the tendency is for the more elastic tax to lead to higher selling outlays (and output) than the less elastic tax.

Chapter 18. *Extension of Results*

In the previous chapters of Part III, the effects of various forms of excise tax on price, output, and selling effort have been studied in the context of monopoly. In this chapter, the limitation of the analysis to *taxes* is removed and the type of tax *or bounty* that would lead to each of eight different combinations of change is shown (Section A). Another way of extending the findings to this point is to consider the circumstances under which the conclusions may hold, even though the assumptions, as stated, are clearly violated. This is done tentatively in certain directions in Section B.

A. *The General Tendencies*

A perusal of Charts 28 through 31 shows a wide variety of reactions to excise taxes of different types. The general tendencies for the taxes so far considered are summarized in Chart 33. For the purpose of this summary, demand functions of type ii are implied, thus neglecting the possibility that the W-E ridge has either a positive or a negative slope. The arrows in the panels show the general direction of change from the pre-tax to the after-tax equilibrium. It will be noted that, as one proceeds to higher numbered panels, the arrows are rotated counterclockwise in direction. It may be observed that the same counterclockwise rotation of the arrows would occur if the separate panels were based on demand functions of type i or iii. The numbers of the panels of the chart correspond to the following types of taxes.

1. HIGHER SELLING OUTLAYS, HIGHER PRICE, LOWER OUTPUT
    a. Highly regressive tax, for example, center panel, Chart 31: $t(p) > 0$;

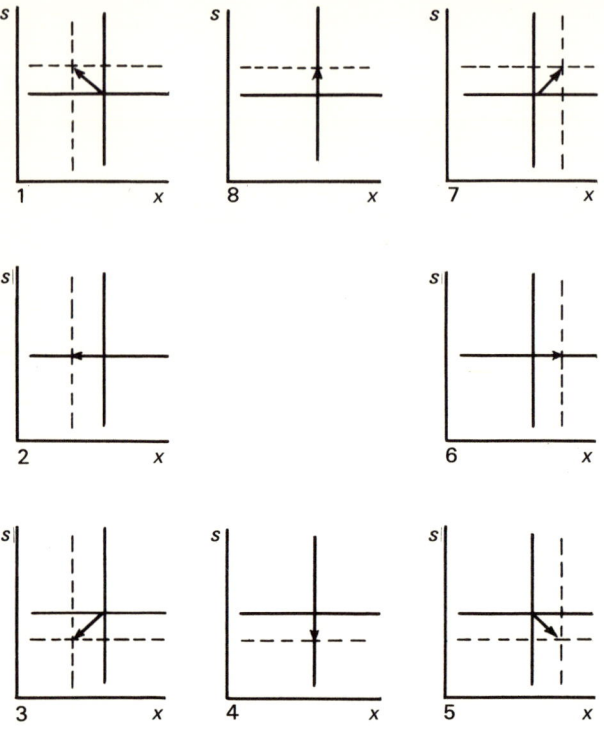

CHART 33.
Effects of various taxes and bounties on selling outlays and output: demand function of type ii.

$t'(p) < 0$, in order that the W-E ridge of the profit surface be *raised*;

$E_t(p) < 0 < -E_x(p)$, which follows from the two previous inequalities, and which shifts the N-S ridge to the *left*.

b. A second possible "tax" function that would lead to the changes shown in panel 1, Chart 31:

$t(p) < 0$, the "tax" is a bounty;

$t'(p) < 0$, the slope of the "tax" function must be negative, that is, the "tax" must decline (the bounty must increase) as price increases;

$E_t(p) > -E_x(p)$, the elasticity of the "tax" function must be greater than the demand elasticity.

This second possibility is treated in more detail below.

Extension of Results 189

2. HIGHER PRICE, LOWER OUTPUT

The specific tax, for example, center panel, Chart 28:
$t(p) > 0$;
$t'(p) = 0$, in order that the W-E ridge of the profit surface not be shifted;
$E_t(p) = 0 < -E_x(p)$, which also follows from these two inequalities, and which shifts the N-S ridge to the left.

3. LOWER SELLING OUTLAYS, LOWER OUTPUT

Ad valorem tax when the demand elasticity exceeds unity, or progressive tax such that the tax elasticity is smaller than the demand elasticity, for example, right center panel, Chart 29:
$t(p) > 0$;
$t'(p) > 0$, which *lowers* the W-E ridge;
$E_t(p) < -E_x(p)$, which shifts the N-S ridge to the left.

4. LOWER SELLING OUTLAYS, LOWER PRICE

Ad valorem tax when demand elasticity equals unity, or progressive tax such that the tax elasticity equals the demand elasticity, for example, left center panel, Chart 29:
$t(p) > 0$;
$t'(p) > 0$, which lowers the W-E ridge;
$E_t(p) = -E_x(p)$, which means that the N-S ridge will not be shifted.

5. LOWER SELLING OUTLAYS, LOWER PRICE, HIGHER OUTPUT

  a. Progressive tax such that tax elasticity exceeds the demand elasticity, for example, center panel, Chart 30:
  $t(p) > 0$;
  $t'(p) > 0$, to lower the W-E ridge;
  $E_t(p) > -E_x(p)$, to shift the N-S ridge to the right.

  b. A second "tax" function also possible in the instance:
  $t(p) < 0$, the tax is a bounty;
  $t'(p) > 0$, the slope of the bounty function must be positive, that is, the "tax" must increase (the bounty must decline) as price increases;
  $E_t(p) < 0$, the elasticity of the bounty function must be negative.

This possibility is also treated below.

It remains to discover, if possible, what kinds of taxes would lead to the combination of changes depicted in panels 6 through 8 in Chart 33.

In panel 6 the tax has not shifted the W-E ridge line; therefore:

$$t'(p) = 0$$

that is to say, the slope of the tax function must be zero.

It has already been established that the shift of the N-S ridge line, at each level of selling outlays, is related to the tax-induced change in marginal revenue, with respect to output. This change has been shown to be measured by expression (27). If (27) is positive, marginal revenue is reduced by the tax and the N-S ridge line is shifted toward lower output; if this expression is negative, marginal revenue is increased by the tax and the N-S ridge line is shifted toward higher output. In the present instance the slope of the tax function, $t'(p)$, must be zero; hence the tax elasticity, given by

$$E_t(p) = t'(p) \cdot \frac{p}{t}$$

must be zero. If this holds, the only circumstance under which (27) can be negative (and the N-S ridge shifted to the right) is that $t(p)$ be negative, that is, that the tax be, in fact, a bounty! In this case the description of the "tax" that would have the effects shown in panel 6 would be as follows:

6. LOWER PRICE, HIGHER OUTPUT
   Specific per unit bounty:

   $t(p) < 0$, the "tax" is a bounty;
   $t'(p) = 0$, the bounty is constant per unit, regardless of price;
   $E_t(p) = 0$, the elasticity of the bounty per unit with respect to price must, if $t'(p)$ equals zero, be zero.

The combined changes shown in panel 7 require that $t'(p)$ be negative, in order to raise the W-E ridge line. Since the N-S ridge line is moved to the right, (27) must be negative; since the demand elasticity, $E_x(p)$, is always negative, the only "tax" formula that will meet the stated requirements is one with the following characteristics.

Extension of Results 191

7. HIGHER SELLING OUTLAYS, HIGHER OUTPUT
   Variable per unit bounty:
   $t(p) < 0$, the tax is a bounty;
   $t'(p) < 0$, to raise the W-E ridge line (the bounty per unit must increase as price increases);
   $E_t(p) < -E_x(p)$, the tax elasticity is smaller than the demand elasticity.

Then the ratio within the brackets in (27) is negative but less than unity; the entire term in brackets is positive; and, since $t(p)$ is negative, (27) is negative, as required. An example of such a "tax" function would be an ad valorem bounty, when the demand elasticity exceeds unity.

Panel 8 shows the results of a "tax" such that the W-E ridge is raised—thus the slope of the tax function must be negative, and the N-S ridge is unaffected—hence (27) must be zero and the tax elasticity must be equal to the demand elasticity. It may be concluded that the "tax" function meets the following requirements.

8. HIGHER SELLING OUTLAYS, HIGHER PRICE
   Variable bounty per unit.
   $t(p) < 0$, for a bounty;
   $t'(p) < 0$, the bounty per unit must increase, as price increases, if the W-E ridge line is to be raised;

$E_t(p) = -E_x(p)$, if the N-S ridge line is not to be shifted. An example of such a function would be an ad valorem bounty, when the demand elasticity is unity, or a progressive bounty such that the elasticity of the per unit bounty is equal to the demand elasticity.

For both panels 1 and 5 a second possible "tax" function was given above. For panel 1 the second type of "tax" can be derived as follows. The W-E ridge is raised; thus the slope of the "tax" function must be negative. The N-S ridge is moved to the left; therefore (27) must be positive. Expression (27) will be positive, even though $t(p)$ is negative, if $t(p)$ is negative *and* if the tax elasticity is positive and greater than the (negative) demand elasticity. The ratio of the elasticities within the brackets is negative and larger, in absolute value, than unity; the entire term in brackets is negative; expression (27), the reduction in marginal revenue with respect to output, is positive; and the N-S ridge line is shifted toward lower outputs. The "tax" which changes selling outlays, output, and price as shown in panel 1 may be *either* a highly regressive per unit tax, such that the tax elasticity is negative, or a highly progressive per unit bounty, that is, a bounty that rises rapidly as price is increased.

For panel 5 the second type of "tax" can be shown by similar reasoning. The W-E ridge is lowered; hence the slope of the "tax" function, $t'(p)$, must be positive. The N-S ridge is shifted to the right; therefore, (27) must be negative. It will be, if the "tax" is negative and if the tax elasticity is negative.

Some comments may be in order concerning the types of taxes or bounties that lead to the various outcomes illustrated in Chart 33. It will be noted that the changes exemplified by panels 2, 3, and 4 can be achieved only by taxes, those shown in panels 6, 7, and 8 can be achieved only by bounties; and those shown in panels 1 and 5 can each result from either a tax or a bounty.

In the upper row, panels numbered 1, 8, and 7, have in common a tax (or bounty) function with a negative slope, that is, increasing the price reduces the per unit tax or raises the per unit bounty. It is clear from the chart and from previous findings of this part that the negative slope of the tax function generally exerts an upward pressure on selling outlays.

The other panels support this conclusion: in panels 2 and 6, the slope of the tax function is zero and the W-E ridge of the profit surface is unchanged by the tax. Although a tax with this characteristic may change the optimum level of selling costs, such a change would result from a movement *along* a positively or negatively sloped W-E ridge (demand function of type i or iii) rather than a movement away from the pre-tax W-E ridge.

Similarly, in panels 3, 4, and 5 the tax (or bounty) functions have a positive slope—the per unit tax increases (the per unit bounty decreases) as price is raised. In each case the W-E ridge line is lowered by the tax, and the tendency, regardless of the type of demand function, is to reduce selling outlays.

Examination of the panels from the point of view of output and price changes shows that output has declined in the left-hand panels 1, 2 and 3. What these three taxes have in common is an elasticity that is smaller than the demand elasticity (or a bounty with an elasticity larger than the demand elasticity). This effect of the

Extension of Results 193

relative sizes of the tax and demand elasticities has already been shown in Chapter 4, where selling outlays were neglected. What has been added here is the possibility that a tax can reduce output and also reduce price (in panel 3, the price change may be zero or up or down). These conclusions hold regardless of the type of demand function.

Similarly, in the center column of panels 8 and 4, the two "taxes" have an elasticity *equal* to the demand elasticity and the output change depends upon the slope of the N-S ridge. If, however, the bounty increases selling outlays (panel 8), price must rise; if the tax reduces selling outlays (panel 4), price must fall.

Finally, panel 5 shows the effects of a tax with an elasticity greater than the demand elasticity; panels 6 and 7 represent the effects of bounties with an elasticity smaller than the demand elasticity. Output rises as a result of the tax, and whether price falls, rises, or remains unchanged depends upon the change in selling costs. In panels 5 and 6, where selling outlays remain unchanged or decline, price falls. In panel 7, where selling outlays rise, price may or may not rise, depending upon the specific nature of the demand function.

B. *Scope of Results*

It is perhaps worthwhile, at this stage, to restate the major assumptions on which the analysis is based, partly to specify the kinds of problems that have not been studied, and partly to see to what extent the results can be extended to situations where the assumptions, as stated, do not hold. The most important assumptions are as follows:

1. The demand for taxed product per time period depends only upon the firm's price and its volume of selling outlays per time period.
2. The firm sells only one product.

The first assumption is simply a verbal statement of the general demand function. Two aspects of the demand function deserve to be mentioned: the market structure of the industry and the dynamic effects of advertising.

If the firm is a sole supplier, the "demand" referred to is industry demand, and the results so far obtained appear to be correct. However, even if there are several firms in the industry, various methods of collusion under which these results would still stand are possible.

At one extreme, if all firms have perfect knowledge, operate under identical cost functions, charge the same price, spend the same amount on advertising (the type of advertising would have to be such that it influences *industry* demand only and not a firm's market share), and market the same output, an excise tax would affect each firm's price, output, and selling outlays in the same way. Somewhat more realistically, if the firms are successful in maximizing industry profit, even though cost conditions vary from one firm to another and if prices are identical, a tax would seem to affect the optimum volume of total selling outlays in the manner described. (A peculiarity of these artificial arrangements is that it makes no difference to the industry which firm pays for advertising outlays!) In any event it is difficult to imagine collusion so perfect that no firm identifies its own products or advertises its own name.[1]

When "competitive" advertising is admitted (i.e., advertising that changes a firm's market share without changing industry demand — many advertising programs are doubtless a mixture of competitive and industry advertising), the effects of an excise tax are less clear. If price collusion, whether overt or not, is effective and price is near the level appropriate to the industry aggregate of advertising outlays,[2] an excise tax, by changing the marginal profitability of that portion of selling outlays that affects industry demand, will lead to the changes described in this section.

In addition, an excise tax is likely to make some change in the profitability of purely "competitive" advertising. Neither the costs of maintaining market share by advertising nor the effectiveness of advertising in physical terms is affected by a tax, but the profitability of a given share is changed. It does not appear unreasonable to conclude that an excise tax will also affect competitive advertising, at least in the directions stated above. It must be admitted, however, that "competitive" advertising has not been formally analyzed, nor has the effect on price and output of a tax been studied if price is not at the level that maximizes *industry* profit.

The second aspect of the demand function involves the element of time. As it stands, the demand equation says that, at each price,

---

[1] The story, authentic or not, of the traveler abroad who encountered a billboard with the two-word exhortation, "Use Soap," illustrates the ultimate in this respect.

[2] There are no a priori grounds for presuming that this price is higher than the price that is appropriate for some lower aggregate volume of advertising expenditures (including zero).

Extension of Results

the sales per time period depend only upon the selling outlays in that same period and that current sales are not affected at all by past selling outlays and prices. Although the general appropriateness of this model can be challenged, it is felt that it has sufficient validity, at least as a first step, to justify some interest in its implications. The selection or development of a dynamic equilibrium model in which to introduce an excise tax is well beyond the scope of the present study.

The second assumption—that the firm sells a single product—is implied in the profit function, in which the total profit of the firm (which is the profit that the firm is assumed to maximize) is derived from the production, advertising, and sale of one product only. In a multiproduct firm, there is one rigidly drawn set of circumstances for which our results still hold.

1. The demand for the taxed product is unrelated to the prices or quantities sold of the other products.
2. Production costs of the taxed product are not affected by the quantities sold of the other products.
3. A part of the firm's advertising program is designed to affect the demand of only the taxed product.

In this case, the tax would modify such a "special" advertising program as stated in this section.

If, as seems more likely, condition 3 does not hold and the advertising program affects the demand for all the firm's products, the influence of a tax on one item on the profitability of all advertising outlays will still be in the *directions* described above, but the strength of the incentive to change the advertising outlay will be attenuated by the unchanged profitability of advertising as it affects the demand for the untaxed products. In other words, if the taxed product makes a large contribution to total profit, the results of this section stand. If the taxed item makes only a small contribution, the effect of the tax, if any, will be slight.

If, furthermore, conditions 1 and 2 are not satisfied, two or more of the firm's products will be related in consumption and/or production, and the problem becomes the one made famous by Edgeworth,[3] with further difficulties created by including advertising in the analysis. This problem is also outside the scope of this study.

---

[3]*Political Economy*, I, 131-35.

Chapter 19. *Summary of Part III*

The conclusions of Part III on selling outlays and excise taxes are, for convenience, summarized here.

The answer to the perennial question, "How does advertising affect price and output?" turns out to be important, not only for its own implications, but also for the light it would shed on the question, "How does an excise tax affect selling outlays, price, and output?" Whether advertising increases output and reduces price, or produces some other combination of changes, can apparently not be resolved by logical operations on accepted premises; rather, we have a question of fact to be answered by empirical research in specific instances. The original question is seen to be nearly equivalent to "What type of demand function attaches to the product?"

The conclusions listed below are those that do not depend on the type of demand function. To a certain extent, these results verify and extend those obtained in Part II.

1. A specific tax must reduce output; price and selling outlay changes are not generally predictable.
2. If the tax elasticity is positive but smaller than the demand elasticity, there is a tendency toward lower selling outlays and lower output.
3. A tax with an elasticity equal to the demand elasticity will reduce selling outlays.
4. If the tax elasticity *exceeds* the demand elasticity, there is a general presumption, not a certainty, that price and selling outlays will fall and output will rise.
5. A highly regressive tax will have a tendency to increase selling outlays and price and to reduce output.
6. The greater the slope of the tax function, the greater is the downward pressure on selling outlays and price.
7. The greater the elasticity of the tax, compared to the demand

elasticity, the greater are the upward pressure on output and the downward pressure on price.
8. If two taxes lead to the same after-tax output, the tax with the greater slope, with respect to price, must lead to lower selling outlays and lower price.
9. If two taxes are equal at the pre-tax price and both taxes *increase* price by the same amount, selling outlays and output will be lower under the more elastic of the two taxes. If both taxes *reduce* price by the same amount, the relative effects are reversed.

Part IV. *Effects of Excise Taxes on Product Quality*

The two following chapters are concerned with the changes induced by an excise tax in the taxed product. These changes may be improvements — in the eyes of most consumers — or the reverse, depending upon the form of the tax (Chapter 20). The possibility that some "improvements" can reduce the time rate of demand and the implications for tax effects are the subject matter of Chapter 21.

Chapter 20. *Before-tax and After-tax Equilibrium*

Among the many matters treated in the literature of tax incidence, the possibility that an excise tax might influence the characteristics of the taxed product itself appears as a minor and undeveloped issue. This neglect is not surprising in view of the relatively recent emphasis by Chamberlin on the "product" as an economic variable.[1] Chamberlin, however, does not introduce excise taxes into his equilibrium models to determine possible adjustments. Some writers mention that taxes might (do) affect product quality.[2] Only a few have attempted to derive a general solution to the problem.[3]

[1]Chamberlin, *Monopolistic Competition*, Chapter IV.

[2]Dalton notes, "The chief practical obstacle in the way of carrying out this policy [a progressive excise tax, or a lump-sum tax with rebate proportionate to output; see footnote 4, Chapter 4] arises from the difficulty of checking the quality of the monopolist's product. For it would obviously pay him, if subjected to such a tax, to sell an inferior [sic] product at a lower price" (*Principles of Public Finance*, p. 61). Dalton presents no proof of his statement. U. K. Hicks, *Public Finance* (New York, 1948), says "...it [the search, according to Hicks, for the "taxpayer"] has unduly narrowed the range of vision; not even quality changes (which are just as likely as price changes) can conveniently be allowed for" (p. 157).

[3]Due, *Incidence of Sales Taxation*. His work touches on product quality in two different ways, both under the heading of monopolistic competition. First, he considers how the existence of product variation may "modify" the amount of price change from a tax. "Where the price for one reason or another—law, custom, etc.—cannot be changed, the increased cost [sic] may render a reduction in quality of product profitable." Also, "...even where price adjustments are possible and are made, it may be profitable to readjust quality; this will in turn lead to further price adjustments until a final equilibrium is reached. The direction and amount of change depends upon the particular circumstances, and any generalizations are impossible" (p. 65).

Second, Due analyzes the possible effect of a general retail sales tax on the quality of service offered by the retailer. "In general, the entire tax is passed onto consumers by quality reduction—with reduced convenience of location, variety of goods, store furnishings, credit and delivery—but with accompanying exodus of firms" (p. 153).

J. Guerin, "Excise Taxation and Quality of Product," *Finance publique*, 15 (1), 21–30, examines briefly the effects of specific and ad valorem taxes. His findings will be discussed below.

Before beginning the analysis, it may be well to emphasize the distinction between selling effort and product quality. Selling effort has been defined in this study (Chapter 11) as "those activities that raise the demand curve for the product without changing the variable costs of production." Similarly, quality of product refers to the attractiveness of the good to the buyers. Clearly the latter concept is unsatisfactory as it stands (since advertising presumably affects "attractiveness"), but it is further qualified: "An improvement in quality is any change ... of the product ... which raises the demand curve of the product and which increases variable production costs ...."[4] Some of the supposed vagueness in the distinction between selling costs and production costs, then, disappears, at least in principle.[5]

Furthermore, the concept of product quality as a variable subject to the control of the firm is primarily a matter of notation, used to shorten the exposition; it is a kind of intermediate logical term that cancels out when a conclusion is reached. Consider, for example, the following: one effect of a progressive excise tax (with an elasticity equal to the pre-tax demand elasticity) is to induce the firm to change the product (if possible) in such a way that price will have to be lowered to sell a given number of units per time period and that the cost of producing a given number of units per time period is lower. There need be no specific reference to "product quality" at all!

The following analysis of the quality equilibrium and of the effects of excise taxes on that equilibrium is formulated in terms of a single quality variable. This suggests either that the overall quality of the product can be measured or that the number of units sold at each price depends upon only a single characteristic of the product which is measurable. The first implication raises difficulties that cannot be resolved here; the second seems to be unnecessarily restrictive.

---

[4]This definition leaves out of account those quality improvements (such as new designs) that result from a one-shot investment but may not change variable production costs. Such improvements are much more important in a context of imperfect knowledge than in the present context of certainty. The producer is presumed to know which specific product will maximize profit.

[5]"There will always be some costs which are difficult to apportion: Should the cost of a cellophane wrapper, for instance, be included among production costs or selling costs?" (Boulding, *Economic Analysis*, p. 717). In the present distinction, such a cost must be considered a cost of production.

Before-tax and After-tax Equilibrium

However, the point made in the previous paragraph is that formal mathematical analysis is a convenient tool. Some, if not all, of the conclusions of this chapter can be derived from a verbal argument in which product quality is not assumed to be measurable.

A. Before-tax Equilibrium

The equilibrium among these three variables can be described in substantially the same manner as that among price, output, and selling outlays. The equilibrium conditions will be restated in summary form, in order to emphasize the context and to specify the distinction between selling effort and product quality. (The following steps may be compared to those given in Chapter 11.)

The price, or average revenue, function involves two independent variables, output per time period, x, and product quality, k (this use of k has no connection with any other meaning that may have been given to it, including that in Chapter 5):

$$p = p(x,k)$$

The corresponding real world circumstances relate to a single-firm industry. This demand function might equally well be expressed in other forms.

The total costs of the firm are treated also as a function of output and quality:

$$c = c(x,k)$$

It is assumed that the firm can and does choose the methods of production that require the least cost for a given output and for a given level of product quality.

Pre-tax profit is given by

$$\pi = x \cdot p(x,k) - c(x,k) \tag{79}$$

The firm is presumed to produce and sell a single product. The first and second-order derivatives of the profit function are

$$\pi^x = x \cdot p^x(x,k) + p(x,k) - c^x(x,k) \tag{80}$$

$$\pi^k = x \cdot p^k(x,k) - c^k(x,k) \tag{81}$$
$$\pi^{xx} = x \cdot p^{xx}(x,k) + 2p^x(x,k) - c^{xx}(x,k)$$
$$\pi^{kk} = x \cdot p^{kk}(x,k) - c^{kk}(x,k)$$

$$\pi^{xk} = \pi^{kx} = x \cdot p^{xk}(x,k) + p^k(x,k) - c^{xk}(x,k) \tag{82}$$

First-order equilibrium conditions are as follows.

(I) $\quad \pi^x = 0 \hfill (83)$

That is, at each quality level, marginal revenue with respect to output variation [the two left-hand terms of the right side of (80)] must be equal to marginal cost with respect to output variation [the right-hand term of (80)]. Since (83) is an implicit function in two variables, x and k, it may be plotted as a line on a two-dimensional graph. This line is the "arbitrary quality" ridge line of the profit surface; if quality is measured on the vertical axis and output on the horizontal axis, this ridge line corresponds to the N-S ridge line, identified in Chapter 11. It may be noted that fixed costs have no effect on the location, in the k-x plane, of this ridge line; an increase in *marginal* cost, $c^x(x,k)$, however, will shift the ridge line toward lower outputs and vice versa, at all quality levels.

(II) $\quad \pi^k = 0 \hfill (84)$

At each fixed level of output, marginal revenue with respect to quality variation [the left-hand term of the right side of (81)] must be equal to marginal cost with respect to quality variation [the right-hand term of (81)]. It is assumed that both quality variation and the effect of quality variation on price and costs are continuous.[6] Since quality is defined so that an increase in quality, at a fixed output, increases total costs, the marginal cost of quality variation, $c^k(x,k)$, must be positive and hence equilibrium is possible only if a quality increase, at a fixed output, also leads to a price increase, that is, $p^k(x,k)$ is positive. Equation (84) represents the "arbitrary output" ridge line of the profit surface, or the W-E ridge line on a k-x graph. An increase, say, in the cost of a quality change, $c^k(x,k)$, for example, the price of cellophane for wrapping, will lower the W-E ridge line at all outputs.

An equilibrium position is indicated by the joint satisfaction of the first-order conditions or, what amounts to the same thing, by the intersection of two of the arbitrary ridge lines of the profit surface. In order to assure that the equilibrium position is a maximum, three

---

[6]For a development of the price-output-quality equilibrium, under conditions of monopolistic competition, where quality variation and its effects are not continuous, see H. Brems, *Product Equilibrium under Monopolistic Competition* (Cambridge, 1951), Chapters 3, 4, and 5.

Before-tax and After-tax Equilibrium

second-order conditions must also be satisfied. These second-order conditions for a maximum are as follows.

(III) $\pi^{xx} < 0$

This condition is equivalent to a requirement that, at a given quality level, the marginal revenue curve (with respect to output) must intersect (condition I) the marginal cost curve (again, with respect to output) from above.

(IV) $\pi^{kk} < 0$

The marginal revenue curve with respect to quality variation, at a fixed output, must intersect the marginal cost curve from above.

(V) $\pi^{xx} \cdot \pi^{kk} > [\pi^{xk}]^2$

This condition is shown in Appendix II to require the N-S (or "arbitrary quality") ridge line of the profit surface to be steeper (on a k-x graph) than the W-E (or "arbitrary output") ridge line.

These requirements shed some light on the question, "Do the conditions for profit maximization provide any assurance that a quality increase will increase the optimum output?" The question may be rephrased: "Must the N-S ridge line of the profit surface (which shows the optimum output for each quality level) have a positive slope at the equilibrium position?" The slope of the N-S ridge line depends upon the second-order cross derivative of the profit function [i.e., expression (82)]. The answer to both questions is "no," for in the only condition in which the cross derivative appears (V) it is squared and thus could satisfy the condition while being either positive or negative. Samuelson's proof[7] that advertising need not increase output can be broadened to cover the effects of product quality. A quality improvement may reduce output, increase it, or leave it unchanged, and the optimum price reaction to a quality change is also unpredictable in the abstract unless considerations other than profit maximization can be brought to bear on the question.

In previous chapters the slopes of the ridge lines served as the basis for classifying *demand* functions; that is, the best level of selling outlays, for each output, may be increasing, remaining

[7] *Foundations of Economic Analysis*, p. 42.

constant, or declining as output increases. Exactly the same type of classification of *profit* functions that combine price, output, and product quality can also be made.

It may be helpful, then, to expand somewhat the terse explanation (Appendix II) of the determinants of these slopes. The slope, in the k-x plane, of the N-S ridge line is given by

$$-\frac{\pi^{xx}}{\pi^{xk}}$$

or

$$-\frac{x \cdot p^{xx}(x,k) + 2p^{x}(x,k) - c^{xx}(x,k)}{x \cdot p^{xk}(x,k) + p^{k}(x,k) - c^{xk}(x,k)} \tag{85}$$

where p^x is the slope of the ordinary demand curve—the amount by which price must be changed to sell an added unit at a fixed quality level. It is negative (although it need not be for a maximum to exist).

p^{xx} is the second derivative of the demand function with respect to output, that is, it is the curvature of the ordinary demand curve. It may be positive, zero, or negative.

c^{xx} is the second derivative of the cost function with respect to output, or the slope of the marginal cost curve. It is positive if marginal costs are increasing, zero if they are constant, and negative if they are declining.

p^k is the slope of the demand (average revenue) function with respect to quality change, at a given output. It is the change in price that can be made on a given output, if the quality (of all units) is increased slightly. If must be positive if a maximum exists.

p^{xk} is a cross derivative of the demand function. It measures the rate of change in the slope of the demand curve (with respect to output) as quality is increased.

c^{xk} is a cross derivative of the cost function, showing the effect of quality change on the level of marginal costs (with respect to output). It is, by definition, positive; that is, an increase in product quality raises marginal costs.

The slope of the W-E ridge line is given by

$$-\frac{\pi^{xk}}{\pi^{kk}}$$

or

$$-\frac{x \cdot p^{xk}(x,k) + p^{k}(x,k) - c^{xk}(x,k)}{x \cdot p^{kk}(x,k) - c^{kk}(x,k)} \qquad (86)$$

where p^{kk} is the curvature of the average revenue function with respect to quality. It may be positive, zero, or negative.

c^{kk} is the second derivative (curvature) of the cost function with respect to quality. It measures the extent to which higher quality affects the cost of increasing quality. There is a presumption, once a specific quality characteristic is identified, that this quantity is positive; for example, if the supply of the factor input used to provide the quality characteristic is not completely elastic, the increased use of that factor would raise its price.

The relation between the slopes of the two ridge lines near the equilibrium position has been shown in Appendix II to be as follows: if the W-E ridge line has a positive slope, the slope of the N-S ridge must be positive; if the W-E ridge is horizontal, the N-S ridge must be vertical; if the W-E ridge line has a negative slope, the N-S ridge line must also have a negative slope. Which of these three conditions holds in any given situation depends entirely upon the *sign* of (82), that is, the signs of the denominator of (85) and the numerator of (86).

Some conclusions follow immediately from the above.

1. The *level* of marginal cost (with respect to output) affects the location of the N-S ridge line but has no influence on the *sign* of the slope or on the slope itself.

2. The slope of the marginal cost curve (at a given level of quality), that is, whether marginal costs are increasing, constant, or declining, cannot affect the *sign* of the slope of the N-S ridge line. But the behavior of marginal cost as output increases does affect the *magnitude* of the slope of the N-S ridge line. By substituting a positive number, then zero, and finally a negative number for c^{xx} in the numerator of (85), it is seen that increasing costs ($c^{xx} > 0$) have a tendency to steepen the N-S ridge line and decreasing costs ($c^{xx} < 0$) to flatten it.

3. The issue of the effect (positive, negative, or zero) of product quality (or of selling effort) on the optimum output and price cannot be resolved by an investigation of cost conditions alone. The direction of the effect is determined by the sign of (82), which in turn

depends upon (*a*) the effect of quality (selling effort) on price, at a given output; (*b*) the effect of quality (selling effort) on the *slope* of the ordinary demand curve; and (*c*) the effect of quality on marginal costs (selling effort, by definition, does not change marginal cost).

4. The amount by which quality (selling effort) changes the optimum output (i.e., the slope of the N-S ridge line) is, however, affected by cost conditions. If marginal costs are declining with output, an increase in quality (selling effort) will lead to a greater output change (up or down) than if marginal costs are increasing.

The minor differences between the treatment of product quality and selling effort are as follows.
1. $c^s(x, s)$, the marginal cost of increasing selling outlay, equals \$1; $c^k(x, k)$, the marginal cost of increasing quality, is positive.
2. $c^{ss}(x, s)$, the *slope* of the marginal cost of selling effort, is zero; $c^{kk}(x, k)$, the *slope* of the marginal cost of product quality, need not be zero.
3. $c^{xs}(x, s)$, the effect of selling effort on the marginal cost curve, is zero;
$c^{xk}(x, k)$, the effect of product quality on the marginal cost curve, is positive.

The *similarities* between the two analyses are as follows.
1. The orientation of the ridge lines of the profit surface can be described in substantially identical terms whether the profit function involves price, output, and selling outlays or price, output, and product quality.
2. The classification of *demand functions* in Chapter 12 can be carried over here to a classification of *profit functions* that is based on the slope of the W-E ridge line. In the former instance that slope depends upon demand conditions only; here, it depends upon both demand and production cost conditions.

B. *After-tax Equilibrium*

It will first be shown that an excise tax shifts the ridge lines of the quality profit surface in exactly the same manner that it shifts the ridge lines of the selling outlay-profit surface. The results of Part III, showing the effects of excise taxes on output, price, and selling effort, can then be translated as they stand into effects on output, price, and product quality.

Before-tax and After-tax Equilibrium

The per unit tax is, as before, a function of price:

$$t = t[p(x,k)]$$

The after-tax profit function is (79) less the tax bill:

$$\pi = x \cdot p(x,k) - x \cdot t[p(x,k)] - c(x,k)$$

The after-tax ridge lines are given by equating the partial derivatives of the profit function to zero:

(I) $\quad \pi^x = 0$

or $\quad x \cdot p^x(x,k) + p(x,k)$
$\quad\quad - \{x \cdot t^p[p(x,k)]p^x(x,k) + t[p(x,k)]\} - c^x(x,k) = 0$

The tax-induced shift in this ridge line depends primarily upon the per unit tax and the ratio of the tax and demand elasticities (as shown in Chapter 4 and as restricted somewhat by assumption in Chapter 12).

If the tax elasticity is smaller than the demand elasticity, the N-S ridge line is shifted to the left; if the two elasticities are equal, it is not shifted; if the tax elasticity exceeds the demand elasticity, it is shifted to the right.

(II) $\quad \pi^k = 0$

or $\quad x \cdot p^k(x,k) - x \cdot t^p[p(x,k)]p^k(x,k) - c^k(x,k) = 0$

or $\quad x \cdot p^k(x,k) \{1 - t^p[p(x,k)]\} - c^k(x,k) = 0$

The W-E ridge line is lowered, at all outputs, in proportion to the slope of the tax function (with respect to price), t^p.

Thus the effects of a tax on the ridge lines of a quality profit surface are identical to the effects on those of a selling outlay profit surface. The conclusions of Part III are equally applicable if "product quality" is substituted for "selling outlay." The major findings of Part III are briefly restated here in terms of the effects of taxes on product quality.

1. A specific tax must reduce output; whether quality is increased, decreased, or left unchanged depends upon the slope of the W-E ridge line; there is a presumption that price will rise, but it need not. Guerin[8] concludes that a specific tax is likely to raise price, to

---

[8] Guerin, *Finance publique*, 15 (1), 26–27.

reduce quality, and [apparently] to lower output. He states correctly, "... it is possible that the best adjustment to the tax involves a product of higher quality than the pre-tax product."[9] He does not specify the other changes that may accompany an increase in quality.

2. If the tax elasticity is positive but smaller than the demand elasticity (e.g., an ad valorem tax when marginal costs are not zero), there is a strong presumption that quality and output will fall; the price change is uncertain. Guerin implies that the effects of an ad valorem tax are the same as those of a specific tax.[10]

3. If the tax elasticity equals the demand elasticity, quality must fall, price will probably fall, and output will fall, remain unchanged, or rise, according to the slope of the N-S ridge line.

4. If the tax elasticity exceeds the demand elasticity, there is a strong presumption that quality will fall (not a certainty—cf. Dalton's comment, footnote 2 of this chapter), that output will rise, and that price will fall.

5. A highly regressive tax will have a tendency to *increase* quality and price and to reduce output.

6. The greater the slope of the tax function, that is the marginal rate of per unit tax, the greater is the downward pressure on quality and price.

7. If two taxes lead to the same after-tax output, the tax with the higher marginal rate must lead to lower quality and lower price.

8. If two taxes are equal at the pre-tax price and both taxes increase price by the same amount, product quality and output will be lower under the more elastic of the two taxes. If both taxes *reduce* price by the same amount, these relative effects are reversed.

Other results in Part III apply here also.

---

[9]*Finance publique*, 15 (1), 27.
[10]*Finance publique*, 15 (1), 26.

Chapter 21. *Durability as a Dimension of Quality*

If the product is one that is consumed, durability is analogous to amount of product contained in the unit offered for sale; that is, a product is more durable if, at a constant time rate of consumption, it lasts longer. In this sense, a two-pound box of sugar is twice as durable as a one-pound box, as long as the sugar does not deteriorate. If the product yields a service, durability is equivalent to lifetime at a given rate of service—again provided that the service remains the same over time.

The possibility exists, then, that a good can be improved, yet the demand in units per time period decline. For surely, if shoes could be made to retain their appearance, style, and usefulness for ten years, the annual demand for shoes would decline. Similarly, if sugar for household use were sold only in twenty-five pound bags, the number of units sold, at one dollar per bag, would be much smaller per time period than the number of one-pound bags at one dollar per bag. Thus the definition of product quality seems to leave out of account a large number of potential product changes that most people would regard as "improvements."[1]

However, it will be shown that, for a monopolist, the range of variation over which increases in durability reduce demand at a given price cannot include the profit-maximizing level of durability. Thus the optimum level of durability must be in the range over which increases in durability *increase* demand, at a given price. Thus

---

[1] See Brems, *Product Equilibrium*, pp. 30 ff., and Lawrence Abbott, "Vertical Equilibrium under Pure Quality Competition," *American Economic Review*, XLIII, 831–32. It is interesting to note that, of these two authors, Abbott treats only the first aspect of durability—the size of a can of tomato juice, the amount of copper in a ton of ore of various degrees of refinement—and Brems deals only with the latter aspect—the lifetime of a pair of stockings, an automobile battery, a flashlight bulb.

product durability is indistinguishable from product quality in its effects, and, in general, the influence of a tax will be the same in either case.

If the effects of an excise tax on product durability are the same as those on quality, the reader is entitled to wonder why this chapter does not end at this point. There are two reasons. First, it is not obvious that the price-output-durability equilibrium is analytically identical to the price-output-quality equilibrium. Second, a closer look at the effect of a tax on the first type of durability—amount of commodity in a taxable unit—reveals some useful implications for the specific formulation of tax legislation.

A. *Before-tax Equilibrium*

An increase in durability (of either kind) is defined to have the following effects (a decrease would have the opposite results):

1. The total cost of producing a fixed number of units is increased, that is,

$$c^d(x, d) > 0$$

where d represents durability, or amount of commodity, and x represents output *per time period*.

2. The price at which a given number of units can be sold *per time period* may rise, remain unchanged, or decline, that is,

$$p^d(x, d) \gtreqless 0$$

If the effect of a durability increase on price is positive, durability is identical to quality [cf. expression (81) in Chapter 20, where $p^k(x, k)$ must be positive at equilibrium] and a tax would affect either in the same way. The question that arises is, "Is equilibrium possible in a single-firm industry at a level of durability such that a durability increase would *reduce* the price at which a given number of units could be sold per time period?" An alternative formulation of the question is, "Is equilibrium possible at a level of durability such that a durability increase *reduces* the output that, at a fixed price, could be sold per time period?" Abbott states that the answer to the latter question is "no."

Just as, in price analysis, profit-maximizing or money-revenue-maximizing firms would never be concerned with prices in that lower range in which the

Durability as a Dimension of Quality

elasticity of demand is unity or less than unity, so, in vertical quality analysis, we can safely ignore the corresponding upper range of vertical quality, *since cost-raising quality improvement would not be advantageous to firms in a fixed-price market unless it induced an increase in the number of units sold* (italics added).[2,3]

Abbott's remarks rest on the assumption that the price elasticity of demand is related to price in such a way that only one price will maximize profit (see Chapter 3). Whether this assumption must also be true with respect to durability is not obvious.

Abbott is, however, correct, as will now be shown. The demand function is given by[4]

$$x = x(p, d)$$

The cost function is

$$c = c(p, d)$$

Total profit is

$$\pi = p \cdot x(p, d) - c(p, d) \tag{87}$$

The durability equilibrium, at a fixed price, is shown by the partial derivative of (87) with respect to durability

$$\pi^d = p \cdot x^d(p, d) - c^d(p, d)$$

and first-order conditions require that

$$p \cdot x^d(p, d) - c^d(p, d) = 0$$

In other words, marginal revenue, at a fixed price, with respect to durability, must equal marginal cost, at a fixed price, also with respect to durability. This condition may hold if both of these margins are positive; on the surface it may also hold if both are negative. For the type of marginal cost at issue can be negative—at a fixed

---

[2] Abbott, *American Economic Review*, XLIII, 832–33.

[3] Brems does not give equilibrium conditions involving durability: "... this chapter deals with consumer behavior, not entrepreneurial reactions...." *Product Equilibrium*, p. 35).

[4] Since Abbott is dealing with a fixed-price market, it is necessary to choose price as one of the independent variables so that it can be held constant. Actually, the first of the two questions on this point given above can be answered more easily if output and durability are chosen as independent variables. The present formulation is preferred because later it will more easily yield results concerning the after-tax equilibrium.

price, increasing the durability of the product has two effects: the variable costs per unit increase, but the number of units sold may decrease. When the latter effect overcomes the former, an increase in durability can lower total cost.

These relations can be shown by diagraming a cross-section (along a price line) of a d-p chart of the profit surface, as in Chart 34. Since this chart illustrates conditions that must hold at *any* fixed price, these conditions must hold at the optimum price. Several levels of durability are shown: some minimum level, d_m, is required to sell any units; as durability is increased, sales per time period increase; at some level of durability, d_1, the output curve is horizontal—at this level, slight durability changes have *no* effect on sales per time period; at levels of durability above d_1, further increases in durability *reduce* sales (in the range below d_1 durability has the same effect on output as quality).[5] The *total revenue* curve is simply the output curve multiplied by price, which is held constant; thus the

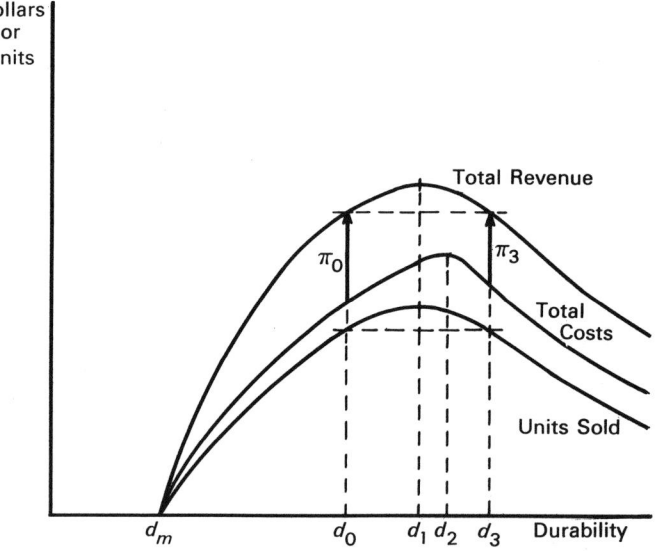

CHART 34.
Cross section, at a fixed price, of revenue, cost and profit surfaces (durability and price as independent variables).

---

[5]The vertical units-sold scale for output is related to the dollar scale via the price-durability-output function. That is, at any given price, the number of units sold per time period depends only upon product durability.

Durability as a Dimension of Quality

total revenue curve also reaches a peak at d_1. Below d_1, the *total cost* curve must rise faster than the output curve, since a durability increase not only is leading to increased output but also is raising the variable cost per unit. At d_1, *the cost curve must be rising*, for, even though output is not increasing, variable costs per unit are. At some higher durability level, say d_2, the per unit costs of a durability increase just balance the decline in output and the total cost curve is horizontal. Above d_2, the cost curve falls, that is, $c^d(p,d)$ is negative.

Equilibrium is indicated at the durability level such that the slopes of the total revenue and total cost curves are equal (i.e., first-order conditions for a maximum; second-order conditions must also hold). Levels of durability between d_1 and d_2 can be immediately ruled out, for the total revenue curve is falling and the total cost curve is rising. Below d_1, some durability level such as d_0 will produce a relative profit maximum. It is not possible that any durability level *above d_2* will yield a greater profit than that given by d_0 (which is greater than any profit for durability levels below d_1). For the output corresponding to d_0 can also be reached by some durability level above d_1, say d_3. At each of these two durability levels, price is the same and total revenue is the same, but by definition total costs are greater at d_3 than d_0. Therefore, the profit at d_0, π_0, must be larger than π_3, the profit at d_3. This inequality holds for any output that can be achieved at two durability levels. The maximum profit position is, then, indicated by d_0, and d_0 and the fixed price constitute one point on the arbitrary price ridge line of the profit surface.[6]

---

[6]Abbott's statement is correct, then, for the single-firm industry. He was, however, analyzing a group equilibrium, and this conclusion does not automatically carry over to a competitive industry.

Brems notes:

"It might be tempting to draw the conclusion that the entrepreneur should avoid increases of the durability factor. But this conclusion is hardly correct. It is true that if increases of the durability factor are undertaken, the *individual*... [buyer] will reduce the time rate of replacements. But a larger *number* of [individuals] may be attracted and the larger share of the market [which implies the existence of several firms in the industry] may well make up for the lower individual time rate of replacements. Increased durability may prove a powerful competitive weapon" (*Product Equilibrium*, pp. 33–34, author's italics).

The introduction in 1963 of stainless steel razor blades by the large American manufacturers would seem, if the makers' claims of increased life are correct, to support Brems' view. At the same time, a reduction in durability may result from a lessening of competition. Brems quotes two company statements which indicate that the firms were at least considering a durability reduction.

B. After-tax Equilibrium

The previous analysis has shown that, at the pre-tax equilibrium, durability is one aspect of product quality, with the same general effect on demand. One more step is needed to show that it also has the same effect at the after-tax equilibrium. If an excise tax is levied such that the per unit tax is a function of price only, in the context of Chart 34 the per unit tax is constant at all levels of durability, since price is constant. Since π_0 and π_3 are achieved at equal outputs, the total tax bill must be the same at d_0 and d_3. Therefore π_0 less the tax bill is still greater than π_3 less the tax bill (the same conclusion holds for any pair of durability levels—one above and the other below d_1—that lead to the same output), and the tax cannot shift the optimum level of durability from d_0 to some level above d_2. The effect of the tax is to lower the W-E ridge of the d-p diagram. *Whether a tax lowers or increases durability depends upon the form of the demand, cost, and tax functions, in exactly the same manner as a tax would affect product quality.*

However, where durability enters only as "amount of commodity," it is possible to make some reasonable judgments concerning the slope of the W-E ridge line of the profit surface and hence concerning the effect of a tax on amount of commodity per unit. For purposes of illustration, assume that a firm has a monopoly on the production and sale of tomato juice and will offer only a single size of can for sale. It seems reasonable to presume that each of the following alternative price-output-can size combinations yields the revenue, cost, and profit shown.

Output per time period:	250 cans	500 cans	1000 cans
Best can size:	16 oz.	8 oz.	4 oz.
Best price:	$0.39	$0.20	$0.10
Total revenue:	$97.50	$100.00	$100.00
Total cost:	$24	$25	$26
Pre-tax profit:	$73.50	$75	$74
After-tax profit:			
5¢ specific tax	$61	$50	$24
50% ad valorem tax	$24.75	$25	$24

These schedules are designed to show a mild preference on the part of consumers for the 4- and the 8-ounce cans, a slight total cost advantage in producing larger can sizes, and a slight profit advantage for the 8-ounce can. The best can size is 8 ounces, although the profit gain over the other sizes is small.

A tax of 5 cents per can would lead to after-tax profit as shown and would cause the adoption of the 16-ounce can. The tax-induced change in can size, and the consequent reduction of the tax bill from the $25 due if the 8-ounce size is retained to $12.50, may or may not be a surprise to the tax authorities.[7] In effect, the change in can size permits the seller to change the per ounce tax, subject only to consumer reactions and cost changes. If, however, the tax is levied per ounce, the firm may well find it desirable to produce and sell concentrated juice!

More generally, when such conditions hold, the W-E ridge of the profit surface will have a negative slope and a specific tax per unit would lead to an increase in amount of commodity per unit (cf. Chart 27, demand type iii).

An ad valorem tax, in the example given, would not lead to any change in amount of commodity per unit, although if other possible levels were shown, the tax could induce such a change.

When the profit surface is, as above, relatively flat over wide ranges of durability (with respect not only to the amount-of-commodity aspect, but also to lifetime as a dimension of durability), the effects of different types of taxes can perhaps be seen better by an extreme example. Suppose the firm to be, not in stable equilibrium with respect to durability, but in a neutral equilibrium. That is to say, for any given level of durability, the best price and output adjustment yields exactly the same profit as that resulting from any other level of durability. How the firm adopts any one level is of no interest, but the reactions to a tax are illuminating.

A neutral equilibrium with respect to durability[8] will exist under the following conditions.

1. Doubling product durability doubles the best price and reduces the best output by half—or, more generally, changing durability by any multiple changes price by the same multiple and output by

---

[7]There are indications that changes of this kind would not be unanticipated. Two such avenues of partial escape from taxation are blocked, in the cigarette tax law, by stating the per package tax according to both the number of cigarettes in a package and their length.

[8]It is not necessary to assume that the firm is in neutral equilibrium with respect to output.

the reciprocal of the multiple. Thus the *total revenue* of the firm is the same, whatever level of durability is chosen.

2. Doubling product durability reduces the best output by half but leaves *total cost* unchanged, or changing durability by any multiple changes output by the reciprocal of the multiple but leaves total cost the same.

It follows, since durability changes affect neither total receipts nor total outlay, that any level of durability is as good as, and no better than any other level, in terms of gross profit. (The schedule given above for can sizes is intended to come close to this extreme.)

If, now, an excise tax is levied, the firm will react by adjusting durability in such a way as to make the tax bill as small as possible. (Gross profit is, by hypothesis, unaffected by durability change; profit net of tax will be maximized when the tax bill is minimized.) These reactions cannot be shown by reference to the ridge lines of the profit surface, for, if a stable equilibrium does not exist with respect to durability, there is no arbitrary output (or arbitrary price) ridge line at all.

However, it is not difficult to see how a tax would affect durability. A specific tax would lead to an increase in durability. An increase in durability would reduce output in number of units and hence reduce the tax bill. If equilibrium is truly neutral, there is no limit to this increase; in fact, a limit would arise eventually either from consumer preferences or cost conditions, or both.

An ad valorem tax would not lead to a change at all. The resulting tax bill can be changed only if total revenue is changed, and under the assumed conditions that is impossible. The tax lowers profit, but there is no inducement to change the durability of the product.

A progressive tax would reduce durability. If the tax is progressive, a given increase in price (due to durability increase) raises the per unit tax more than proportionately and reduces output only proportionately—then the tax bill rises; conversely, the tax bill can be reduced by lowering both durability and price.

Although this example is not intended to reflect any actual situation, it does indicate the direction of the pressure that an excise tax may exert on the durability or amount of a product per taxable unit. It may also show, in general, that the best form of tax depends upon the nature of the product and the producer's alternatives. The lack of an effect of this kind from an ad valorem tax adds somewhat to

Durability as a Dimension of Quality

the relative desirability of this tax vis-à-vis the specific tax, as shown on other grounds by Musgrave and Suits.[9]

Of course, a pure monopolist is unlikely to find that profit is maximized when only a single quality of his product is offered for sale. Consumer preferences are doubtless not identical, and offering a range of qualities may well enable consumers to match their preferences more closely and in turn yield a higher profit to the producer.

[9] Musgrave and Suits, *Quarterly Journal of Economics*, LXVII, 601, 604.

Part V. *Conclusion*

Some of the possibilities for using progressive excise taxes to achieve specific goals are explained briefly. The general nature of the problems that are likely to be encountered is also noted.

Chapter 22. *Implications of the Results*

In the foregoing pages the optimum adjustments of price, output, and selling outlays (or product quality) to the imposition of an excise tax are examined under several different market structures. The method of analysis is general and will yield answers to the broad questions posed in this study for any excise tax function or schedule that may be devised, as long as the per unit tax liability is determined by price alone. No attempt is made to examine a large variety of possible excise taxes, but several uncommon forms of tax functions are selected for special study in order to show the extent to which their effects may be similar to or different from those of the more usual excises.

Without repeating the details of the findings, it may be noted that widely accepted beliefs concerning the adjustments to the usual excise taxes are not correct for some types of tax. In addition, the inclusion within the scope of this study of tax-induced changes in selling outlays or product quality has led to some unsuspected results for the ordinary taxes—the specific and the ad valorem tax.

Although important general problems remain to be investigated (and a decision to tax a particular commodity would give rise to a number of specific problems), the conclusions presented in the previous chapters suggest a number of implications for tax policy that pertain to the formulation of an excise tax to achieve certain goals. The wide gap between the abstract level of this study and the manifold difficulties of tax administration inevitably means that the enumeration of some of the possibilities is to be interpreted as tentative and exploratory, rather than as constituting a series of proposals for legislative action. These possibilities are discussed in two sections, depending upon whether the primary purpose of the tax is (A) to raise revenue, or (B) to achieve non-fiscal goals. In Section C some of the new problems created or existing ones intensified by new kinds of taxes — in particular, progressive excises — are mentioned.

A. *Excise Taxation for Revenue*

The consideration of the amount of revenue raised by a tax has been generally neglected throughout the previous chapters for one reason: in principle at least, tax authorities have a great variety of revenue-raising devices at their disposal, and it was not intended in this study to discover new ones. The primary interest here is in the other effects of the tax. However, since any tax must make some change, either for the taxed firm(s) or for buyers, apart from the collection of taxes, the desirability of these other changes must have a bearing on the choice of a tax for raising revenue.

A comparison of the relative amount of price (and output) change resulting under monopoly from the specific and ad valorem tax has already been made by Musgrave and Suits. They showed that, if a given amount of revenue is raised by each tax, the price rise will be smaller under the ad valorem tax. This conclusion can be extended somewhat if it is supposed that the total tax bill to be collected is not larger than the monopolist's excess profit. In this case the tax revenue can be raised without causing any price or output change at all, by levying the appropriate progressive tax. Consumers would benefit from such a tax (compared to an ad valorem tax) and, surprisingly, so would the taxed firm. If the firm was maximizing profit before the tax was imposed, any price-output change must reduce the profit from which the tax bill is to be paid; if the tax bill is to be the same in either case (e.g., ad valorem versus progressive tax), the firm is better off under the tax that leaves price and output unchanged. Furthermore, it appears that, where some excess profit is being earned by a firm or industry (for the argument applies equally well to, say, a collusive oligopoly), it is possible to raise some amount of revenue with a progressive tax that would increase price by a smaller amount than would the ad valorem tax yielding the same total of collections.

But progressive taxes — particularly, highly progressive ones — are not likely to be substantial revenue producers.[1] If these taxes lower price significantly, collections can be small or even zero (as with a proportional tax on excess price when price falls to the level of the parameter c).

Potential revenue-producing taxes could also be compared on the basis of still other side effects. To a certain extent, this was done in Chapter 17 in terms of changes in selling outlays, and these results apply equally well to changes in product quality.

B. *Excise Taxation for Non-fiscal Purposes*

The general recognition that all taxes have effects other than raising revenue has led to numerous attempts to utilize excise taxes for regulatory purposes.[2] Although the use of taxes for such purposes has not been achieved without strong opposition in the United States, the federal government and many state governments have imposed excise taxes that were clearly regulatory in intent. Some examples are the tax on state bank notes, which, as desired, drove these issues out of circulation; the special tax on colored oleomargarine; and taxes on chain stores and other forms of business organization.[3] In view of the effects that progressive taxes may have on price and non-price variables, such taxes deserve consideration as regulatory devices for certain purposes.

Among the many non-fiscal goals that taxes may serve is the control of monopolized or near-monopolized industries. In the past, such control (apart from public utilities) has never been extended to the point of interference in the terms of sale. Penalties imposed on parties found guilty of antitrust regulations may be fines, revocation of licenses, dissolution, divorcement or divestiture orders, injunctions prohibiting certain practices, the exaction of promises to discontinue certain practices, or the payment of triple damages to

---

[1] Except, possibly, when levied on goods in competitive markets. But in this case their other effects are not substantially different from those of other excises (see Chapter 9).

[2] "Taxes disturb free enterprise, since they always have some influence on economic activity. From this point of view, one of the secondary aims in choosing among taxes would be to keep restrictive or distorting effects to a minimum. In sharp contrast, governmental control as a primary aim for taxation is designed to influence economic activity in certain specific ways, regardless of revenue" [C. Shoup, *Facing the Tax Problem*, (New York, 1937), p. 130].

[3] Shoup, *Facing the Tax Problem*, pp. 144, 145, 153–54.

injured parties.⁴ In general the attack on monopoly has been against activities that are indicative of monopoly or the attempt to monopolize. Among such activities are combinations and conspiracies, acquisition of stock or assets of competitors, making exclusive or tying contracts, and discriminating among buyers on a price basis. Implicit in the rationale of the antitrust laws is the belief that the penalties imposed will make a firm act more competitively or will prevent the creation of monopoly—more specifically, that there will be an immediate or eventual downward effect on price.

Other instruments that have been suggested to control monopoly price have included the prohibition of "excessive" price or the setting of a maximum price, the lump-sum tax and rebate plan mentioned in Chapter 8, a graduated tax on price, proportional or progressive taxes on advertising outlays, and various types of taxes based on the rate of return to invested capital.⁵ Direct intervention in the market by a progressive tax could achieve more closely the correct price adjustment and at the same time render useless the predatory or defensive activities required for the creation and maintenance of a monopoly position.

It should be pointed out that a tax designed for the control of monopoly price is not a tax on "big" business per se. If the tax lowered price, output would increase; and, if the monopolist had permitted the presence of a few small rivals (attracted by high prices), the lowered price could put them out of business and the monopolist would become bigger. The tax would not adversely affect the combination of firms seeking cost savings; it would deter combinations with a view to monopolization.

In certain instances the imposition of a progressive tax could serve as a penalty, or as remedial action, following a conviction for antitrust violations. In effect, this was one suggestion made by W. H. Nicholls when the major cigarette manufacturers in the United States were convicted for such violations, and the courts imposed no remedies.⁶ The existing specific tax on cigarettes reduced price competition and acted as a barrier to the entry of firms that might have sought a foothold in the industry by marketing lower-price

⁴C. Wilcox, *Public Policies toward Business* (Homewood, Ill., 1955), 64–69.
⁵Higgins, *Canadian Journal of Economics and Political Science*, IX, 408–28; W. H. Nicholls, *Price Policies in the Cigarette Industry* (Nashville, 1951); A. C. Pigou, *The Economics of Welfare*, (4th ed.; London, 1952).
⁶Nicholls, *Price Policies*, pp. 415 ff.

Implications of the Results

cigarettes.[7] At a minimum Nicholls proposed that the specific tax be changed to an ad valorem tax.

Other remedies considered by Nicholls were dissolution and a tax on advertising outlays, graduated upward according to the dollar volume of the outlays.[8] Either of these programs would change the structure of the industry: dissolution, if it were possible to break up the loyalties to the major brands, would increase the number of independent firms; advertising taxes, by reducing the heavy volume of advertising expenditures, would presumably ease entry into the industry by lowering the outlays that a new firm would have to make to compete successfully with the established companies.

To some extent a progressive excise tax would have effects similar to those of dissolution. New firms would find entry somewhat easier in either case: after dissolution, the more numerous firms would find it harder to keep rivals out; after a progressive excise tax, new firms offering low-price goods would pay little or no tax and the collusive efforts of the oligopoly would be less effective.

The proposed tax on advertising would have a tendency to reduce such outlays (see Appendix III), but it is likely that an ad valorem or progressive tax on cigarettes would do the same. Since some taxes on various forms of advertising have not withstood challenges in the courts, progressive excise taxes would seem to be potential alternative devices to further the same purpose. Added difficulties with an advertising tax arise from the problem of determining the volume of advertising expenditures per time period, from the probable stimulative effect of such a tax on other forms of selling outlays, and from the apparent lack of a legal basis for selecting the advertising expenditures of a single industry as a base for taxation. These difficulties would either disappear or be less serious if an ad valorem or progressive excise tax were imposed.

C. Problems Associated with Progressive Excise Taxes

In view of the tentative nature of the suggestions for possible uses of progressive excise taxes for non-fiscal purposes, it would be inappropriate to attempt to anticipate all problems that could

---

[7]In Appendix V it is shown that the elasticity of industry demand with respect to the price net of tax must be reduced by a specific tax, left unchanged by an ad valorem tax, and increased by a progressive tax.

[8]*Price Policies*, pp. 408–15.

conceivably arise from the imposition and administration of such taxes. However, some difficulties would be encountered in any case and clearly warrant some mention, although none of them is "new" —they have already been encountered in one form or another in regulatory or tax administration.

1. DETERMINATION OF THE APPROPRIATE TAX FORMULA

When a regulatory tax is intended to stop an activity, the design is comparatively simple: the tax may be just heavy enough to succeed in its purpose or heavier to any degree—in either case, it achieves the desired purpose. If, initially, the tax is too light and the activity does not cease, the weight of the tax can be increased.

But, if a tax is intended to modify the extent of an activity *by a certain amount* (as in inducing a monopolist to increase output to the corresponding competitive level), the tax will not be easy to devise for at least two reasons. First, the corresponding competitive level of output and price will not be obvious.[9] Second, the type of tax function and the values of the parameters in the function that must be chosen to yield this price and output will also not be known.[10] The values of these parameters could, in principle at least, be based on demand and cost studies of the industry in question.

If, however, the purpose of the tax is only to modify an activity *in a certain direction*, the determination of the tax formula will be much simplified. Information concerning the elasticity of demand, or marginal cost, at the current level of activity would be sufficient, within a range of appreciable error, for determining the tax parameters.

It will, nonetheless, generally be more difficult to design a progressive tax for regulatory purposes than a tax to raise revenue. More intensive studies of demand and cost conditions would be necessary in the former instance, before the imposition of the tax. However, just as the record of collections from a revenue tax and the performance of the taxed industry yield valuable information

---

[9]Pigou discussed this problem at length in *The Economics of Welfare*, pp. 365–78.

[10]Generally speaking, a progressive tax function must have at least two parameters. These parameters, taken together, will determine the weight of the per unit tax at each price; one of the parameters will determine the tax elasticity. Tax functions with two or more parameters are not novel. A bracketed tax with only two brackets has three parameters: the price that defines the brackets and the tax rate or the per unit tax in each bracket.

Implications of the Results

concerning demand and costs, the experience under a regulatory tax would be equally informative. A trial and error approach is not necessarily inappropriate to taxation for either purpose.[11]

2. DETERMINATION OF PRICE AND THE TAXABLE UNIT

Two existing but separate problems arise under a progressive excise tax. If the per unit tax is a function of price (i.e., any tax except the specific tax), the price that fixes the tax is generally intended to be the true transaction price, that is, the price at which the seller is willing to relinquish ownership and the buyer to assume it.[12] But any excise tax that varies with the actual transaction price will encourage arrangements that give rise to a difference between the actual and true transaction prices. A common tax that fits this description is the ad valorem tax, and such arrangements have been discovered.[13] The imposition of a progressive tax would provide a greater incentive (than does the ad valorem tax) to such arrangements, since a given discrepancy between true and actual transaction prices could yield a greater saving in taxes.

A second problem arises under any tax except the ad valorem; the definition of the unit whose transaction price determines the tax must be very precisely drawn. Otherwise the seller may be able to change the "price" and the tax bill substantially by altering the units in which the product is sold. It is for this reason that the cigarette tax regulations specify both the number and the length of the cigarettes in a taxable package. Similarly, if a progressive tax were levied on cigarettes, the same type of specifications would be necessary; otherwise the producer could reduce the price, the size of

---

[11]The problems that are created under progressive excise taxation by general price level changes are not different in substance from those arising under other forms of excise tax. "When an attempt is made to introduce progression into ad valorem excise taxation by grading the taxed commodities according to price and imposing higher ad valorem rates on the higher-priced grades, falling prices will tend to counteract the effect of the grading, and rising prices will tend to accentuate it" [J. Viner, "Taxation and Changes in Price Levels," *Journal of Political Economy*, XXXI, 494–520, reprinted in Viner, *The Long View and the Short* (Glencoe, Ill., 1958)]. Rising prices will increase the weight of a progressive tax (perhaps to a prohibitive extent) but may or may not change the tax elasticity, depending upon the form of the tax function.

[12]The problem of verifying that the tax is paid on the *actual* transaction price is, given the accounting and auditing practices in modern business, not insuperable.

[13]B. U. Ratchford, "The Measure of Consumption Taxes," *Law and Contemporary Problems*, VIII, 567–68; Firms subject to an ad valorem tax levied at the manufacturer's level found it profitable to "sell" the product to their distribution subsidiaries at artificially low prices in order to lower the tax bill.

230   Conclusion

the package, and the tax bill—thereby successfully avoiding the tax to a great extent.

Both of the problems just discussed are combined under a progressive tax, for the total tax bill depends upon the number of "units" sold (like the specific tax) and upon the price per unit (like the ad valorem tax). But an awareness of the potential difficulties exists, and some methods of meeting them have already been developed.

3. QUALITY REACTIONS

Although changes in product quality may well result from a progressive excise tax, these changes may or may not be considered a "problem."[14] The purpose of the tax may be to reduce quality.

There are several considerations to be borne in mind before concluding, with Dalton, that the downward quality change is a decisive objection to progressive taxes. First, a very commonly used tax — the ad valorem — will also reduce product quality, given the same circumstances. So this disadvantage (if it is one) does not apply to progressive taxes alone.

Second, there is no a priori reason for the belief that a reduction of quality from the level that maximized monopoly profit and a reduction in price would leave consumers any worse off. High quality of product is not necessarily better when accompanied by a high price than lower quality at a lower price.

Third, the extent of quality change depends in part on the reaction of consumers to the change. If the change is substantial, there is an indication that the higher quality level was not greatly advantageous to consumers.

Finally, if the quality reaction to a tax is considered to be undesirable and if objective methods of measuring quality are devised, separate tax functions could be applied to each quality class in a manner that would keep the quality change small.

---

[14]Dalton regarded quality change as the "chief practical obstacle" to the levy of a progressive tax (see footnote 2, Chapter 20).

Appendixes

Appendix I. *Joint Maximization and Marginal Revenue*

One implication of the interdependence among several action variables in a joint maximization problem is that it is impossible, in general, to describe the "path" from a disequilibrium position to an optimum position, even though the marginal gains of each of the action variables may be known to be positive (or negative or zero) at the disequilibrium position. When there is a single independent action variable, it is true that, to increase profit to a maximum from a position of less than maximum profit, the action variable must be increased in value if its marginal gain is positive and reduced in value if its marginal gain is negative.

When there is more than one action variable, following the simple rule will not assure that profit will be maximized; it will only assure that profit will be increased. Consider a firm operating at the point marked A on Chart 24. The marginal gain from increasing selling costs (and price) while holding output constant is positive; profit can be increased by raising selling costs (and price); yet, compared to the optimum level of selling outlays ($\sqrt{s} = 33\frac{1}{3}$), outlays at A are *too high* and should be reduced, not increased, if profit is to be maximized. In addition, output should be reduced.

Furthermore, the concept of "marginal revenue" in a joint maximization context requires qualification. There are, for example, two different marginal revenue curves for selling outlays: one representing the gain from added selling outlays with output held constant (and price varying), and the other representing the gain from added selling outlays with price held constant (and output varying). The distinction is important since a given excise tax will affect these two types of marginal revenue in different ways. An advantage of the graphic device introduced in Chapter 11 is that it makes possible the visualization of the sign of either of these two marginal revenue functions, as well as the marginal revenue associated with price or output changes. For example, at any point below the W-E ridge line, the marginal profitability of selling cost (and price) increases is positive; at any point to the left of the N-S ridge line, the marginal profitability of output increases (and price decreases) is positive; and so forth.

Appendix II. *Relation between Slopes of the Ridge Lines*

The implicit equation of the N-S ridge line is given by

$$\pi^x = 0$$

or
$$x \cdot p^x(x,s) + p(x,s) - c^x(x,s) = 0 \qquad (48)$$

The slope of this function in the *s-x* plane (with respect to the *x* axis) is given by

$$-\frac{\pi^{xx}}{\pi^{xs}}$$

At equilibrium π^{xx} must be negative (the second-order partial derivatives of profit must be negative if a maximum exists). Thus the *sign* of the slope depends upon the *sign* of π^{xs}: the N-S ridge will be positively sloped if $\pi^{xs} > 0$, negatively sloped if $\pi^{xs} < 0$, and vertical if $\pi^{xs} = 0$.

The equation of the W-E ridge line is given by

$$\pi^s = 0$$

or
$$x \cdot p^s(x,s) - 1 = 0 \qquad (50)$$

The slope of this function is given by

$$-\frac{\pi^{sx}}{\pi^{ss}}$$

At equilibrium π^{ss} must be negative (for the same reason that π^{xx} must be); hence the slope of the W-E ridge line (to the *x* axis) also depends upon the sign of π^{sx}, which may be positive, zero, or negative.[1]

[1] It may be noted that for continuous functions $\pi^{sx} = \pi^{xs}$ (Allen, *Mathematical Analysis*, p. 301).

The various possibilities are tabulated as follows.

Sign of π^{sx}	Slope of W-E Ridge Line	Slope of N-S Ridge Line
Positive	Positive	Positive
Zero	Zero	Vertical
Negative	Negative	Negative

The statements made in the text concerning the relation between these two slopes are proven.

It may be added that the third of the three second-order conditions for a maximum to exist given above may be rewritten to show that the N-S ridge line of the profit surface must always be *steeper* than the W-E ridge. The condition is

$$\pi^{xx} \cdot \pi^{ss} > (\pi^{sx})^2 \tag{52}$$

or

$$\frac{\pi^{xx}}{\pi^{sx}} \cdot \frac{\pi^{ss}}{\pi^{sx}} > 1 \tag{88}$$

Assume first that the slopes of both ridge lines are positive, that is,

$$\pi^{sx} > 0$$

But

$$\pi^{ss} < 0$$

so that

$$\frac{\pi^{ss}}{\pi^{sx}} < 0$$

Dividing (88) by π^{ss}/π^{sx} — a negative quantity — will reverse the direction of the inequality and yield

$$\frac{\pi^{xx}}{\pi^{sx}} < \frac{\pi^{sx}}{\pi^{ss}}$$

Multiplying by −1 will again reverse the inequality, giving

$$\frac{-\pi^{xx}}{\pi^{sx}} > \frac{-\pi^{sx}}{\pi^{ss}} \tag{89}$$

This is equivalent to the requirement that the slope of the N-S ridge line [the left-hand side of (89)] be greater than the slope of the W-E ridge line [the right-hand side of (89)].

If, on the other hand, both ridge lines have negative slopes (as in Chart 27), then

Relation between Slopes of the Ridge Lines

$$\pi^{sx} < 0$$

and

$$\frac{\pi^{ss}}{\pi^{sx}} > 0$$

Now, dividing (88) by π^{ss}/π^{sx} — a positive quantity — will yield

$$\frac{\pi^{xx}}{\pi^{sx}} > \frac{\pi^{sx}}{\pi^{ss}}$$

Multiplying by -1 will reverse the inequality:

$$\frac{-\pi^{xx}}{\pi^{sx}} < \frac{-\pi^{sx}}{\pi^{ss}}$$

Thus the slope (negative) of the N-S ridge line must be smaller (i.e., a larger negative number) than the slope of the W-E ridge line.

In either of the above cases, as well as in the third case, where the N-S ridge is vertical and the W-E ridge horizontal, it is clear that the N-S ridge line must be the more steeply sloped of the two.

Appendix III. *Effects of a Tax Based on Advertising Outlays*

[In 1949 Professor William H. Nicholls suggested two measures to] ... encourage competition in the tobacco industry. First, a sharply progressive tax might be imposed upon the individual firm's total expenditures on advertising.... A second measure ... would be the sharp reduction or elimination of the federal and state cigarette taxes..... If cigarette taxes are not eliminated, however, at least they should be based on value rather than quantity of product.[1]

B. Higgins also raises the possibility of taxing advertising:

Where monopoly is based solely on differentiation through incurrence of selling costs, one is tempted to suggest a high tax on selling costs. However, the effect of such a tax in itself is to reduce sales as well as selling costs, so that excess capacity is increased rather than diminished.[2]

Higgins' demonstration (p. 318 and figure 2) that sales must fall and his implication that price would not change are not convincing, especially in view of the analysis below.

Nicholls and Higgins are, of course, correct in assuming that an advertising tax of the form suggested would tend to reduce advertising outlays (as the sequel will show), but the usefulness of the attempt to inhibit advertising directly has been questioned. G. W. Stocking and M. W. Watkins comment as follows:

Either procedure [i.e., a direct limit on advertising or a graduated excise tax imposed on advertising] would encourage price competition in the sale of cigarettes. But any limitation on advertising as a means of increasing the effectiveness of competition would no doubt be politically inexpedient. For the bare proposal alone would arouse the vehement opposition of practically

---
[1] Nicholls, *American Economic Review*, XXXIX, 294–95.
[2] Higgins, in Musgrave and Shoup, *Economics of Taxation*, pp. 312–21.

Effects of a Tax Based on Advertising Outlays 239

every newspaper and periodical in the country. Editors and publishers would defend the cigarette manufacturers and fight their battle for them, probably under the slogan of "freedom of the press." So the idea of curbing the cigarette monopoly by limiting advertising expenditures must be dismissed as quixotic.[3]

It is the purpose of this appendix to show (1) what the effects of a tax based on advertising would be, and (2) that there is an excise tax, based on both quantity and price, that would have substantially the same effects as the advertising tax (plus, perhaps, some added ones, as noted below).

For the present it will be convenient to redefine one variable. The letter T still represents the total tax bill, but s now represents only advertising expenditures (and not all selling outlays).

1. The pre-tax equilibrium has been described above. It is now further assumed that price depends upon output and advertising outlays only.

$$\pi = x \cdot p(x,s) - c(x,s) \qquad (47)$$

The pre-tax N-S ridge line of the profit surface is

$$\pi^x = x \cdot p^x(x,s) + p(x,s) - c^x(x,s) = 0$$

The pre-tax W-E ridge line is

$$\pi^s = x \cdot p^s(x,s) - 1 = 0$$

and the after-tax profit function is now

$$\pi = x \cdot p(x,s) - T(s) - c(x,s)$$

The after-tax N-S and W-E ridge lines are, respectively,

$$\pi^x = x \cdot p^x(x,s) + p(x,s) - c^x(x,s) = 0$$

$$\pi^s = x \cdot p^s(x,s) - T'(s) - 1 = 0$$

---

[3] G. W. Stocking and M. W. Watkins, *Monopoly and Free Enterprise* (New York, 1951), p. 164. The writers appear to have been first-rate prophets. "Baltimore City's special taxes on advertising have been declared invalid by the Baltimore City Court.... The taxes were: (1) a 4 per cent tax on the gross sales price of space sold through the various advertising media and on time sold in connection with any intrastate radio or television program; and (2) a 2 per cent tax on the gross receipts of persons selling advertising space and time.... The court held that the taxes violated the constitutional guarantee of the freedom of the press...." (A. S. Abell Co. v. Mayor and City Council of Baltimore) (*Tax Administrators News*, XXII, 81).

The N-S ridge line is not changed by the tax; that is to say, at a constant level of advertising, the same level of output is optimum as before the tax. Of course, if advertising is held constant, the tax bill is also constant, and the tax is a fixed charge that does not change the optimum price or output.

If the tax function has a positive slope (i.e., the tax bill increases as advertising increases), the W-E ridge is lowered at all outputs. The argument that explains the *lowering* of the W-E ridge is similar, with slight modifications, to that given above for the ad valorem tax.

A tax (with a positive slope) based on advertising leaves the N-S ridge unchanged and lowers the W-E ridge. These changes are illustrated in the left panels of Chart 29. The advertising tax will reduce advertising expenditures; may reduce price, but need not; and will affect output differently according to the slope of the N-S ridge line.

Hahn's analysis[4] yields results that are similar to these. Advertising is reduced by the tax, and price may or may not rise. However, one discrepancy is difficult to account for: "It is easily seen that the result of the tax will normally be to lower output."

2. Apart from the difference between advertising and the more inclusive concept of selling effort, these are precisely the effects of an excise tax with an elasticity equal to the demand elasticity. The excise tax would lower the dollar expenditure on selling effort as a whole and, unless the decreased selling effort changed drastically the marginal productivity of advertising per se, would also lower advertising expenditures.

Furthermore, if the proponents of taxes on advertising are correct that a reduction in advertising alone by a tax would "encourage competition" (it would, however, also stimulate other types of selling effort not subject to tax), then a reduction in the total of selling outlays would encourage competition more than a reduction in advertising alone. The excise tax has another important advantage in that it can be directed to specific industries.

It might be added that a regressive tax on advertising, that is, a tax whose total amount decreases as advertising expenditures increase [and $T'(s) < 0$] would *raise* the W-E ridge of the profit surface and hence increase the amount of advertising (as in Chart 33, panel 8).

[4]Hahn, *Economic Journal*, LXIX, 308–9.

Effects of a Tax Based on Advertising Outlays 241

The analysis in this appendix presumes a sole supplier producing a single product. The brief comments made in Chapter 18 concerning the possible extension of the results to other market situations apply here also.

Appendix IV. *Relation between Classifications of Demand Functions*

In Chapter 12, demand functions were classified by two different criteria, according to the way the best level of selling outlays changes as (1) output changes or (2) price changes. The first class consists of three types: i, ii, and iii, and the second also includes three types: 1, 2, and 3. That these two criteria of classifications are not independent is indicated by the table on p. 144. To see that the relation between the two criteria must be as stated, consider first a demand function of type ii, that is, the best level of selling outlays is the same at all outputs and the W-E ridge of the profit surface is horizontal. Chart 35 is a slightly modified version of Chart 26, illustrating the profit surface resulting from such a demand function when production costs are zero. A constant price line for the equilibrium price of $75 has been added, as well as a heavy line, R-R', which will be explained.

The chart shows (at the point marked A) that, *at a fixed output of approximately 35 units per time period*, the greatest profit ($2900) can be obtained by spending $625 ($\sqrt{s} = 25$) per time period on selling activities and charging a price of $100 per unit. This profit is, of course, not the maximum that can be earned; it is, however, the most that can be earned if output is fixed at 35 units. Thus, selling outlays of $625 and a price of $100 may be said to be optimum for an output of 35 units. A natural question at this point is, "Is $2900 the most profit that can be earned *at a fixed price of $100 per unit?*" The answer is clearly "no," as can be seen by moving along the $100 price line toward higher profit contours: keeping the $100 price and increasing both output and selling outlays will raise profit. These

Relation between Classifications of Demand Functions 243

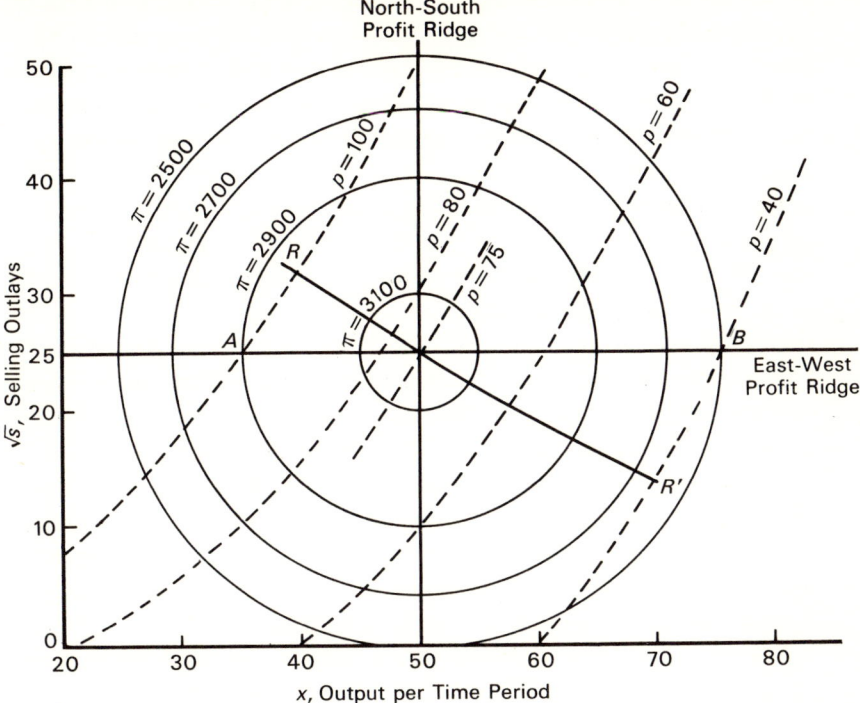

CHART 35.
Contours of profit surface, three ridge lines, constant price lines: demand function type ii.

increases should be continued until the price line is tangent to a profit contour, for example, at point R, where profit is greater than $2900. Since (1) the profit contour through point A is vertical (these contours are vertical at any point on the W-E ridge), (2) *all* price lines have a positive slope, and (3) at points to the left of the N-S ridge movements to the right represent increases in profit, point R must be above (i.e., represent higher selling outlays) and to the right of (at a higher output than) point A.

The same argument applies to *any* fixed price larger than the equilibrium price of $75, and a series of points corresponding to R for outputs less than 50 units could be identified. All of these points would lie north of the W-E ridge and would represent a third type of ridge line, showing, for each arbitrarily fixed price, the best level of selling outlays (and output). The $75 price is peculiar, however, in the sense that arbitrarily adopting an output of 50 units and maximizing profit yields values of $625 for selling outlays and $75 for price, whereas arbitrarily fixing price at $75 and maximizing profit yields $625 for selling outlays and 50 units for output. This symmetry of results occurs *only* if an optimum value of one of the variables is selected in the first place.

The continuation of the third ridge line to outputs greater than 50 units (and to prices below $75) is determined in essentially the same way. Point B represents the best level of selling outlays ($625) and price ($40) for a fixed output of approximately 76 units. Yet the slopes of the profit contours and of the $40 price line make it apparent that fixing price at $40 and reducing selling outlays (and output) will increase profit. The best profit for this price is indicated by point R', which must be below and to the left of point B.

Therefore, the "arbitrary price" ridge line, R-R', must be above the W-E (or arbitrary output) ridge at outputs below x_0, must intersect it at x_0, and must lie below it at outputs greater than x_0. In other words, *the slope of the ridge line R-R' must be smaller (taking its sign into account) than the slope of the W-E ridge.*

But the ridge line R-R' simply describes the relation between (1) price and (2) the best level of selling outlays. Since a movement (along R-R') upward and to the left must represent a price increase and an upward movement represents an increase in selling outlays, the best level of selling outlays must, in this example, be rising as price rises. It follows that, if the demand function is, as here, type ii (i.e., the best level of selling outlays remains the same regardless of output), the demand function must also be type 1 (i.e., best level of selling outlays is rising as price rises).

Similarly, if the demand type is iii (as, for example, in Chart 27), the W-E ridge is declining, the R-R' ridge must be declining too, and such a demand function must also be type 1.

If, however, the demand function is type i and the best level of selling outlays is higher at high outputs and vice versa (as in Chart 24), it is impossible to say without selecting a specific demand curve how the best level of selling outlays is related to price. Depending upon the slope of the price lines, the R-R' ridge could be declining (type 1), horizontal (type 2), or rising (type 3). None of the given data provides any clue concerning which of these situations obtains. In particular, the slope of the price lines is not determined

Relation between Classifications of Demand Functions 245

by the slope of the W-E (or the N-S) ridge lines. The slopes of the ridge lines depend on second-order derivatives of the profit function (Appendix II), whereas the slopes of the price lines depends upon first order derivatives of the demand function, and there is no necessary connection between these first- and second-order derivatives.

Appendix V. *Effect of an Excise Tax on the Elasticity of Industry Demand with Respect to Price Net of Tax*

It will be simpler to work out first the effect of a tax on the flexibility of price, the reciprocal of the demand elasticity.[1]

Given the industry demand function

$$p = p(x)$$

and the per unit tax function

$$t = t[p(x)]$$

let p_n = price per unit net of tax; then

$$p_n(x) = p(x) - t[p(x)]$$

The pre-tax price flexibility is given by

$$E_p(x) = \frac{dp}{dx} \cdot \frac{x}{p(x)} = \frac{p'(x) \cdot x}{p(x)}$$

The after-tax price flexibility will be

$$E_{p_n}(x) = \frac{dp_n}{dx} \cdot \frac{x}{p_n} \tag{90}$$

But

$$dp_n/dx = p'(x) - t'[p(x)] \, p'(x)$$
$$= p'(x)\{1 - t'[p(x)]\}$$

---

[1] Allen, *Mathematical Analysis*, p. 255.

Excise Tax and Elasticity of Industry Demand

Therefore (90) becomes

$$E_{p_n}(x) = p'(x)\{1 - t'[p(x)]\} \cdot \frac{x}{p(x) - t[p(x)]} \tag{91}$$

The elasticity of demand with respect to the price net of tax is the reciprocal of (91) or

$$E_x(p_n) = \frac{p(x) - t[p(x)]}{x \cdot p'(x)\{1 - t'[p(x)]\}}$$

This may be rewritten as

$$E_x(p_n) = \frac{p(x)\left\{1 - \frac{t[p(x)]}{p(x)}\right\}}{x \cdot p'(x)\{1 - t'[p(x)]\}} \tag{92}$$

where $p(x) > 0$
$t'[p(x)] < 1$

Apart from the portions of the numerator and denominator that are in large brackets, (92) is the *pre-tax* demand elasticity; the bracketed terms consist of characteristics of the tax function:

1. The average rate of tax:

$$\frac{t[p(x)]}{p(x)}$$

2. The slope of the tax function: $t'[p(x)]$

The effect of a specific tax is seen by noting that the slope of the specific tax function is zero; the numerator of (92) is reduced by the tax, but the denominator is unaffected. Therefore a specific tax makes the industry net demand curve less elastic.

The ad valorem tax has an elasticity, that is,

$$E_t(p) = \frac{t'[p(x)] \cdot p(x)}{t[p(x)]}$$

equal to unity, so

$$t'[p(x)] \cdot p(x) = t[p(x)]$$

or

$$t'[p(x)] = \frac{t[p(x)]}{p(x)}$$

The slope of the tax function (i.e., the marginal tax rate) equals the average tax rate.

But then the two bracketed terms in (92) must be equal to each other, and the before- and after-tax elasticities are the same! An ad valorem tax does not change the industry net demand elasticity. (A tax of this type *does* change marginal revenue — unless marginal revenue happens to be zero.)

An excise tax with an elasticity exceeding unity (i.e., a progressive tax) will make the net industry demand curve more elastic. For if the tax elasticity exceeds unity, that is,

$$E_t(p) = t'[p(x)] \cdot \frac{p(x)}{t[p(x)]} > 1$$

then

$$t'[p(x)] > \frac{t[p(x)]}{p(x)}$$

The slope of the tax function (the marginal tax rate) exceeds the average tax rate. It follows that the bracketed term in the denominator of (92) must be smaller than the bracketed term in the numerator the ratio of the two terms must be larger than unity, and the tax increases the demand elasticity.

It may be emphasized that the demand at issue is *industry* demand. If there is more than one firm in the industry, a tax may lead to changes in the number of firms and perhaps to a change in the elasticity of demand facing any one firm.

Bibliography

Abbott, Lawrence. "Vertical Equilibrium under Pure Quality Competition," *Americal Economic Review*, XLIII (December 1953), 826-45.
Allen, R. G. D. *Mathematical Analysis for Economists*. London: Macmillan, 1953.
Bain, Joe S. *Price Theory*. New York: Henry Holt, 1952.
———. "Pricing in Monopoly and Oligopoly," *American Economic Review*, XXXIX (March 1949), 448-64. Reprinted in Richard B. Heflebower and George W. Stocking (eds.). *Readings in Industrial Organization and Public Policy*. Homewood, Ill.: Richard D. Irwin, pp. 220-35.
Boulding, Kenneth E. *Economic Analysis*. Rev. ed. New York: Harper, 1948.
Brems, Hans. *Product Equilibrium under Monopolistic Competition*. Cambridge: Harvard University Press, 1951.
Chamberlin, Edward Hastings. *The Theory of Monopolistic Competition*. 6th ed. Cambridge: Harvard University Press, 1950.
Cournot, Augustin. *Recherches sur les principes mathematiques de la theorie des richesses*. Paris: Marcel Rivere, 1938.
———. *Researches into the Mathematical Principles of the Theory of Wealth*. Translated by Nathaniel T. Bacon with notes by Irving Fisher. New York: Augustus M. Kelly, 1960. (Reprint.)
Dalton, Hugh. *Principles of Public Finance*. 3rd ed. rev. London: Routledge and Kegan Paul, 1951.
Dorfman, Robert, and Peter O. Steiner, "Optimal Advertising and Optimal Quality," *American Economic Review*, XLIV (December 1954), 826-36.
Due, John F. *The Theory of Incidence of Sales Taxation*. New York: Kings Crown Press, 1942.
———. *Sales Taxation*. Urbana: University of Illinois Press, 1957.
Edgeworth, Francis Y. *Papers Relating to Political Economy*. 3 vols. London: Macmillan, 1925.
Folliet, P. *Les tarifs d'impots*, Lausanne: Librairie Payot, 1947.
Garver, Raymond. "The Effect of Taxation on a Monopolist," *American Economic Review*, XXII (September 1932), 463-65.
Guerin, J. "Excise Taxation and Quality of Product," *Finance Publique*, No. 1 (1960), pp. 21–30.

Hahn, Frank H. "The Theory of Selling Costs," *Economic Journal*, LXIX (June 1959), 293-312.

Hicks, Ursula K. *Public Finance*. New York and London: Pitman, 1948.

Higgins, Benjamin H. "Post-war Tax Policy (Part I)," *Canadian Journal of Economics and Political Science*, IX (August 1943), 408-28. Reprinted in slightly condensed version in Richard A. Musgrave and Carl S. Shoup (eds.). *Readings in the Economics of Taxation*. Homewood, Ill.: Richard D. Irwin, 1959.

Marshall, Alfred. *Principles of Economics*. 8th ed. New York: Macmillan, 1949.

Musgrave, Richard A. *The Theory of Public Finance*. New York: McGraw-Hill, 1959.

———, and C. S. Shoup (eds.). *Readings in the Economics of Taxation*. Homewood, Ill.: Richard D. Irwin, 1959.

———, and Daniel B. Suits. "Ad Valorem and Unit Taxes Compared," *Quarterly Journal of Economics*, LXVII (November 1953), 598-604.

Nicholls, William H. *Price Policies in the Cigarette Industry*. Nashville: Vanderbilt University Press, 1951.

———. "The Tobacco Case of 1946," *American Economic Review*, XXXIX (May 1949), 284-96. Reprinted in Richard B. Heflebower and George W. Stocking (eds.). *Readings in Industrial Organization and Public Policy*. Homewood, Ill.: Richard D. Irwin, pp. 220-35.

Pigou, Arthur Cecil. *A Study in Public Finance*. 3rd ed. rev. London: Macmillan, 1951.

———. *The Economics of Welfare*. 4th ed. London: Macmillan, 1952.

Ratchford, B. U. "The Measure of Consumption Taxes," *Law and Contemporary Problems*, VIII (1941), pp. 567-68.

Robinson, Joan. *The Economics of Imperfect Competition*. London: Macmillan, 1950.

Scott, Maurice Fitzgerald. "A Tax on Price Increases?", *Economic Journal*, LXXI (June 1961), 350-66.

Shoup, Carl S. *Shifting and Incidence Theory: Taxes on Monopoly*. Rev. New York: Columbia University, September 1950. (Mimeographed.)

———. *Facing the Tax Problem*. New York: The Twentieth Century Fund, 1937.

Stigler, George J. "Notes on the Theory of Duopoly," *Journal of Political Economy*, XLVIII (August 1940), 521-41.

———. *The Theory of Price*. Rev. ed. New York: Macmillan, 1952.

Stocking, George W., and Myron W. Watkins. *Monopoly and Free Enterprise*. New York: Twentieth Century Fund, 1951.

Sweezy, Paul M. "Demand under Conditions of Oligopoly," *Journal of Political Economy*, XLVII (August 1939), 568-73. Reprinted in George J. Stigler and Kenneth E. Boulding (eds.). *Readings in Price Theory*. Homewood, Ill.: Richard D. Irwin, 1952, pp. 361-83.

Tax Administrators News, XXII (July 1958), 81.

Von Mering, Otto. *The Shifting and Incidence of Taxation.* Philadelphia: Blakiston, 1942.
Wilcox, Clair. *Public Policies toward Business.* Homewood, Ill.: Richard D. Irwin, 1955.

Index

Abbott, L., 211, 212, 213, 215
Ad valorem tax, average rate, 17
  effects on product quality, 210, 218
  effects on ridge lines, 153–55
  effects on selling outlays, 155–59
  elasticity, 18
Advertising, 127–28
  taxes on, 238–41
Allen, R. G. D., 16, 21, 27, 29, 48, 131, 136, 235, 246
Amount of price change, and increasing vs. decreasing costs, 45–46
  and tax elasticity, 49–50
  and weight of tax, 46–48
Average rate of tax, 4, 16–17

Bain, J. S., 111, 118, 119, 120
Boulding, K. E., 140, 158, 202
Bounties, 99–101
  combined tax and bounty, 44, 73
  elasticity of per unit bounty, 99–100
  price and output effects, 100–101
Bracketed tax, 87–97
  ad valorem 12, 92–94
  definition, 22
  specific, 12, 89–92, 94–95
Brems, H., 204, 211, 213, 215

Chamberlin, E. H., 111, 113, 127, 128, 201
Cournot, A., 11, 34, 41, 153, 155

Dalton, H., 44, 201, 210, 230
Demand functions classified by
  selling outlay-output relation, 141–43, 242–45
  by selling outlay-price relation, 144, 242–45
Dorfman, R., 127, 131

Due, J. F., 97, 108, 110, 111, 115, 116, 117, 128, 201
Durability, *see* Product durability

Edgeworth, F. Y., 3, 7, 42, 46, 195
Elasticity of per unit tax, definition, 17–18
  price effects, 19, 39–44
Elasticity of total tax bill, definition, 21
  price effects, 21
Equal taxes compared, equal at after-tax price, 49–50, 64, 185
  equal at pre-tax price, 65–71, 81–85, 178–84, 210
  taxes lead to same output, 177–78, 220
Equilibrium conditions, 26–27, 129–31
Excise tax, amount of price change, 45–50
  analytical formulation, 33–35
  as control device, 5–6
  as revenue source, 5
  direction of price change, 37–44
  effects on product quality, 208–10
  effects on selling outlays, 139–41
  graduated, 4, 11–12, 22
  major criticism of, 3
  price and output effects, 37–45
  see also Tax functions

Flatness of profit function near equilibrium, 31–33
Folliet, P., 89

Garver, R., 54, 55, 56
Guerin, J., 201, 209, 210

Hahn, F. H., 138, 158, 240
Hicks, U.K., 201

253

Higgins, B. H., 101, 226, 238
Highly regressive tax, 22
  effects on product quality, 210
  effects on ridge lines, 173–74
  effects on selling outlays, 174–76

Marshall, A., 18, 42
Monopolistic competition, 111–16
Monopoly, 25–50
Monopsony, 103–108
  effects of excise tax, 106–108
  proportional tax on price deficiency, 107
Musgrave, R. A., 34, 49, 81, 83, 101, 111, 153, 219, 224, 238

Nicholls, W. H., 128, 226, 227, 238

Oligopoly, 116–20

Pigou, A. C., 9, 226, 228
Power tax, amount of price change, 64–71
  average tax rate, 17
  definition, 14, 51
  direction of price change, 52–64
  elasticity, 18–19
  examples, 51–53
Price theory, monopolistic competition, 111–13
  monopoly, 25–30, 128–44, 203–208
  monopsony, 103–105
  oligopoly, 116–20
  pure competition, 108–109
Product durability, 211–19
  definition, 211
Product quality, 201–10
  definition, 127
  tax effects neglected, 4, 5, 201
Progression, per unit tax functions, definition, 19
  discontinuous tax, 20
  effects of tax, 19, 20
Progressive tax, definition, 22
  effects on product quality, 210, 218
  effects on ridge lines, 163–66
  effects on selling outlays, 166–68
Proportional tax on excess price, amount of price change, 80–85
  average tax rate, 17
  definition, 13
  direction of price change, 76–79
  effects on price and output, 76–85
  elasticity, 18, 74

  examples, 75
Proportional tax on price deficiency, 107
Pure competition, 108–10

Quality, *see* Product quality

Ratchford, B.U., 229
Regression, per unit tax function, definition, 19
  price effects, 19
Regressive tax, definition, 22
  highly regressive tax, 22
Ridge lines of profit surface, 134–36
Robinson, E. A. G., 101
Robinson, J., 75, 101, 111

Samuelson, P. A., 134, 205
Scott, M. F., 74
Selling effort, definition, 127
  effects of tax neglected, 4, 5, 128
  pre-tax equilibrium, 128–38
  selling outlay-output profit surface, price lines 136–137
  profit contours, 134
  ridge lines, 134–36
Shoup, C. S., 20, 101, 111, 153, 225, 238
Specific tax, effects on product quality, 209–10, 218
  effects on ridge lines, 145–46
  effects on selling outlays, 146–49
Steiner, P. O., 127, 131
Stigler, G. J., 118
Stocking, G. W., 238, 239
Suits, D. B., 34, 49, 81, 83, 219, 224
Sweezy, P. M., 74

Tax functions, definition, 9–10
  continuity, 15–16, 20
  progression, 19
Tax policy, 223–27
  monopoly control, 225–26
  revenue taxation, 224
  taxation of advertising, 227, 238–41

Viner, J., 229
Von Mering, O., 111

Watkins, M. W., 238, 239
Wilcox, C., 226